Skulls to the Living, Bread to the Dead

To my Jane, a poetic soul, very much alive

Skulls to the Living, Bread to the Dead

Stanley Brandes

© 2006 by Stanley Brandes

BLACKWELL PUBLISHING
350 Main Street, Malden, MA 02148-5020, USA
9600 Garsington Road, Oxford OX4 2DQ, UK
550 Swanston Street, Carlton, Victoria 3053, Australia

First published 2006 by Blackwell Publishing Ltd

7   2012

Library of Congress Cataloging-in-Publication Data

Brandes, Stanley
Skulls to the living, bread to the dead : celebrations of death in
Mexico and beyond / Stanley Brandes
     p.   cm.
Includes biographical references and index.
ISBN 978-1-4051-5247-1 (hardback : alk. paper)
ISBN 978-1-4051-5248-8 (paperback : alk. paper)
1. All Souls' Day.   2. All Souls' Day–Mexico.   3. Mexico–Social life
and customs.   4. Mexico–Religious life and customs.   I. Title.

A catalogue record for this title is available from the British Library.

Set in 11/13.5pt Dante
by Graphicraft Limited, Hong Kong
Printed and bound in Singapore
by Ho Printing Singapore Pte Ltd

For further information on
Blackwell Publishing, visit our website:
www.blackwellpublishing.com

CONTENTS

Feliz Día de Muertos

"Happy Day of the Dead"

Storefront banner, Cuernavaca, Morelos

October–November 2000

FIGURES AND PLATES

ACKNOWLEDGMENTS

I carried out the research for this book in three different countries—Mexico, Spain, and the United States—over a period of three decades. As I review the many years that I have been engaged, off and on, in studying the Day of the Dead, I cannot help but conclude that it would be easier to compile a list of people who have had no part in this project rather than to name those who have. The totality of colleagues, friends, and family who in some way have contributed to this project possibly outnumber those who, through no fault of their own, have not. I suffer a serious risk in trying to specify precisely which friends, colleagues, and family members deserve to be thanked. I am sure to overlook someone or another. Hence, prior to citing anyone in particular, I wish to extend an apology to those individuals who deserve to be mentioned, but whom I have inadvertently forgotten. As for the others, none can be blamed for errors contained in the final product. The responsibility for data and interpretations found in this book rests upon a single person: me.

Although research on the Day of the Dead began in the late 1970s, it was in 1988, during a semester sabbatical leave at Project Zero in the Graduate School of Education at Harvard University that I began to think about and write the book. I want to thank Howard Gardner and others at Project Zero for hosting me and providing me access to rich intellectual resources necessary for advancement of this project. Other organizations that offered me wonderful settings in which to read and write include the John Carter Brown Library at Brown University and the Center for U.S.–Mexican Studies at the University of California, San Diego. In both cases, I could not have asked for more luxurious or favorable circumstances in which to carry out my work.

Although I gathered a considerable amount of information for this book through fieldwork, at least an equal portion—and perhaps more—was garnered through documentary research. Librarians at Harvard University, Brown University and the University of California, San Diego, were exceptionally helpful in facilitating my search for data. No less helpful were those at my home institution, particularly Suzanne Calpestri at the University of California, Berkeley, as well as at institutions abroad, including most importantly the Colegio de México in Mexico City, and the Archivo de Indias and the Escuela de Estudios Latinoamericanos in Seville. Librarians at the Larchmont Public Library aided with Chapter 7.

I was fortunate to earn funding for this project from several granting agencies. At the University of California, Berkeley, I more than once received assistance from the Committee on Research and the Center for Latin American Studies, as well as from a Humanities Research Fellowship. Additional financial aid also came, at various points in the writing of this book, from the John Simon Guggenheim Foundation, the National Endowment for the Humanities, and UC-MEXUS. I express my gratitude to all of these organizations for the crucial role that they played in facilitating my research and writing.

Over the years, I have delivered a good number of colloquia and informal presentations on themes that, in revised and expanded form, eventually became incorporated into this book. I wish to thank my hosts—both the scholars who invited me as well as their institutions. They include the University of Caracas, Venezuela; the Department of Anthropology at the University of Seville, Spain; Project Zero and the Department of Anthropology, Harvard University; CIESAS, Mexico City; the Instituto de Antropología, Universidad Nacional Autónoma de Mexico, Mexico City; the Universidad Autónoma del Estado de Morelos, Cuernavaca, Mexico; the Watson Center for International Studies and the John Carter Brown Library, Brown University; and the Department of Anthropology at the University of California, Riverside. At all of these institutions, scholars and students who attended these talks offered insightful comments and questions which inspired me to seek new information or reframe my findings. I am grateful for the opportunities they provided me to air my ideas publicly prior to publication. Some of that publication consists of earlier versions of articles and book chapters that have been worked into this volume in revised and expanded form (Brandes 1988, 1997, 1998a, 1998b, 2003; and Narvaez 2002:221–238).

Finally, there are the scholars and students who have helped me directly with every possible phase of research and writing, from bibliographic advice and editorial assistance to providing moral support and posing challenging questions about my interpretations. I received most aid from graduate student research assistants. Jorge Duany helped me launch the historical research phase and Beatríz Reyes-Cortes was there to help me two decades later, on the eve of the book's publication. In between, I counted on assistance from two other trusted graduate students, Jonathan Xavier Inda and Jeff Juris. Jeff carried out the enormous task of interviewing key respondents in the San Francisco Bay Area and thereby provided much of the material upon which Chapter 8 is based. I owe him and the other student assistants—who by now have become productive, independent scholars in their own right—an enormous debt of gratitude. At least one undergraduate student at UC Berkeley also provided essential material for this book: Katherine Sheets, whose research uncovered the lawsuits that I discuss in Chapter 7.

A host of historians, anthropologists, and related scholars have added to my bibliographic knowledge and understanding of specific aspects of the Day of the Dead. These include Liza Bakewell, Douglas Cope, George M. Foster, David D. Gilmore, John Graham, David Kertzer, Nora Jiménez, Jorge Klor de Alva, Claudio Lomnitz, Larissa Lomnitz, Cheryl Martin, Jesús Martínez, Guillermo de la Peña, Elena Poniatowska, Jesús Rodríguez Velasco, James Taggart, and William Taylor. I am very grateful for all the assistance received from these knowledgable associates. My late colleague, Alan Dundes, a scholar more keenly attuned to cultural paradoxes than anyone I have ever known, first posed the question which led me on the journey which has become this book: why are sweets so important to the Day of the Dead? For this contribution, as for so many others, I owe him an especially deep debt of gratitude. Finally, I offer my wife, Jane Brandes, hearty thanks for perceptive editorial advice and sustained encouragement.

Unless otherwise noted, all photographs and translations contained in this volume are those of the author.

PART 1

INTRODUCTION

1

THE DAY OF
THE DEAD, PROBLEMS
AND PARADOXES

Inscribed in my memory are two disturbing incidents concerning death in Mexico. The first occurred when, having just graduated from college, I spent a summer exploring the country and, as part of the normal tourist route, visited the celebrated *momias* or mummified bodies stored in a cave in the small city of Guanajuato. I was struck not only by the exoticism and morbidity of transforming these objects into a tourist attraction, but even more so by the commercial exploitation of the anonymous dead. Vendors situated at street corners and kiosks throughout town hawked mummy-shaped lollypops and trinkets to curious foreigners, and it was the mummies, rather than the colonial mines for which the city owed its existence, that most attracted visitor attention. Like other tourists, I remained completely mystified by the candies and figurines, fashioned in the form of cadavers, and speculated on what they might indicate about a possible Mexican death fetish.

Three years after the visit to Guanajuato, I found myself back in Mexico, this time in the role of graduate student researcher. It was literally on my first official day of anthropological fieldwork when another disturbing encounter with death occurred. This was still at a time when I barely knew Spanish, had never actually lived among Mexicans, and, at 23 years of age, wanted more than anything to become a successful ethnographer. The fateful event took place in the small town of Tzintzuntzan, located on the shores of Lake Pátzcuaro in the west-central state of Michoacán. It was early summer, a season of heavy afternoon electrical storms. Word had arrived at the house where I settled that a neighbor— a middle-aged man in the prime of life with wife and young children—had been struck dead by lightning while caught unprotected in a far off cornfield. The man's wake took place that evening. At the suggestion of my host family, I did as any responsible neighbor in Tzintzuntzan would: I attended. The following morning, I received a surprise visit from several mourners, who invited me to attend the burial and take pictures of the deceased. The year was 1967, the end of that era when many Tzintzuntzan households still lacked plumbing, electrical service, and telephones, not to mention television sets and cameras.

The aggrieved wife of the deceased had heard about my recent arrival and assumed, correctly, that I had brought a camera—at that time a cherished and rare possession in that town of humble farmers and potters.

Later that day, camera slung over my shoulder, I followed the funeral party on foot to church for requiem mass and afterwards to the town cemetery, where the grave had been dug and prepared. At the graveside, the casket was opened and the deceased's family gestured for me to take pictures. I squirmed inside at the thought of carrying out the appointed task. It seemed to me nothing short of disrespectful, a serious violation of etiquette, an unwelcome invasion of privacy, and an intrusion into the solemnity of the occasion to take pictures of the deceased, particularly at the moment of burial. And yet everyone stood in silence, staring into space, waiting patiently for me to proceed.

To carry out the job well, I should have hovered over the head of the deceased and, pointing the lens downward, taken several shots from directly overhead. Unable to assume this posture, both for fear of offending the mourners and because I found the task unpalatable, I bent down and took pictures first from one angle, then from another. Through the viewfinder, I could see a distorted vision of the man's face. When the pictures were developed a week later, I was not surprised to discover that the subject's face was barely recognizable. The family said nothing to me of this outcome and seemed grateful for what I had accomplished. Only later did I realize that that my hesitation about taking photographs during a burial ceremony had been misguided. At the time, I could not accept what later became obvious to me: the mourners sincerely wanted me to take a portrait of their departed relative and would have done anything I asked in pursuit of a good shot. My own emotions and cultural suppositions, not those of the mourners, were what got in the way. I was confronted for a second time with an attitude towards death that seemed distinct from my own.

Apart from this incident, what I most remember about the occasion was that it was pervaded from beginning to end by a deep sadness and solemnity. At the wake, women wept and men spoke softly. The mass and burial were entirely subdued. The life of the deceased had been cut short abruptly, while he was strong and able bodied. This funeral did not commemorate the death of an elderly citizen, who had lived out his life and seen his family grow and thrive. Nor was it held in honor of an *angelito*, literally "little angel," the word used to describe a child who dies in sexual innocence and therefore is destined to go directly to heaven, without having to pass through Purgatory. In Tzintzuntzan, as in the United States, funerals for the elderly are sad, to be sure; but they are also tempered by the recognition that the inevitable has come to pass. When an *angelito* dies, mortuary rites in Tzintzuntzan are more animated, less mournful, and often accompanied by live music. Nonetheless, in my experience, and contrary to how Tzintzuntzeños might describe such occasions if asked about them in an interview, these events tend to be cheerless and distressing. However young the deceased, however quickly the child ascends to Heaven, the mourners feel and demonstrate a deep sense of loss.

In fact, in Tzintzuntzan, as throughout Mexico, people react to death in most ways exactly as do people elsewhere in the world, that is, by profound grieving. In this respect, funerals belie the popular image of Mexicans as unafraid of death, jocular when confronted by death, and maintaining an intimate, almost cozy relationship to death. The casual, even humorous, attitude towards death often attributed to Mexicans forms an integral part of most portrayals of Mexican national character, an attitude that this book examines thoroughly, particularly in the concluding chapter. This reputation of what I term the morbid Mexican is in large part undeserved. And yet it is a reputation expressed freely by foreigners and Mexicans alike.

Two aspects of the reputation must be differentiated from one another. Consider first the casual attitude towards death, the recognition of the inevitability of death, its naturalness and frequency, together with the awareness of death as a great social equalizer that commands all of us to the same fate. These dispositions probably pertain to the vast majority of developing societies, possessed of high birth rates, elevated death rates, and limited access to effective health services. Philippe Ariès (1974) long ago identified their presence in early modern Europe; Nancy Scheper-Hughes (1992) has described how they manifest themselves in contemporary northeast Brazil. The request that I photograph the deceased at his Tzintzuntzan graveside was also possibly a product of this point of view, emanating from a specific combination of economic and demographic circumstances with which I, as a typical middle class urban American, was unfamiliar. And yet, Jay Ruby's fascinating historical exploration of photography and death in the United States (Ruby 1995) makes me question whether class affiliation or economic conditions have anything at all to do with the desire to capture images of the deceased. His study demonstrates conclusively that, from the time that photography was invented in the mid-19th century down to the present day, Americans, like Europeans, have had a predilection for taking pictures of dead relatives. This custom is neither a relic of the past nor limited to the Third World.

A second aspect of the stereotype of the morbid Mexican—the reputation for looking death straight in the eye and laughing at it, for being contemptuous of death, and for playing with death verbally and artistically—derives from neither economic conditions nor class affiliation but rather from a different source: the Day of the Dead. The annual celebration of the Day of the Dead, with its elaborate and often expensive decoration of altars and gravesites (see Plate 1.1), the ubiquitous skull and skeleton toys and candies, and widespread publication in newspapers and magazines of humorous epitaphs which poke fun at political and artistic celebrities—this is what is mostly responsible for the popular portrayal of Mexicans as being inured against the normal, devastating personal impact of death. Throughout the final quarter of the 20th century, the Day of the Dead became permanently emblematic of Mexico. It is indisputably Mexico's most famous holiday, the holiday that Mexicans invest most time and money in celebrating. Mexicans celebrate the Day of the Dead in a radically different manner from the way in which they observe funerals. Apart from its undisputed status as a major mortuary ritual, the Day of the Dead has over the course of modern history been transformed into an ostentatious display of art, poetry, and creative energy. The ultimate paradox is that the very holiday responsible for producing a stereotype of the stoic Mexican, who longs for death, is actually a powerful affirmation of life and creativity.

Although this book focuses squarely on the Day of the Dead, and explores the multiple transformations that this holiday has undergone over the course of five centuries, it is necessary to provide a description—however brief and schematic—of this ritual. The Day of the Dead is a specifically Mexican term referring to the Mexican version of a pan-Roman Catholic holiday, All Saints' and All Souls' days, observed on November 1 and November 2 respectively. Strictly speaking, the Day of the Dead—known in Spanish as *el Día de Animas* [Souls' Day], *el Día de los Finados* [The Day of the Deceased], or *el Día de los Fieles Difuntos* [The Day of the Faithful Departed]—refers to All Souls' Day, which normally falls on November 2. Only when November 2 happens to coincide with Sunday is All Souls' Day observed on November 3. The Day of the Dead includes such a range of interlocking activities that in colloquial speech it has come to denote not only November 2, but also, and more usually, the entire period from October 31 through November 2. The Day of the Dead is in actuality a sequence of Days of the Dead. Hence, we occasionally also encounter the term *Días de Muertos*, or *Días de los Muertos*—that is, Days of the Dead, in the plural. In some parts of Mexico—for reasons explored in chapter 4—the holiday has come to be known as *la Noche de Muertos*, or the Night of the Dead, rather than the Day of the Dead. And, in Oaxaca, the holiday is so central to community life that it has come to be called by the simple shorthand term *los Muertos* (Norget 2005:194).

Note that, despite the elaborate manner in which the Day of the Dead is celebrated, the Roman Catholic Church requires only the observance of special Masses on November 1 in honor of all the saints and on November 2 in honor of the souls in Purgatory. These Masses, which originated as early as the 11th century (Cornides 1967:319; Smith 1967:318), three centuries later assumed a permanent place of importance in the liturgical calendar, nearly equivalent in significance to Christmas and Easter (Gaillard 1950:927–932). Nowadays, at the beginning of the 21st century, the Church requires parish priests to recite one special Mass on November 1 and another on November 2, although three Masses on November 2 are more common: one in honor of the departed souls, a second dedicated to a cause designated annually by the Pope, and the third in recognition of persons or principles selected individually by each parish priest. These special Masses constitute the only official, obligatory part of All Saints' and All Souls' days celebrations throughout the Roman Catholic world, including Mexico.

Most observers would agree, ironically, that, at least in Mexico, Mass is the least salient part of the holiday. Come the end of October, a multitude of foreign visitors descend upon Mexico to witness colorful—some would say carnivalesque —ritual performances and artistic displays. Decorated breads, paper cutouts, and plastic toys, most of them playing humorously on the death theme, are evident everywhere. Sculpted sugar candies in the form of skulls, skeletons, and caskets suggest an almost irreverent, macabre confrontation with mortality. During October 31 through November 2, Mexicans clean, decorate, and maintain vigil over relatives' graves. Everything from expensive tombstones to simple earthen mound graves are adorned with flowers, candles and food, aesthetically arranged in honor of the deceased (see Figure 1.1).

In Mexico, most of the activities and artistic displays connected with this holiday—including special food offerings, cemetery vigils, home altars, and the like—are a folk elaboration entirely separate from liturgical requirements. The origin of these folk practices is a source of scholarly and popular debate. What is clear is that, for Mexicans, foreigners, and peoples of Mexican descent, the holiday has come to symbolize Mexico and Mexicanness. Within Mexico, it is a key symbol of national identity. In the United States, where the holiday is also widely observed, it symbolizes ethnic identity, which to some celebrants means

Fig. 1.1 Cleaning a grave in Mexico City, October 31, 1995

Mexican identity, to others Latino identity, and to still others local community identity. Throughout this book, these themes, and others bearing on the ethnographic content and symbolic meanings of the Day of the Dead, are fully scrutinized and elaborated.

For many—perhaps most—of the faithful, the Day of the Dead is first and foremost a sacred occasion, directed towards recognizing, honoring, and even nourishing deceased ancestors through creating conditions which promote a kind of spiritual communion with them. It is a mortuary ritual, which aims to satisfy both the alimentary and emotional needs of departed souls. Celebrants who re-member to provide properly for their ancestors on the Day of the Dead can, after death, expect to receive the same treatment from their descendents. Hence, children, during this holiday as in all holidays, are fully incorporated into the proceedings and thereby learn, as an anthropologist does—through both observa-tion and participation. It is expected that in the years ahead, at least once annually, during the Day of the Dead, these children will provide for their deceased parents in the way that their parents provide for their own departed relatives.

The spiritual dimension of the Day of the Dead is central to the experience of most celebrants. The Vatican defines the official side of spirituality, incorporated within the required Masses. Whether or not people actually attend the special Masses in honor of saints and souls, they are fully aware that at least the calendrical timing of the event on November 1 and 2 is regulated by church doctrine. The sequential celebration of first one category of deceased and then another is defined more by popular custom than by church doctrine, however. Hence, there exists no official rule stating that November 1, and the eve of November 1, should be devoted to honoring *angelitos*, a category of departed beings which is defined differently from one region of Mexico to another and which remains unrecognized by the Roman Catholic Church. November 2, which throughout most of Mexico is dedicated to the memory of the adult deceased, is officially aimed at honoring departed souls generally.

To these two, universally celebrated days, people in some parts of Mexico add a third day, which precedes November 1 and 2, and bears no recognition whatsoever to church doctrine. A three-day commemoration occurs most notably among the Nahua, descendents of the ancient Aztecs who occupy numerous communities throughout central Mexico. The Nahua and their relatives celebrate a day known variously as *el día de los accidentados* ("the day of those who died an accidental death") or *el día de los matados* ("the day of those who were murdered"). This third holiday, unrecognized by the Vatican, commemorates a category of deceased inscribed in pre-Columbian thought: one's fate in the afterlife depended more on the manner of death than on one's deeds while alive. Those who died unnatural deaths, through murder, warfare or accident, shared a similar destiny, different from that of people who expired through disease or other natural processes.

Although this book includes discussion of the spiritual and cosmological dimensions of the Day of the Dead, this theme must be approached with particular caution. Ideas regarding cosmology and spirituality vary enormously not only by region, class, and ethnicity, but even more dramatically from one individual to another. Even within the same family, much less the same community, there exist few consistent beliefs regarding the nature of the afterlife and the fate of souls. It may well be that these matters in many respects constitute the essence of the holiday. But Mexico is changing so rapidly, and throughout history has been subject to such radical shifts in the control over purse and power, that it would seem odd to discover any fully consistent set of beliefs. For this reason, I have found the spiritual and cosmological dimensions of the Day of the Dead to be the most elusive.

The broad scope of this study, ranging over centuries and across continents, favors a focus mainly, if by no means exclusively, on behavior, that is, on ritual action. This study is above all an exploration of the politics and economics of the Day of the Dead, with a particular emphasis on ritual changes that have occurred through culture contact and globalization. I am interested mostly in how culture contact and globalization have given rise to particular forms of ceremony, and how people in both Mexico and the United States draw upon religious rites to define themselves, to help sculpt an identity, to create a sense of we and they. Political and economic processes have shaped the interpretation of ritual such that particular forms of behavior have assumed symbolic import. That is, to participate in the Day of the Dead is to affirm symbolically that one belongs to a certain group, accepts a particular definition of self and other. To that extent, this book largely explores symbolic behavior and meaning. That people who celebrate the Day of the Dead derive a sense of inner peace from participating in ritual almost goes without saying. That this ritual provides solace and peace to saints and souls is also obvious and of central importance to many of the faithful. Nonetheless, the emotional components of this holiday, processed internally and idiosyncratically by each individual, living or deceased, do nothing to negate the outward expressions of devotion, which provide the main subject matter of this study.

This focus, and the specific topics explored in this book, derive from field experiences that initially aroused within me a great deal of doubt. In the late 1970s, I began a long-range study of the ritual cycle in Tzintzuntzan, eventually published as *Power and Persuasion: Fiestas and Social Control in Rural Mexico* (1988). The research, carried out over a period of years, took me to Tzintzuntzan during major religious holidays, including Christmas, Holy Week, Corpus Christi, and the Day of the Dead, among others. In the course of this investigation, I came to realize that there were certain rituals that I appreciated, admired, and enjoyed and others that I looked on with utter disfavor. I also instinctively knew that I would learn an important lesson about myself and about ritual behavior from acknowledging these feelings and struggling to understand them.

Try as we might to be objective and non-judgmental when carrying out fieldwork, no ethnographer can avoid liking or disliking particular people, places, situations, and events. The advisable way to proceed is, first, to recognize one's feelings by accepting them as normal and inevitable. Once this difficult step has been achieved, there are two possible courses of action, which are by no means mutually exclusive: either to incorporate emotional reactions creatively into one's research as a form of reflexivity or to rise above them in an attempt to eliminate personal bias in the reporting and interpretation of events.

In Tzintzuntzan, I was immediately captivated, even charmed, by several holidays: Holy Week, with its colorful passion play, solemn processions, and dramatic acts of penitence; Christmas with its repeated representations of the holy family's search for a manger and its joyful piñata competitions; Corpus Christi, with its fabulous fireworks displays, public enactments of past and present occupational pursuits, and lavish distribution of fruits and cooking implements. In the case of the Day of the Dead, my reaction was the opposite. The first time I observed this holiday, I returned home confessing how disappointed I was in what I had seen and vowing never to attend a Day of the Dead celebration again. When time had passed and I could analyze my experience fairly, I realized the reason why.

Simply put, the Day of the Dead in Tzintzuntzan did not conform to my preconceptions, derived from academic and popular reports as well as from my prior experiences with Mexican ritual and expectations as to what such ritual can and should be. On that initial visit, literally thousands of tourists swarmed through the streets, stomped through the cemetery, clogged and littered the city streets, and crowded into public spaces to observe cultural performances put on by professional actors and dancers imported from outside the town. Everywhere I turned, there seemed to be constant noise and commotion. The worst was the presence of floodlights, garishly illuminating the cemetery in the middle of the night for the purpose of televising the event. At around three in the morning, the cemetery vigil, which theoretically lasts without interruption until the next day, was cut short by a sudden rainstorm. The vigil at the tombs of the ancestors, together with the beautiful arrangements of candles, flowers, and food decorating the graves—all of this was completely destroyed. In the state of Michoacán, the Day of the Dead falls at the very end of the rainy season. Most years it does not rain, but on this occasion it poured, thereby completely aborting the entire final portion of the celebration.

I had hoped for something better, something purer and more authentic. What I observed instead was an almost intolerable cultural hybrid, with urbanites, foreigners, busloads of elderly pensioners, and other unlikely people participating as actors and audience. By my reckoning, these outsiders did not properly belong at the event. Surrounding me I found an incongruous mixture of comportment, mood, and ritual paraphernalia that seemed inappropriate to any mortuary celebration. I was a modernist ethnographer confronted by a post-modern world. Once I recognized the rich combination of elements, the hybridity celebrated by Nestor García Canclini (2001), which was brought together in this event, I could appreciate the enormous opportunity that the Day of the Day presented as subject for study. At that moment I could then view the presence of tourists as intellectually interesting rather than as a contaminant that distorted the authentic ritual proceedings. I could recognize and appreciate creative adaptations to radical political and economic change. I could see what confronted me rather than what I wanted to observe. By maintaining this point of view during field expeditions, and projecting it into my reading of documents from the past, I came to interpret the Day of the Dead as a product of changing political agendas and economic circumstances. I began to understand the symbolic value of this holiday for those who might draw upon it to define personal and collective identity.

The main goal of this book, then, is to understand how and why the Day of the Dead has assumed an emblematic status as symbol of Mexico itself. It also explores the process through which this holiday has become transformed into a marker of ethnic identity within the United States. The Day of the Dead, both in Mexico and the United States, has become a kind of cultural capital—invoked, transformed, and promoted for the economic, political, and social benefit of towns, regions, ethnic groups, and most importantly the nation state. The Day of the Dead is a symbol as much as an event and as such has been subject to manipulation and image management. It has been reinvented many times, by church and state, as well as in the press and through mass communications systems. The book aims to describe and explain this process of invention and reinvention and thereby contribute to the general understanding of ritual change and, most importantly, the politics of identity.

My analysis of the Day of the Dead proceeds largely through the exploration of cultural paradoxes—that is, the simultaneous presence of phenomena that we normally do not think of as co-existing. By analyzing the counter-intuitive combination of elements that mark the Day of the Dead, we can begin to understand the centrality of the Day of the Dead to Mexican identity today. In this fashion, too, we can perceive the ways in which great moments of Mexican history are refracted through the lens of a single religious ritual. The Day of the Dead not only reflects important historical currents but also has influenced them.

The Day of the Dead incorporates at least four paradoxes or counter-intuitive elements, which yield important insights not only about this holiday but also about religious ritual in general. Consider first the reasonable assumption that people would become increasingly obsessed with death, and that death rituals would become more elaborate and central, as mortality rates increase. A decrease in mortality rates, by this reasoning, should bring a corresponding decline in the ritual celebration of death. In Mexico, however, the opposite seems to have occurred. Mortuary ritual, in the form of the Day of the Dead, has become more important within Mexican society during a period when the country's death rates have dropped precipitously, life span has steadily increased, and rates of infant mortality, once tragically high, have approached those found in post-industrial societies. Simultaneous with these favorable demographic changes, the Day of the Dead has gained in popularity. Now, at the turn of the 21st century, the Day of the Dead is celebrated over a wider territory and among a greater range of social classes than has ever before been the case. This experience deserves explanation. It belies the common assumption that Mexican attitudes towards death have been conditioned by the omnipresence of death, that Mexicans are hardened against death because it is an everyday occurrence.

Contrary to what one might expect from a mortuary ritual, the Day of the Dead is replete with expressions of humor, lightheartedness, and jocularity (see Plate 1.2). This is a second paradox that requires explanation. Much of the humor that emerges during the Day of the Dead is political in nature. In fact, during the colonial and national periods, playfulness at cemeteries in central Mexico occasionally reached such raucous proportions that church and state felt threatened enough to ban cemetery vigils, a normal facet of Day of the Dead proceedings today. Some of the humor is fundamentally social as well, grounded in the structure of friendship, which requires a periodic testing of the bond through teasing. And much of the humor emerges in graphic and plastic arts, which are created for the amusement of the public and sale in the open marketplace. Why is humor such an integral part of one Mexican mortuary ritual, the Day of the Dead, and not another, the garden variety funeral? This book addresses this perplexing issue.

Closely related to the unexpected (if not unprecedented) combination of death and humor is the importance of sugar in the Day of the Dead. Sweet breads, found for sale in every Mexican bakery and marketplace at around the time of the Day of the Dead, and jokingly referred to in the United States as "dead bread," are just one common item. Equally evident are small skulls and skeletons, sculpted of sugar paste, chocolate, amaranth seed dough, and other sweet substances. The association of sweets with death, as found in the Day of the Dead, is a third counter-intuitive element that requires explanation.

The Day of the Dead incorporates yet a fourth apparent paradox in that this holiday has become ever more popular within Mexico as tourism and modern communications systems have increased. This development belies a common assumption that societies and cultures become more homogenous as contact among them increases. We are all too ready to believe that tourism destroys cultural authenticity, contaminates the purity of customary behavior and traditional beliefs, and over time eventually obliterates indigenous culture. As a major tourist attraction, the Day of the Dead provides an opportunity to examine these suppositions.

In addition to proceeding through an analysis of presumed cultural paradoxes, this book explores one of anthropology's major themes: culture contact and globalization. The Day of the Dead was born of the colonial encounter, the 16th-century meeting between Europe and America. There is no known society that entirely lacks mortuary ritual; certainly, prior to the Spanish conquest, both Spain and Mexico were home to elaborate funerary ceremonies. However, the Day of the Dead assumed the beginnings of its current configuration only after considerable contact and exchange between these two imperial powers. In the domain of ritual and religion, the consequences of culture contact were radical and profound from the moment that Spaniards landed on the coast of Veracruz in 1519. The European colonization of the Americas produced an exchange of ideas, products, and technology that permanently altered life and thought on both continents. And yet, the pace of culture contact and the movement of populations advanced very slowly when compared with the era in which we find ourselves today. During the course of four or more centuries, as this book demonstrates, the Day of the Dead underwent irreversible transformation through the exchange of peoples and ideas. But, insofar as documentary evidence reveals, changes occurred at a measured pace.

This situation changed notably in the late 20th century, precisely the period when investigation for this volume was underway. In the last quarter of the past century, we entered a period of what has come to be known as globalization, which Inda and Rosaldo have summed up as "the intensification of global interconnectedness" (Inda and Rosaldo 2002:2). To these authors, the term globalization suggests "a world full of movement and mixture, contact and linkages, and persistent cultural interaction and exchange, . . . a world where borders and boundaries have become increasingly porous, allowing more and more peoples and cultures to be cast into intense and immediate contact with one another" (ibid.). With regard to the Day of the Dead, up until the mid-20th century, it was the contact between Europe and Mexico that provided the main impetus for ritual change. Afterwards, with the intensification of contact between Mexico and the United States, the rapid growth of tourism, and increasing U.S. reliance on migrant labor, the mutual effect that these two countries began to have on one another eclipsed all other influences. Globalization has increased the speed and depth of contact among all countries, but the impact on neighboring countries, such as Mexico and the United States, has perhaps been greatest of all.

This volume explores the impact on the Day of the Dead of the forces of globalization. The most dramatic impact has come from domestic and international tourism, radio and television broadcasts, and the flow of labor and capital across the U.S.–Mexican border. The advent of the North American Free Trade Association (NAFTA) has exerted a decided influence on the Day of the Dead, particularly with regard to the massive introduction of Halloween commercial products and symbolism into Mexico. A counterpart to this process has occurred as the Day of the Dead begins to become incorporated into US school curricula, museum programs, and community-wide celebrations during the Fall season.

Hence, in order to understand the Day of the Dead today, we must examine what Arjun Appadurai (2002:51) has termed "ethnoscapes," that is "the landscape of persons who constitute the shifting world in which we live" including tourists, refugees, and migrant laborers. No less important for our purposes are what Appadurai calls "ideoscapes," that is, "concatenations of images," which "are often directly political and frequently have to do with the ideologies of states and the counter ideologies of movements explicitly oriented to capturing state power or a piece of it" (ibid.). As a direct result of globalization, the Day of the Dead, in both Mexico and the United States, has assumed definite political meaning and ideological symbolism far beyond its original religious essence (see Plate 1.3).

This volume is divided into five major sections, three of which which connect chapters according to historical era and processes of change. Part 2, Historical Foundations, examines two topics. The first concerns the significance of sweets and death in the colonial era, and demonstrates why, in that period of the country's history, the Day of the Dead should have assumed a religious role of major importance. In the following chapter, the book traces the origins and meaning of the striking iconography associated with the Day of the Dead, particularly skulls and skeletons. Although this chapter delves deep into prehistory, it focuses mainly on the 19th century through the mid-20th century. The question of the origins of the Day of the Dead becomes significant not in and of itself, but rather because the holiday itself has become cultural capital, a symbol of Mexican cultural independence and national identity. Mexicans and others today invoke the history of the Day of the Dead as a means of affirming who they are and what their country represents. The processes through which the Day of the Dead has come to symbolize Mexico are complex and involve political, economic, and artistic developments, among others. The chapters on sweetness and death and on skull and skeleton iconography not only illuminate aspects of Mexican history previously ignored in the literature but also highlight general features of ritual change.

Part 3, Contemporary Transformations, examines a variety of 20th-century political influences on the Day of the Dead. The first and perhaps major trans-formation is that created by the governmental promotion of tourism. Against a background of comparative ethnography, I focus in this chapter on the town of Tzintzuntzan, singled out by the state government for tourist development and symbolically significant to politicians because of its former position as capital of the pre-Columbian Tarascan Empire. Following this chapter, I consider literary humor associated with the Day of the Dead, particularly *calaveras*, or jocular epitaphs, which change from one decade to another according to the political profiles and artistic preferences of the day. The analysis of *calaveras* demon-strates the opportunities that religious ritual provides for expressing what I have elsewhere called "peaceful protest" (Brandes 1977). Part 3 concludes with an exploration of the recent incorporation of Halloween symbols and practices within

Mexico's Day of the Dead. The Mexican response to this development has been uneven, embraced by some, vehemently opposed by others who see in it yet another expression of American imperialism. The debate over the importation of Halloween into Mexico demonstrates the centrality of the Day of the Dead to Mexican national identity.

Part 4 examines the counterpart of Halloween in Mexico, that is, the introduction of the Day of the Dead into the United States, where in the 21st century the holiday has become increasingly prominent. Environmental and social circumstances in the United States have transformed the Day of the Dead into an emotionally charged event of overriding political significance. The Day of the Dead, which in Mexico has long emphasized family ties, in the context of the United States assumes symbolic importance in terms of ethnic and community affiliation. In one chapter dealing with this holiday north of the border, I explore how children have become introduced to the Day of the Dead through literature and public school education. A second chapter, focusing on the San Francisco Bay Area, shows different routes that the Day of the Dead has taken in the United States, and the variety of meanings that this holiday has acquired for people of Mexican descent and others living outside the country where it originated.

The concluding chapter assesses what the Day of the Dead can tell us, if anything, about the meaning of death to those who celebrate the holiday. The chapter confronts and challenges the stereotype of the morbid Mexican and demonstrates the variety of social and symbolic meanings this holiday has assumed in both Mexico and the United States. There is and never has been an authentic Day of the Dead. Through vast expanses of space and time, there have emerged many different Days of the Dead, each responding to the needs and aspirations of local celebrants.

PART 2

HISTORICAL FOUNDATIONS

2

THE SWEETNESS
OF DEATH

A pleasurable aspect of any annual holiday, in Mexico or elsewhere, is the inevitable presence of special foods. One of the most impressive features of the Day of the Dead is the prominence of unusual delicacies, which can be purchased only at this time of year—or even of ordinary, everyday food prepared and arranged in special fashion. The Day of the Dead features food in two ritual contexts: (1) placed on gravesites during the cemetery vigil, and (2) displayed on home altars. Home altars are open to the view of family and anyone who visits the family. When placed on the home altar, all *ofrenda* objects are on public display, and families, for their own benefit and that of others, try to arrange offerings as artistically as possible. In the case of the graveside *ofrenda*, food and drink tend to be transported to the cemetery in covered baskets and containers, where they remain out of public view throughout the cemetery vigil. Whether openly displayed or covered beneath cloth, Day of the Dead food is called *ofrenda*, or offering, because it is set out as a commemorative gift to the deceased relatives who are being honored on this occasion. In both cases, too, the symbolic significance of the food is transformed through its display in a ritual context. An orange resting on the kitchen table is placed there to be peeled and eaten. Put the same orange on a home altar, or leave it nestled among other fruit in a covered ceramic bowl on top of a relative's grave, and it becomes a sacred object.

An incident that occurred to me in Tzintzuntzan illustrates this principle. I was chatting to a married couple in their outdoor kitchen, right next to a small decorated table, which served as the family's Day of the Dead altar. As a natural gesture of hospitality, the wife offered me some fruit that was sitting on a simple sideboard. When I raised my arm to reach for a banana, the woman instantaneously extended her hand to prevent me from reaching for the fruit set out on the altar. "Not from there," she said with nervous laughter. "That one is for the deceased." Then, pointing to the sideboard, she said, "Help yourself to a banana from over there." To eat fruit from the altar is equivalent to stealing fruit from the deceased. It would in fact constitute an act of sacrilege. Only after the Day of the Dead has passed can the fruit be removed from its ritual setting—be it altar or gravesite—and thereby symbolically transformed back into food for human consumption. From that moment, it may be eaten with no offence to the departed souls.

The *ofrenda*, in fact, is food that facilitates the relationship between living and deceased relatives. Mexicans decidedly do not believe that the returning souls actually eat the fruit, bottled drinks, and other comestibles that are set out in their honor. They do believe, however, that deceased relatives are spiritually present and aware that their living kin have gone out of their way to remember them. They also believe that the spirits derive some nourishment and contentment from the smell of the food displayed in their honor. The situation that Ochoa Zazueta (1974:97) describes for the town of Mizquic, just south of Mexico City, seems typical of central and southern Mexico generally: "It is believed that the departed relative visits the home and takes pleasure in the foods that in real life pleased him or her. The visitor, since he or she is a spirit, can only aspire to enjoy the aroma of the *ofrenda*, with which they remain satisfied." The aroma is all they can hope for because, as the people of Mizquic say, "the souls are [made] of wind and cloud, without either teeth or palate, without eyes and without hair" (ibid.; English translation mine).

Ethnographic reports elsewhere in Mexico also indicate no belief in the actual consumption of *ofrenda* foods. In the state of Oaxaca, it is said that "the dead do not actually consume the *ofrendas* left for them, as those who are alive would . . . Rather, it is the ephemeral 'essences' of the food set out for them—the flavor and the aroma—that the dead take from their offerings" (Norget 2005:219). Villagers of San Juan Totolac, in the state of Tlaxcala, "try to put out as ofrenda recently prepared mole, tamales, and sweets, as well as the freshest flowers and fruits, since it is believed that the souls carry off only the essence [that is, the aroma] of these items so situated" (Scheffler 1976:97). Cándido Reyes Castillo, from Huaquechula in the state of Puebla, states that, "of course, there are those who say the dead do not return, but I know they do. I feel sure of this, because when we offer food to the deceased it loses its aroma and taste" (quoted in Carmichael and Sayer 1991:99). Among the Mixe, when a relative dies during All Saints' Day itself, this departed soul cannot partake of the food set out that very year. Rather, it is said to wait around either in the house itself or in the resting place of the dead until the following year, when it returns for its share of the *ofrenda* (Lipp 1991:139).

There is evidence, then, that insofar as food for the dead is concerned, we are confronted with a widespread, probably ubiquitous phenomenon: the spiritual presence of the recently deceased. This phenomenon, as we have seen in the previous chapter, was recognized and brilliantly analyzed by Robert Hertz (1907) at the beginning of the last century. In fact, altars and tombstones which are prepared in honor of deceased relatives more often than not bear photographs of kinfolk who died in the relatively recent past, say, within four or five years of the commemorative date. This practice might indicate that, once this amount of time has passed, the liminal mourning period is over. Of course, a home altar in theory is dedicated to all the deceased relatives of the family that erects it. Members of the family will automatically attest to the fact that the altar belongs to all of their departed souls. And, in fact, those whose parents died a decade or more before the erection of the altar will continue dedicating the altar to those departed souls. Nonetheless, if specific relatives are singled out for commemoration, through photographs or otherwise, the date of death tends to fall closer rather than further from the commemorative ritual itself.

Before explaining the origin and symbolic meaning of the *ofrenda*, let us take account of its varied composition. The two most common *ofrenda* ingredients are candles and fresh flowers or flower petals. In fact, these are the only items without which an *ofrenda* would be considered incomplete and inadequate. In the household where I reside in Tzintzuntzan, the elderly couple who for many years served as my hosts would sprinkle marigold petals in the form of a cross on the floor at the foot of their bed. They would soften the wax at the bottom of two candles so that they could stand up on the floor as well. This simple arrangement, though far from being an altar, constituted their home *ofrenda*. Many residents of Tzintzuntzan, especially in past decades, have done nothing at gravesites but place jars of freshly picked flowers and several candles on the graves of their departed relatives. This, too, constitutes an *ofrenda*, albeit a simple one. It is an arrangement that can be found at tombs and graves all throughout Mexico and Latin America. It is, in fact, the only *ofrenda* practicable where there are *nichos* or above-ground burial chambers, which usually contain narrow ledges, protected by glass windows, where candles and flowers can be placed.

However, much more common throughout Mexico—particularly central and southern Mexico—is the *ofrenda* that consists of breads, candies, and other foods. These comestibles, in fact, have become world famous, a symbol of Mexico itself, as one *New York Times* report (November 4, 1993) demonstrates:

> From bike repair shops in rural villages to fashionable burger joints in Mexico City, the dead's annual homecoming brings forth the designer in everybody. Across the country, bakers fashion *pan de muerto* [in the United States, whimsically termed "dead bread"] the special bread that looks like twisted bones glistening with white icing. The markets are filled with rows of sugar skull candies with tin-foil eyes and gold grins, sugar coffins in which serape-clad corpses holding liquor bottles are tipsy with Bacardi.

Liquor is a common feature of home altars, although generally not graveside *ofrendas*. Given that a home altar is a public display, liquor is offered exclusively to deceased male relatives (Brandes 2002:110). If a deceased male relative was known to like a particular brand of beer, a bottle of that beer becomes part of the home *ofrenda* in his honor; likewise tequila or brandy. Living relatives would probably prefer to forget or hide the alcoholic preferences of a deceased female relative, which pretty well assures that altars erected in their honor are devoid of alcoholic beverages.

Ordinary foods, too, are a regular feature of the *ofrenda* honoring all departed kin. These include oranges, bananas, squash and other fresh produce of the season, as well as cooked items such as tamales and chicken or turkey *mole*. Everywhere that altars are erected, family members take account of the individual tastes of deceased relatives in deciding which foods to include in the *ofrenda*. A potter from Tzintzuntzan explained to me, "The custom here is to take to the dead whatever they enjoyed in life . . . fruit and such things, . . . *corundas* [a kind of *tamal* prepared throughout the state of Michoacán], tortillas, beans, pork, a duck, if the deceased liked fish, whatever, whatever the deceased liked most." In Mizquic, famous throughout Mexico for particularly elaborate Day of the Dead celebrations, food offerings include "tamales, oranges, sugarcane, bananas, different types of *pan de muerto*, salt, water, candy, corn on the cob, lard, *atole* [a corn gruel drink], squash, *tejocotes* [a small, yellow, plum-like fruit], lemons, sugar, chocolate, *mole*, cinnamon, corn kernels, tangerines, tall candles [*cirios*], votive candles, and flowers. Among the Mizquic offerings, too, figure rum, pulque, and bunches of fresh herbs" (Ochoa Zazueta 1974:96). The typical *ofrenda* in the central Mexican town of Tlayacapan includes "sweets, chocolate, chayotes, *jícamas*, special breads, oranges, peanuts, green *mole* with fish, flowers, tamales, and figurines" (Ingham 1986:137). It is safe to say that everywhere seasonal availability exerts some influence over the composition of offerings, especially in the case of fruit and flowers.

It is unremarkable that seasonal availability and the food preferences of the deceased should affect the nature of the *ofrenda*. What is surprising, however, is the prominence of sweets on this occasion. After all, fruit is inherently sweet. *Pan de muerto* is always a sweetbread, molded from a sugary dough which is not normal for daily fare (see Figure 2.1).

Of course, chocolate is sweet, as is the squash set out on Day of the Dead altars, which is often cooked with brown sugar—a common dessert. Then, too, there is a proliferation throughout Day of the Dead season of sculpted sugar candies in the form of skulls, skeletons, and caskets, not only used as altar decorations, but also presented as gifts to friends and relatives. Mortuary rituals in the west are sometimes associated with sweets. Visitors who pay condolence calls to mourners in the United States often bring boxes of candy. But candy is no particular feature of funerals in Mexico. Nor is it likely that sweets achieve the degree of centrality in mortuary rituals anywhere that they do during Mexico's Day of the Dead. The presence of sugar and sweets during the Day of the Dead

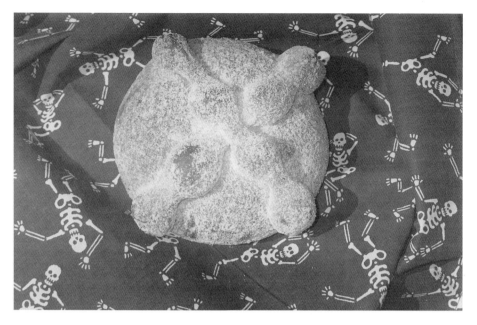

Fig. 2.1   *Pan de muerto*, Mexico City, 1996

is sufficiently noteworthy that we must ask whether there exists in Mexico a special relationship between sweets and death.

Consider, first, the possible historical origins of sweet offerings during the Day of the Dead. Insofar as ancient Mesoamerica is concerned, a necessary point of departure is the testimony of the great 16th-century chronicler, Fray Bernardino de Sahagún. Sahagún, whom some scholars see as a "pioneer ethnographer" (Klor de Alva, Nicholson, and Quiñones 1988), tells us that the Aztecs fashioned sacred images out of wood, which they covered with *tzoalli*, or amaranth seed [*Amaranthus hypocondriacus*] dough. The dough was shaped anthropomorphically. Take as an example Sahagún's account of what the Aztecs did with a *tzoalli* image of the great deity Uitzilopochtli during Panquetzalitzli, the fifteenth month of the Aztec calendar (Sahagún 1978, Book 3:5–6):

> And when he died, thereupon they broke up his body, the amaranth seed dough. His heart was Moctezuma's portion. And the rest of his members, which were made like his bones, were disseminated among the people . . . And when they divided among themselves his body of amaranth seed dough, it was only in very small [pieces] . . . The youths ate them. And of this which they ate it was said, "The god is eaten." And of those who ate it, it was said, "They keep the god."

On the 16th month of Atemoztle, *tzoalli* mountain images were made during the feast of the rain god, Tlaloc. The mountain images were apparently anthropomorphic, for Sahagún's account (ibid.: Book 2:29) declares that "they made eyes and teeth on them and worshipped them with music . . . They opened their breasts with a tzotzopatztli [a weaving sword] . . . and they took out their hearts and struck off their heads. And later they divided up all the body among themselves and ate it." The goddess Tzapotlan tenan, who was the turpentine deity, also had her image fashioned on amaranth dough (ibid.: Book 1:17), as did the god Omacatl (ibid.), of whom it was said, "He who ate the god first made a sacred cylinder [of dough]: this was the bone of the god. Only a priest . . . [made it]. Then the sacred roll was shared, broken in pieces, divided among them."

During the thirteenth month of Tepeilhuitl (ibid., Book 2:131–133) amaranth dough images took on a specific mortuary meaning, according to Sahagún's account:

> All the [wooden] serpent [representations] which were kept in people's houses and the small wind [figures] they covered with a dough of [ground] amaranth seeds. And their bones were likewise fashioned of amaranth seed dough . . . Either fish amaranth or ash amaranth [was used]. And [for] whoever had died who had not been buried, they also at this time made representations of mountains. They made them all of amaranth seed dough. Thereupon they dismembered the amaranth seed dough [figures] . . . little by little they went taking some of it when they ate it.

As indicated in this passage, these dough images commemorated only specific classes of deceased, namely, those who had drowned or who had died in such a way that they had to be buried rather than cremated. Food offerings were set out in honor of these images.

Sahagún continues:

> They . . . placed these images of the dead on . . . wreaths of grass, and then at dawn placed these images in their oratories, on beds of grass, rush, or reed; having placed them there they offered them food, tamales, and *mazamorra* [a dessert made of maize gruel and fruit], or stew made of fowl or dog meat, and later burned incense to them in a pottery incense burner like a big cup filled with coals . . . And the rich sang and drank pulque in honour of these gods and their dead: the poor can only offer them food.

It is tempting to interpret the dough figures as precursors of the special breads and sugar candies manufactured nowadays in the form of skulls and cadavers. The Aztec food offerings, too, seem like erstwhile gravesite ofrendas. Especially noteworthy in Sahagún's accounts, of course, is how the Aztecs incorporated anthropomorphically shaped food into their rituals, including some kinds of mortuary ritual.

However, before attributing the origin of contemporary Mexican sugar skulls, cadavers, and the like to the Aztecs, a cautionary note is in order. For one thing, Mexicans today make sculpted breads and candies specifically to be presented as gifts and offerings. During the Day of the Dead, candy images bear the names of particular living people to whom they are given as a playful token of affection. All these sweets are eventually consumed. Sahagún's Aztecs, by contrast, offered food to the amaranth figurines, which were treated as holy objects (although they were apparently eaten after ritual purposes had been served). Moreover, sculpted food images today do not delineate distinctions among the deceased according to how they died or the manner in which the body was disposed, as was the case before European contact. If any distinction is made at all—and certainly there is no salient one—it is based on age. Candy skulls presented nowadays to young children are sometimes called *muertitos* ("little dead people") in specific reference to the youth of the recipients, whereas those destined for adults are simply *muertos*, or "dead people".

But the problem of indigenous origins goes deeper than just the presence or absence of analogues. It extends to the nature of the source material itself. Sahagún and other Spanish chroniclers had as their main goal the conversion of indigenous peoples, not the preservation of accurate information about pre-conquest culture. As Louise Burkhart (1989:5) has stated, the contemporary historical reconstruction of the pre-conquest period often boils down to a "quest for the authentic Indian." She continues (ibid.), "The use of colonial sources to reconstruct pre-conquest culture is symptomatic of a general tendency within anthropology to place other cultures into an 'ethnographic present' in which they are described as static, self-perpetuating systems." Sahagún, like other 16th-century chroniclers, must be read for what he reveals about the contact situation during the period in which he lived and wrote. Burkhart wisely points out (ibid.:6–7):

> The Nahuas [i.e., Aztecs] reinterpreted their own culture and their own past in the light of new experiences and pressures; their own image of the "ancient Aztec" was in part a colonial artifact.
>
> In discussing their culture, the colonial Nahuas did not speak freely, for Europeans created the context within which the information was set down. They sought answers to particular questions, determining not only what matters would be recorded but the form the records would take. Investigators, especially those who were priests, tended to respond to what they learned about indigenous religion with shock or zeal, depending on their own values. Even if the Indians were encouraged to be honest, they soon understood what their interlocutors thought about some of their most cherished traditions.

Burkhart's cautionary analysis casts some doubt on the degree to which Aztec ceremonial practices are lineal ancestors of Day of the Dead customs today. Her caution would extend, of course, to the matter of how food was incorporated into religious ritual.

It is critical, when assessing any early colonial sources, to bear in mind that what we know of the ancient Aztecs is largely the product of information extracted from indigenous peoples under tumultuous circumstances and that, moreover, these circumstances were fraught with clear-cut power relations. The Chroniclers were representatives of Church and Crown, hence at the pinnacle of the colonial hierarchy. "Their ultimate goal," states Burkhart (ibid.:9), "was to silence indigenous voices, to resolve dialogue into monologue, to replace cultural diversity with conformity." With particular respect to Sahagún, it has been said (Klor de Alva et al., 1988:5) that, "his primary mission was to replace the 'mission of the devil' with Christianity." Even Klor de Alva (1988:46), who manifests utmost respect for Sahagún's ethnographic accomplishments, recognize that "the more details he gave, the more the text could be useful for eradicating idolatrous beliefs and practices." At the same time, given the number of instances of amaranth figurines reported by Sahagún, as well as the extreme detail of the reports, it would be difficult to deny their importance in Aztec religious ritual. It is entirely possible that the missionaries were anxious to eradicate the practice of manufacturing consumable amaranth idols. If so, the missionaries were largely unsuccessful, judging by the enormous popularity of eatable figurines in Mexico today. (And though they are not anthropomorphic in shape, amaranth seed candy, made with seeds and honey and known popularly as *alegría*, can be purchased nowadays at virtually every outdoor stand throughout the Republic.) All things considered, there can be no doubt that anthropomorphic foods were a significant part of pre-Columbian sacred tradition in the Valley of Mexico.

The conquest literature, too, indicates that foods in general were an integral part of Aztec mortuary ritual. Perhaps the most complete account comes from the Dominican friar, Diego Durán (1964:171–172), who arrived in New Spain from Seville as a five-year-old child in 1542. In 1581, he described the Aztec ritual honoring military officials who died in war:

> Four days after the ceremony had taken place, images of the dead were made from slivers of firewood, each one with feet, arms and head. Faces were placed upon them—eyes and mouth—and paper loincloths and mantles also. On their shoulders were put wings of hawk feathers, as it was believed that in this way they would fly before the Sun every day. The heads of these bundles were feathered and pendants for the ears, nose and lips were placed upon them. These statues were taken to a room called *tlacochcalco*. The widows then entered, and each one placed in front of her statue a dish of stew called *tlacatlacualli*, which means "food of human flesh," together with some maize cakes called *papalotlaxcalli*, which means "butterfly bread," and a little flour made of toasted maize dissolved in water as a drink. After this food had been offered, the drum began to sound again, and the singers began their hymns which told of mourning and tears . . . Each carried a gourd vessel of the white native wine [*pulque*] and placed it in front of each statue . . . In front of the statues were also placed flowers and tobacco and thick straws for

drinking . . . The chanters of the dead then took the gourds of wine in their hands and raised them twice, thrice, in front of the statues. After this they poured the wine in the four directions around the statue.

It is important to recognize the integral role of food and drink in Aztec mortuary ritual, although it is impossible to evaluate the extent to which these comestibles might be precursors of the Day of the Dead *ofrenda*. There is probably no funerary rite anywhere in which food does not play some role. The offerings that Durán describes for the Aztecs are certainly no closer in substance or function to that which occurs during the Day of the Dead than are food offerings in other times and places.

If we consider early reports of All Saints' and Souls' days in Mexico, there exists scattered evidence regarding food. Fray Toribio de Benavente [Motolonía] (1951:144–145) reported of 16th-century Tlaxcala that, "on the feast of All Souls in nearly all the Indian towns, many offerings are made for the dead. Some offer corn, others blankets, others food, bread, chickens; and in place of wine they offer chocolate." About a century later, Fray Francisco de Burgoa (1674:2) described daily life in and around Oaxaca, writing unappreciatively of "these Indian nations, in which drunkenness is so powerful, as are their gentile rites; in the funerals of their kin, friends, and family they make superstitious banquets . . . and drinks . . . for guests and singers, and this superstitious custom is so strong that the best Christians adapt to its use." Apparently, by the end of the 17th century, when Burgoa published his account, at least some Spaniards and Indians shared funerary customs in the Oaxaca Valley.

The first really detailed report of sculpted images in Mexico dates from the mid-18th century, by which time the Day of the Dead in the Valley of Mexico clearly had acquired its present-day flavor. The relevant testimony belongs to Francisco de Ajofrín (1958:87), a Capuchin friar:

> Before the Day of the Dead they sell a thousand figures of little sheep, lambs, etc. of sugar paste [*alfeñique*], which they call ofrenda, and it is a gift which must be given obligatorily to boys and girls of the houses where one has acquaintance. They also sell coffins, tombs, and a thousand figures of the dead, clerics, monks, nuns and all denominations, bishops, horsemen, for which there is a great market and a colorful fair in the portals of the merchants, where it is incredible [to see] the crowd of men and women from Mexico City on the evening before and on the day of All Saints.

Noteworthy in this account is the use of the words Day of the Dead in a Mexican context, as well as the implication that the figurines were used as toys, hence, that they were probably humorous or at least whimsically conceived objects, not unlike those in Mexico today. Ajofrín (ibid.) goes on to explain that the sugar figurines and other "cute little things" (*monerías*) are made in rapid succession by "clever" artisans who sell them cheaply. However, he warns the innocent consumer against advance payment, which would result, he says, in the receipt of second-class goods delivered late.

The references to corn, chickens, banquets, and the like that we encountered in the 16th-century and 17th-century literature also suggest possible continuity with Aztec customs. However, Ajofrín's 18th-century description resonates in every respect with contemporary Day of the Dead patterns. It is important to note that early colonial observers themselves made no claim for indigenous origins of the Day of the Dead. To them, All Saints' and Souls' days seemed to be of little note at all. It is, rather, later writers, mainly contemporary scholars and literati, who used scattered conquest sources to assert pre-Columbian origins. It is also essential to note that of all colonial writers, only Burgoa and Ajofrín actually mention All Saints' and All Souls' days. The remainder of the accounts describe either Aztec rituals that were very remote in virtually every respect from Roman Catholic ceremonies or post-conquest funerals, and different as well from a collective, annual commemorative event such as the Day of the Dead.

An examination of the colonial period in Spain and, indeed, throughout Europe reveals countless analogues to the food offerings in contemporary Mexico. Consider the Castilian province of Zamora, located in west-central Spain. From the 1500s, All Souls' Day celebrations required a catafalque, situated in the main chapel of any given church, surrounded by a variety of candles as well as by "twenty-five rolls of bread" (Lorenzo Pinar 1991:95). Historian Lorenzo Pinar (ibid.:165) states that in Zamora,

> ofrendas and banquets formed an habitual part of funerals. The ofrenda consti-tuted—according to those who treated of it—one more of the multiple efforts made on behalf of the souls in Purgatory, and the church insisted that [*ofrendas*] be installed on the days of Easter, during principal annual festivals, and during All Souls' Day."

In the town of Madridanos, again in the province of Zamora, it was stipulated that women "give offerings [*ofrenden*] in church for their parents, ancestors, and elders . . . that Food orders especially the days of Easter and principal fiestas, and in particular the Day of the Commemoration of the Souls" (quoted in ibid.:165).

Comparable evidence comes from the Basque country. An important docu-ment from 18th-century Guipúzcoa (Aguirre Soronda 1989:350) describes how funerals were conducted: "They carry out funeral services . . . with obligations of bread and wax, apart from . . . veal and lamb, and the customary ofrenda of all the women of the land." The document concludes with a moral commandment from San Tobias: "*Pon sobre la tumba del justo pan y vino*" [Put on the tomb of the just one, bread and wine]. We can assume that, at least at the level of Catholic religious orthodoxy, the bread and wine mentioned here represent the body and blood of Christ. The association between bread and death rituals persists in the Basque country to the present day. As recently as 1987, a Basque priest (quoted in ibid.:355–356) reported that for a full year after a death in the family, the relatives put on the tomb "candelabras with candles tied about with black ribbon, on top a black cloth and resting on the cloth a basket filled with bread." "Formerly on All Saints' Day," continues the priest, "the aggrieved family brought a [loaf of] bread to church, which was divided among the priest, sacristan, and altar boys."

Consider the vast northeast region of Catalonia as well. Curet (1953:288) writes that in 18th-century Barcelona, "on the afternoon of All Saints' Day and well into the night, the animation along the Ramblas and streets flowing into it was extraordinary." Food stands sold special seasonal sweets called *panellets dels morts* [little bread-like dead], and the people at large held chestnut roasts, a custom that I observed as recently as 1969 during All Saints' and All Souls' days in the central Spanish province of Avila. A document from the Barcelona silversmiths' guild dated October 15, 1671, stipulates that on All Souls' Day two *corteres* of *pa dels morts* [dead bread, in Catalan] be offered to the deceased. What is astounding about this document, aside from references to dead bread, is the use of the term *Diada dels Morts*, that is, Day of the Dead, to refer to All Souls' Day. This, to my knowledge, is the earliest use of the term. Equally relevant is Joan Amades's observation (1956:611) that in 18th-century Barcelona, during All Saints' Day, *panellets* and chestnuts "were combined and distributed in such a manner that they formed whimsical designs and figures." *Panellets* are still the All Saints' Day sweet of choice in Catalonia. For generations they were made of marzipan (sweetened almond or walnut paste) and covered outside with pine nuts. By the 1990s, candies using these ingredients were still available, although a version containing natural fruits (lemon, strawberry, pineapple, and the like) has also become popular. According to one Barcelona baker, the newer fruity sweets agree more than do the rich nuts of the past with contemporary preferences for "light cuisine."

Several revealing testaments from late medieval Mallorca conclusively document the convention of placing bread on tombs during All Souls' Day. In a will dated December 13, 1344, Jaime Corbera stated, "I wish and arrange . . . that my heirs should give each year, on the Day of the Deceased [*Día de Difuntos*] on my sepulcher, five *sueldos* of bread, candles, and other obligatory objects, in such manner as on this day is custom to do" (quoted in Gabriel Llompart 1965:96–97). A century later, this Mallorcan practice was still flourishing, as witnessed in another will, stating that "my . . . brother Pedro Juan be obligated for life on the Day of the Deceased [*día de difuntos*] each year to carry to the sepulcher of the Betnassers . . . a *cuévano* of bread worth 10 sueldos, as well as a tall candle [*cirio*] to burn while the holy office is celebrated, as is customary" (ibid.:96).

Throughout the late Middle Ages and early modern period, bread was not only placed on tombs during All Souls' Day but also was distributed to the poor and crippled. In present-day Mallorca, confectioners sell small circular cookies on All Saints' and All Souls' days, which, in Mallorcan, are called *panetets de mort* ("little dead breads"). Gabriel Llabrés Quintana (1925) believes that *panetets*, small sweet breads that were strung like rosary beads as a seasonal gift to children, were originally the large round breads annually given to the poor on this occasion. As recently as the 1920s, sweet rosaries were still being produced, although the beads were by that time fashioned, not out of pastry dough, but rather out of candied egg yolk or marzipan.

There is thus an abundance of evidence from the Middle Ages to the present of offerings of breads and sweets on All Saints' and All Souls' days. The evidence, moreover, derives from diverse parts of the Iberian Peninsula. Food, candles, and flowers seem for centuries to have been essential ingredients in funerary ritual and All Saints' and All Souls' days celebrations. Among foods, bread is the earliest and most widely reported offering. However, even in the case of sweets not based on wheat dough, the vernacular name of the sweet tends to derive from the word for bread: *pa* in Catalan and Mallorcan, *pan* in Castilian. Hence, *penellet* and *panetet* both mean approximately "little bread-like substance." The earliest references, scant but highly significant, specify the custom of carrying bread to the very tombs. From the early modern period on, bread offerings occur in many forms and on diverse occasions throughout the year but principally as a means of aid to clergy and the poor.

In addition to *panellets* and *panetets*, there are nowadays plenty of European analogues to the Mexican sweets offered during the Day of the Dead. The clearest case of all is the presence of so-called *huesos de santo* ("saint's bones"), the single most characteristic Spanish sweet sold during the season of All Saints' and All Souls' days (see Plate 2.1). The central Spanish provinces of Burgos and Avila are particularly well known for *huesos de santo*, although they are found in cities and towns throughout the country. At Foix de Sarriá, one of the most elegant and traditional pastry shops in Barcelona, *ossos de sant*, the Catalan version of *huesos de santo*, are still sold during the end of October and beginning of November. *Huesos de santo* are little cylinders of marzipan, perhaps two inches long. They are filled inside with *marrón glasé*, or crushed chestnuts and sugar and are often sold in varying flavors. Generally, they are glazed with a sugar coating. *Panets de mort* are produced in Mallorca during the same time of year. Enrique Casas Gaspar (1947:362), one of Spain's most encyclopedic folklorists of the postwar period, claims that the *panets de mort* displayed on All Souls' Day in Palma de Mallorca "symbolize the embalmed cadaver." However, these candies, rather than being iconographic, bear only an abstract resemblance to dead bodies.

Sweets of an unambiguously anthropomorphic character, such as those produced in Mexico around the time of the Day of the Dead, are not characteristic of

Spain during All Saints' and All Souls' days. However, this does not mean that they have not been produced at all. Violant y Simmora (1956) presents evidence that little loaves of bread in human and animal form were made especially for children throughout Catalonia at the beginning of the 20th century. Every week or two, when mothers prepared dough for the family bread, they molded small images of nuns or Gypsy women to amuse their children. In Galicia, located in the extreme northwest of the Iberian Peninsula (Epton 1968:186), "the crude figures of a man, a woman and a serpent are sold among other universal symbols." Anthropomorphic designs in food presentation, though not necessarily specific to All Saints' and All Souls' days, exist throughout the Iberian Peninsula. This situation is apparently not universal. I have been told that in France, it is unthinkable to eat an identifiable human form; to some peoples, the practice of eating anthropomorphic dough figures has sadistic, even cannibalistic overtones.

And yet, throughout Europe, France included, sweets are common during All Saints' and All Souls' days. The great folklorist Arnold Van Gennep (1953:2808– 2818) reports, for example, that in the region of Haute-Saône, young boys and girls jointly bake cakes out of nuts and apples during this holiday. There are at least half a dozen Portuguese pastries and candies designed for All Saints' and All Souls' days as well. These include the Azorean specialty, *maminhas do preto* ("little dark breasts"; Adelina Axelrod, personal communication). Italy produces a variety of regional sweets for the occasion. Consider the island of Sardinia, where "they make *papassinos*, which are compounded of bruised almonds, nuts, and walnuts, mixed with sugar and grape-juice into a kind of stiff paste or pudding" (Vansittart 1990:327). On Sardinia, too, on All Souls' eve, church sacristans, "having armed themselves with bells and baskets, go from door to door in their respective parishes, begging for *su mortu, su mortu*, and dried fruit, almonds, papassinos, and bread, are put in their baskets" (ibid.). Think of the way that children in the United States go begging on All Hallows Eve, or, of even greater significance, the way that Mexican children today commonly solicit candies and breads from one another by asking in a jocular tone for *mi muerto, mi muertito*.

The presence of such clear European analogs casts doubt on pre-conquest roots to the Day of the Dead in Mexico. So, too, does the presence of Mexican-style celebrations in other parts of Latin America, most notably the Andean region, which was conquered very shortly after Mexico. There exist several publications that indicate how All Saints' and All Souls' days are celebrated by the Bolivian Aymara. Hans Buechler's description (1980:80–81) is detailed and apt:

> First they shape an arch out of two sugar canes . . . over a table . . . and place two candles on either side; then they heap the table with bananas, oranges, bread, agricultural produce, and quinoa of *k'espiña* dough figures and sometimes milk, alcohol, and coca. The bread and *k'espiña* are prepared specially for the occasion.

A few families in the community own ovens used on All Saints. Each family forms some dough into wreaths (to represent flower wreaths), ladders (for souls to climb out of purgatory), and men and babies (symbolizing respectfully the world of old persons and of infants) and animals (standing for the deceased's herd). The bread figures are then baked in the available ovens. Some families also bake bread for sale on this occasion. Returned migrants . . . prepare *k'espiña* figures. First they grind the roasted quinoa and mix it with lime, water, and a little lard to make a dough. Then they shape the dough into the form of llamas to carry the food offerings to the land of the dead . . . dogs to herd the llamas; eagles; etc. Finally they steam the figures and place them on the "altar."

Joseph Bastien's (1978:171–187) description of what his respondents call "The Feast with the Dead"—the Aymara All Souls' Day—provides a variation of Buechler's account. Bastien's respondents set up home altars, which, in the course of the holiday, are moved from home to the gravesites of deceased relatives. The altars are decorated with *chicha* (maize beer), flowers, fruit, coca, potatoes, candy, oranges, and an item called "bread babies."

To judge from Bastien's photograph, bread babies are beautifully sculpted figurines made of wheat dough (ibid.:183–187). Each is about a foot and a half long and portrays a hooded infant wrapped snuggly in a blanket. The bread babies undergo a mock baptism, after which they are set on an altar. Subsequently they are broken into pieces by an officiating officer who says, "This is the death of these babies, eat their bodies!" Each "baby's" parents, godparents, and other members of the community then consume pieces of the dough body. Clearly, from both Buechler and Bastien's renderings, anthropomorphic food offerings are an essential part of All Souls' Day ritual for the Aymara. So are other foods similar to those employed in Mexico, such as oranges, bananas, beer, and eatable animal figures.

If we turn north of Mesoamerica to the pueblos of New Mexico, there exists convincing evidence of parallels with Mexico and Bolivia. In an early 20th-century account, Elsie Clews Parsons (1917:495–496) reported that on All Souls' Day groups of young Zuñi boys go from house to house, crying out, "*Tsale'mo, tsale'mo.*" At each threshold, they made the sign of the cross and received presents of food—usually bread or meat—from the residents. According to Parsons, too, at Acoma pueblo, which is more observant of Roman Catholicism than is Zuñi, food was taken to the cemetery and placed around the foot of the cross marking each grave. In the pueblo of Laguna, November 2 was called *shuma sashti* ("skeleton day"). Laguna offerings included "the fattest sheep and the best pumpkins and melons" (ibid.:496). Parsons (ibid.), states "On *shuma sashti*, candles are set out on the graves. A little ball made up of a bit of everything served to eat is also put on the fire." The boys who beg for food call out, "*Sare'mo, sare'mo!*" (ibid.). Parsons reports that people of the pueblos themselves could not explain the meaning of the terms used by the young boys on their village rounds.

Superficially, the words seem like nonsense versions of the Anglo-American "trick-or-treat." And yet, folklorist Aurelio Espinosa (1918:550–552) suggests that *tsale'mo* and *sare'mo* are both derived from the Spanish *oremos* (let us pray).

During All Saints' and All Souls' days in Spain, as well, young boys make the village rounds, begging from house to house for food. They also engage in bell-ringing and other noisemaking. In 1969, I observed these practices in the small village of Becedas in west central Spain (Brandes 1975:135). The same practices exist and have long existed in Mexico, too. In Tzintzuntzan, young boys still go from house to house on All Souls' eve to collect donations of food and drink. They then carry these contributions to the churchyard, prepare them over an open fire, and spend the night there in feasting (Brandes 1988:88–109). As for Bolivia, Bastien reports that on All Souls' morning, in the Aymara community he studied, "About forty . . . ritualists were making the rounds, praying for the dead. They carried large sacks filled with bread and fruit. Those who prayed were given beautiful bread figurines, oranges, and bananas." This custom is nearly identical to what occurs nowadays in Tzintzuntzan, where on All Souls' eve, a brotherhood of villagers goes round the graveyard, praying over the tombs and asking for donations of food in return (ibid.). It is also a reminder of our sources from early modern Europe in which distribution of food to the needy was an integral part of All Saints' and All Souls' Day ritual.

The evidence speaks for itself. Throughout southern Europe and Latin America—particularly the parts of Latin America such as Mexico, the Andes, and the American Southwest, which were all settled around the time of the Spanish conquest—special food displays are an important part of All Saints' and All Souls' days proceedings. So is the ritualized distribution of food, whether by begging or other means. The particular foods that are placed on altars or distributed through-out the populace depend largely on local conditions. Hence, *chicha* (maize beer) is the preferred beverage in Bolivia, while it is pulque in Mexico. With such widespread distribution of ceremonial practices all being carried out on a single Roman Catholic holiday and with all of them analagous to what we know of Europe before and during the conquest, it would be hard to deny that the Mexican Day of the Dead does have a prominent, though not exclusive, Spanish origin.

Can we identify anything unique about food offerings in Mexico? Based on comparative historical and ethnographic evidence, it appears that in Mexico, and perhaps only in Mexico, does there exist an elaborate, widespread, and world-famous array of molded sugar and sweet breads on the Day of the Dead. As far as I can tell, Mexico is also the only country in which sugar is the principal substance out of which Day of the Dead figurines are sculpted, rather than being made of sugar, flour, and nuts (see Figure 2.2). In its proliferation and ever-increasing variety of sugar skulls, animals, cadavers, caskets, and the like, Mexico stands alone. At least one key source—Ajofrín—indicates that this

Fig. 2.2 Sales booth with chocolate and sugar skulls, Toluca, October 30, 2000

tradition existed in the mid-18th century. We do not know how widespread its distribution was at that time. Nowadays, of course, the tradition has spread throughout the Mexican Republic and northward to the United States, where it has become a marker of Chicano identity and artistic creativity (see Chapter 8).

The existence of sugar cane figurines in the colonial era brings up the undeniable connection between sugar and colonialism. Sidney Mintz's ground-breaking research on this topic conclusively demonstrates that, from the 16th century onward, the taste for sugar-cane based sucrose increased rapidly. Food preferences were changing simultaneously with the rise of European military might and economic power. "What the metropolises produced, the colonies consumed," says Mintz (1985:xxv). In fact, although it did not become part of the European workers' diet until the 19th century, sugar was already widely consumed by Indians throughout the 16th century. A study of *pulperías* (small grocery stores) in 18th-century Mexico City shows that sugar by that time had become a regular stock item (Kinsbruner 1987:2–3). "The desire for sweet substances spread and increased steadily" throughout the colonial era, continues Mintz; many different products were employed to satisfy it" (Mintz 1985:25). Included among these products, we may surmise, were sugar figurines produced for ritual occasions. Mintz points to marzipan as one of the earliest and most visible products of the revolution in culinary taste that took place during the colonial era, claiming that "it was possible to sculpture an object out of this sweet preservable 'clay' on nearly any scale and in nearly any form" (ibid.:88). Indeed, in Spain's first published cookbook, dated 1778, Francisco Martínez Montiño listed no fewer than eight recipes for molded marzipan. What Europeans, including Spaniards, fabricated out of marzipan, the Mexicans created with sugar itself.

If the connection between sugar and colonialism is indisputable, the relation between colonialism and death is even more so. In the first century after European contact, numerous major and minor epidemics afflicted the indigenous people of the Valley of Mexico and their neighbors. The first major epidemic, a virulent attack of smallpox, came to Mexico from the island of Hispaniola and decimated the Aztec capital of Tenochtitlán. It is generally agreed that this decisive event favored the Spanish Conquest (McNeill 1976:183–184). Subsequent severe and widespread disease occurred in the years 1545–48, 1576–81, and 1736–39. As Charles Gibson (1964:136–137) points out, many lesser epidemics caused traumatic destruction in limited parts of Mesoamerica as well. Throughout the 16th century and the early 17th century, large-scale depopulation occurred both during and between epidemics. Although it is uncertain which pathogens were responsible for the three major epidemics, the most likely candidates are smallpox, measles, typhus, and typhoid (ibid.). Spanish methods of treatment, based largely on bloodletting, only served to exacerbate the effects of disease. In the plague of 1576, for example, the viceroy distributed medical instructions to all affected towns; the principal method was prompt bleeding. The same remedy applied during an epidemic that occurred in 1659 (ibid.:499).

Estimates of population decline are by no means definitive. The most conservative figures put the decline at 22 percent, while others go as high as 80 or even 95 percent (Lomnitz 2005:68). Sherbourne Cook and Woodrow Borah's figures, though among the most radical, are also among the most widely cited. Based on their exhaustive research into the source of royal revenues, they calculate that from 1519 to 1532, the population of central Mexico shrank from 25.2 million to 16.8 million (Cook and Borah 1979:1). In 1548, the population stood at about 6.3 million and in 1605 at 1.075 million. By the 1620s, only about 730,000 Indians remained (ibid.:100). According to Gibson's (1964:136) summary of colonial sources, "excessive labor requirements, excessive tributes, mistreatment, drunkenness, the Indians' *flaca complexión* ["weak constitution"], starvation, flood, drought, disease, and divine providence were all mentioned . . . as causes." John Super (1988:52) refers to this loss as "a demographic catastrophe perhaps unequalled in the history of the world." Claudio Lomnitz (2005:68) calls it "a veritable holocaust for the native population."

Spanish observers of the era were understandably concerned about the decimation of the populace, although, as Lomnitz (ibid.:67) puts it, "most of them were eager to paper over the immensity of the disaster they wrought." From the vantage point of a 16th or 17th-century observer, however, the full extent and impact of this massive loss of life could not have been recognized. The one early chronicler who faced up to the severe demographic catastrophe was

Fray Bartolomé de las Casas. In *The Devastation of the Indies*, first published in Seville in 1552, Casas (1992:58) wrote:

> Thus, from the beginning of their discovery of New Spain, that is to say, from the eighteenth of April in the year one thousand five hundred and eighteen until the year thirty, a period of twelve whole years, there were continual massacres and outrages committed by the bloody hands and swords of Spaniards against the Indians living on the four hundred and fifty leagues of land surrounding the city of Mexico, which comprised four or five great kingdoms as large as and more felicitous than Spain. Those lands were all more densely populated than Toledo or Seville and Valladolid and Zaragoza all combined, along with Barcelona. Never has there been such a population as in these cities which God saw fit to place in that vast expanse of land having a circumference of more than a thousand leagues. The Spaniards have killed more Indians here in twelve years by the sword, by fire, and enslavement than anywhere else in the Indies. They have killed young and old, men, women, and children, some four million souls during what they call the Conquests . . . And this does not take into account those Indians who have died from ill treatment, or were killed under tyrannical servitude. Whether through warfare, debilitation, or disease, the enormous destruction of life suffered by the Indians of sixteenth-century Mexico is incomprehensible to the human mind or, if comprehended, immediately repressed as a defense against deep, paralyzing agony and sorrow.

Under the circumstances, it seems realistic to posit that the Day of the Dead became ritualistically elaborate in Mexico as a consequence of the enormous loss of life during the 16th and the 17th centuries. Not only did people die in staggering numbers in this period, but also they were also uprooted and forcibly resettled in unfamiliar territory. For taxation purposes and to assure civil obedience, people were herded into hundreds of new grid-plan towns (Foster 1960:34–49). The anguish that these changes must have wrought is incalculable.

Sugar, death, and the irreversible destruction of a civilization—no, of many distinct civilizations—were among the clear outcomes of the Spanish colonial regime. As for the connection between sugar and death, a connection flamboyantly displayed during Mexico's Day of the Dead, causation is less easily established. We may gain some insight by looking briefly at sugar, colonialism, and death elsewhere in the Americas during the colonial era. The sugar cane-rich islands of the West Indies are one obvious point of comparison. Certainly, Hispañola, Cuba, and even the English-speaking islands were much the same as Mexico in that they suffered serious population decline. But in their case the decline was so serious that it meant virtual obliteration of the native population. As in the case of Mexico, population figures are inexact and continually under revision. European diseases bore most of the responsibility for the demographic catastrophe in the Caribbean region. However, "massacres and other brutalities on the part of the conquistadores . . . food shortages, overwork, worry, grief, suicide, infanticide, and flight (Fagg 1965:2) were contributing factors. Cook and Borah (1971, vol. 1:376–410) estimate the original population of Hispañola to have declined from nearly four million in 1496 to some 125 souls in 1570. Taking Cuba and Hispañola together, John Fagg (1965:3) states that, "within two generations after Columbus's first voyage to the islands, scarcely any Indians were left."

For several centuries after that, according to Fagg (ibid.), "both islands languished." The Spaniards introduced sugarcane production to the islands in the 16th century and imported African slave labor to work the fields (Mintz 1985:32–33). But, for the most part, these islands were long ignored by the Crown. They were "underpopulated and poorly developed" (ibid.), mainly used as stepping-stones for the colonization and development of richer population centers on the American mainland. To be sure, by the end of the 18th century the West Indian islands were, together with cane-producing northeast Brazil, among the richest agricultural lands in the Amercas. But the slave population that drove the economy, in the Portuguese (Scheper-Hughes 1992:31–64) and Spanish Caribbean (Florescano 1975) alike, was overworked, underfed, and downtrodden. In the words of Richard Dunn (1972:224), "Slavery in one form or another is the essence of West Indian history." The care that Church and Crown took to nurture the Indian population of Mesoamerica in a European style of life and religion was far from replicated in the Indies.

Sugar, colonialism and death were all present in the Caribbean. But, during the colonial period at least, an essential ingredient present in Mesoamerica—concern for the salvation of souls and the militant propagation of Roman Catholicism— was missing in this region. The West Indies existed for the single purpose of economic exploitation. Like Northeast Brazil (Scheper-Hughes 1992:31–64), the West Indies conformed to Wolf and Mintz's (1977:39) model of plantation economies in which "the plantation produces for a mass market. It subordinates all other considerations to the desire to meet the demands of this market." With virtually no disposable income among the slave population, and given the single-minded exploitation of slave labor, sweet bread and sugar candy would hardly have gained a foothold in such societies.

Although sugar, colonialism, and death were also present in colonial Peru, we find nothing there comparable to the elaboration of sweets related to the Day of the Dead in Mexico. In Peru, to be sure, there existed the kind of energetic imposition of Catholicism that characterized New Spain as well as a severe (if not quite as severe) population decline. Burga (1976:56–58) estimates that between 1525 and 1571 the population of Peru declined by some 75 percent. Despite striking parallels with Mesoamerica, we may hypothesize, however, that in Peru it was the character and distribution of sugar plantations that made sugar and sweets less prominent than in the viceroyalty to the north. In the Conquest period and for some time thereafter, the Peruvian population was concentrated high in the Andes. The Spaniards established haciendas in the area around Cuzco, for example (Mörner 1975:360–365), but these estates specialized in the production of cattle, sheep, coca, and European cereals and fruits rather than sugar, for which the high altitude was clearly unsuited. Initially, sugar production became economically important on the north coast (Gonzales 1985) as well as in the area around Lima (Mancera 1974:xiii). However, these regions were, as Mancera puts it, marginalized (*arrinconada*) during the colonial era (ibid.:xi–xii). "The development of these plantations was, even by the end of the 18th century, very much less than that of other American lands. By that time its sugar production . . . was very much less than . . . Brazil had attained two centuries before and five times less than that of Cuba" (ibid.). The marginal role of sugar in colonial Peru was exacerbated by two disastrous floods on the north coast, in 1720 and 1728. The floods proved to be calamaties "from which growers never completely recovered" (Gonzales 1985:18). In examining the relatively minor role that sugar played in colonial Peru, we must also consider the fact that sugar was a plantation, rather than an hacienda-type, crop, to use Wolf and Mintz's (1977) terms. Sugarcane estates were worked almost exclusively by imported black slave labor. "Since the stated purpose of the conquest had been to convert the natives to Christianity, not to exterminate them," African slaves were generally exploited in their place: "This was one of the few domains where Indians were actually spared" (Gonzales 1985:14). The plantations, unsuccessful as they were, oriented themselves insofar as possible toward the external economy. Overall, the marginal economic role of sugarcane in colonial Peru was not conducive to bringing sugar to the culinary prominence that it attained in Mexico.

In Mexico, to be sure, black slaves were an important, often prevalent, presence on sugarcane haciendas (Martin 1985:199); but free labor did exist in Mexico, unlike the exclusive use of slaves in Brazil—a most significant point of contrast that Barrett and Schwartz (1975:571) discerned in assessing the differences between the sugarcane economies of Morelos, Mexico and Bahia, Brazil. These authors (ibid.:558) claimed that they discovered "at least one case in Morelos of a small sugar plantation (*ingenio*) [that of Santa Rosa Cocoyotla] which functioned during the 18th century with few or no slaves; in Bahia not a single such case is known."

Further, sugarcane production in Mexico, unlike Peru, was concentrated in areas of relatively dense colonial population such as Morelos (Martin 1985), Oaxaca (Taylor 1976) and Michoacán (Huerta 1993). In Oaxaca, sugarcane was planted in virtually every part of the Valley (Taylor 1976:78). Ward Barrett's work (1976, 1977) in Morelos demonstrates that sugarcane remained a prominent crop in that area throughout the colonial period, and, moreover, that sugarcane haciendas "developed within a setting of previously established indigenous towns with their own claims to land and necessary water, a very different case from the Greater Antilles, where the aboriginal population had not survived and the land was more or less empty" (Barrett 1976:171). The Morelos sugar estates were populated by "groups of people organized in urban ways" (ibid.). Further, the sugar produced in Morelos, situated close as it was to the capital, furnished this product to Tenochtitlán-Mexico City, the heart of Mexican society and economy.

Cheryl Martin emphasizes the economic link between Mexico City and sugarcane growers and merchants in Morelos. Equally significant is her observation that "for most of the colonial period Mexican production was oriented toward domestic consumption, with sugar-producing enclaves, each tied to a specific city or mining region, scattered throughout New Spain and New Galicia" (Martin 1985:7). Despite the fact that sugarcane production never attained the importance in Mexico on the world market that it did in Brazil (see, e.g., Furtado 1977) or the Caribbean—in the Valley of Oaxaca, for example, it achieved only "modest results" (Taylor 1976) due to the temperate climate—it was prominent locally in areas of dense population and political and economic centralization. This combination of factors probably accorded sugar a culinary role in Mexico that it lacked elsewhere.

And, unlike the Caribbean, sugar became important here in an area of intense religious concentration and activity, where ritual and belief were critical instruments of social and economic control. In fact, Martin (1985:38) underscores the financial involvement of convents and monasteries in the sugar industry. The greater part of loans to the expanding sugarcane haciendas in Morelos came from religious institutions such as these. Eventually, because of default on loans, "leading ecclesiastical institutions in Mexico City acquired sizable perpetual liens on most of the region's haciendas" (ibid.). In such a religious and economic climate, together with the spatial and demographic characteristics that prevailed in central Mexico, it is reasonable to conclude that sugar should play a large role in popular Catholic ritual and ceremony. Indeed, convents have always been and continue to be producers of valued sweets in Mexico, but apparently never more so than during the colonial regime.

If we accept these arguments to explain why sugar should be more prominent in Mexico than elsewhere during All Saints' and All Souls' days, the connection between sweets and death must still be addressed. Although speculative, we cannot avoid confronting symbolic insights when considering this matter. Imagine a visit to a Mexican market around the end of October. We encounter a multitude of wooden tables upon which rest hundreds of colorfully decorated sugar caskets, no two exactly alike. In each casket lies a little cadaver made of sugar, which can be resurrected and made to sit up at the pull of a string. Later the casket and cadaver are consumed, the sugar and colored icing—along with the death that they represent—melting in the consumer's mouth. Can there be a clearer image of the denial of death or, to put it another way, of the affirmation of life? Is there a more concrete way of acting out a fantasy that the processes of death could be reversed or made to disappear altogether?

Of course, the consumption of dead bread, or any bread for that matter, is itself an act that is certain to stave off death, not only symbolically but also biologically. One of the oldest and most widespread Spanish sayings (Arora 1980), *El muerto al hoyo y el vivo al bollo* [To the grave with the dead and bread to the living], assumes particular relevance in this context. Or consider the very chemistry of food offerings. Bread dough rises, an inherent assertion of vitality. Sugar provides a quick rush of energy and is, in essence, "energy in concentrated form" (Poleszynski 1982:8). In fact, sucrose is as rich in energy as protein, a more or less pure source of energy in that it causes no associated bodily "pollution," given that, as Beidler points out (1975:14), "Sucrose is broken down into carbon dioxide and water, both easily eliminated. Moreover, there is some indication that sugar, when combined with fat (in sweet breads, for example), is a source of oral pleasure." Cantor and Cantor (1977:441–442) speculate that combining fats and sugar results in "numerous pleasant associations that relate to early life experiences as well as to continuing experiences that may reinforce the pleasures. The proper combination of fat and sugar that produces the taste of richness is not only enhanced by associated richnesses sensed differently but also revives infantile pleasure of suckling. Textual enjoyment must also have important sexual associations." There is every indication, then, that the chemistry of both bread and sugar—the two most distinctive and prevalent Day of the Dead food substances—inspires a negation of death.

To the question of European versus indigenous origins, there can be no simple resolution until more extensive colonial sources come to light. For now, evidence indicates that the Mexican Day of the Dead is a colonial invention, a unique product of colonial demographic and economic processes. The principal types and uses of food on this holiday definitely derive from Europe. After all, there is no *tortilla de muertos* but rather *pan de muertos*, just one highly significant detail. Nor did cane sugar exist in the Americas prior to the Spanish conquest. The existence of special breads and sugar-based sweets, the custom of placing these and other food substances on gravesites and altars, and the practice of begging and other distributive mechanisms all derive from Spain. At the same time, the particular anthropomorphic form that Day of the Dead sweets assume is part of both Spanish and Aztec traditions. This combination of Spanish and indigenous culinary habits and tastes no doubt culminated in the *ofrenda* patterns we observe today.

The *ofrenda* itself is probably Spanish, although it has long assumed significance in Mexico that far outstrips that in the mother country. One measure of the relative insignificance of All Saints' and All Souls' days in Spain, even as long ago as the 18th century, comes from news bulletins relaying information from Spain to Mexico about the catastrophic earthquake that shook the Iberian Peninsula in 1775. This is the earthquake that flattened Lisbon. It cost many lives and wreaked terrible damage there and in other cities throughout the south of the Peninsula. This tragedy occurred on November 1, All Saints' Day. And yet, reports coming from the Andalusian cities of Granada, Córdoba, Sevilla, Ayamonte, and Huelva (Anonymous 1756) completely ignore even the merest mention of All Saints' and All Souls' days. Only the report from the province of Jaén even mentions All Saints' Day by name, and then simply as a calendrical marker ("*El día de todos los Santos, experimentamos aquí, a las 10 menos quarto de la mañana, un formidable Terremoto*"; ibid.). The bulletins did, in fact, attribute some religious significance to the event. Miraculous occurrences were reported in Jaén, and in Sevilla the earthquake was explained as divine retribution for profligate living. In no case, however, were All Saints' and All Souls' days linked causally or even metaphorically to the earthquake.

There is evidence, in fact, that the Spaniards tried to eradicate, or at least tone down, the popular celebration of this holiday during the colonial era. Historian Juan Pedro Viqueira (1984) believes that, together with Carnival, the Day of the Dead presented a threat to civil authorities, and that, at least during the 18th century and beginning of the 19th century, both of these ritual occasions were suppressed to varying degrees:

> The nocturnal visit which village men, women, and children made to the cemeteries, the festivities and drunkenness that took place there, could only scandalize and above all horrify the illustrious elites, who looked to expel death from social life. This fiesta, which drew boundaries between the living and the dead and partially inverted their roles, showed up the presence of death in the midst of life in an era in which the elite of New Spain . . . tried to forget its existence (Viqueira 1984:13).

It is not surprising, continues Viqueira, that in October 1766 the Royal Criminal Chamber (Real Sala de Crimen) prohibited attendance at cemeteries and also imposed a prohibition on the sale of alcoholic beverages after nine in the evening (ibid.). To the Spanish colonist, death and the celebration thereof apparently were dangerous precursors of civil disorder. Viqueira demonstrates, then, that the Day of the Dead, with its culinary, iconographic, and other flamboyant symbols of death, became a form of resistance against official ideology and social practices.

At the same time, it is also clear that the festival of All Saints' and All Souls' days in Mexico more than survived throughout the colonial era. It was during that time, in fact, that it acquired the distinctive cultural cast that it bears still today. Is it any wonder that this fundamentally Spanish Catholic ritual, which is really a vast collective mortuary rite, should have developed a unique flavor during the colonial period? The devastating impact of death and suffering during the 16th and 17th centuries was enough to assure this outcome. The acute suffering, too, can explain why the Day of the Dead is basically European, rather than indigenous, in origin. Just listen to the words of Motolonía, one of the original

12 Franciscans—the so-called apostles—sent by Spain to carry out missionary work in Mexico in the 1540s (Benavente 1951): "All the feasts with the ceremonies and solemnities which the Indians observed . . . ceased to be held when the Spaniards began waging war. The reason is that the Indians were so absorbed by their afflictions that they forgot their gods and even themselves. They had such hardships to bear."

3

SKULLS AND SKELETONS

Hayden Herrera's biography (1983) of Mexican painter Frida Kahlo, shows a photograph of the artist lying in her sick bed, looking straight into the camera and holding in both hands a colorfully decorated sugar skull with her name scrolled on the forehead. Although the photograph bears no date, it was probably shot around November 1 and 2, when Mexican shops and street stalls are filled, as one traveler put it (quoted in Haberstein and Lamers 1963:587), with "gleaming gay skulls, sugary-white and with splendid gold trimmings." It is common at this time of year for sugar skulls, or *calaveras*, with people's names written on them to be sold in stores and on street corners. A similar product is made out of chocolate as well. People present these candy skulls to friends or relatives, just as they do written verses, also known as *calaveras* (see Chapter 5) and cast in the form of short, satirical epitaphs.

Representations of full-body skeletons are also common at this time of year. Perhaps the most prevalent skeletal form is the soft, spongy, shapeless kind fashioned out of bread dough and known as *pan de muerto*, or, humorously in American English, as "dead bread" (see Chapter 1). In Tlaxcala, for example, bakers produce a wide range of such breads, many of which "are representations of human males and females" (Nutini 1988:170–171). But there also exists throughout the Republic an enormous variety of skeleton toys of all sizes and materials, with the skeleton displayed as naked or clothed, holding a recognizable object such as a pipe or musical instrument, and usually showing some indication of age, gender, occupation, and the like. During the end of October and the beginning of November, too, the newspapers publish images of political or other well-known personalities, anatomically drawn as skeletons but draped with the recognizable trappings of their office. The skeleton figures might also be grouped into little scenes taken from everyday life, installed in tiny painted boxes like dioramas; or they might assume the form of a party of funeral-goers, bus-riders or mariachi musicians.

Fig. 3.1   Ceramic toy casket, Jalisco, October 2000

Other than skulls and skeletons, the most common death-related toys are small caskets, usually made out of chocolate, sugar, or ceramics, and sometimes painted or decorated with multicolored icing (see Figure 3.1). Like the skulls, these caskets might or might not contain an individual's name inscribed in sugar icing. A popular type of casket has a little plastic window at the top through which you can view a little sugar cadaver, set prone at the base. When a string is pulled, the cadaver tilts upward at the waist, as if resuscitating (see Chapter 1).

Probably more than any other single element, it is the prevalence of skulls and skeletons and caskets of all types that has made the Mexican Day of the Dead famous throughout the Western world. The ornamentation on these figurines and funerary objects is almost always colorful; it is occasionally detailed and aesthetically impressive as well. Far from evoking feelings of morbidity, the Day of the Dead toys and candies are filled with charm and humor. Like other Mexican artisan crafts—for that is what in essence they are—Day of the Dead figurines have awakened interest in this holiday abroad and, through this interest, stimulated tourism. Among foreigners, they invariably appeal to the collectors' instinct. They are sold in cities throughout the United States as if to provide evidence that Mexicans really are different from mainstream Americans.

The plethora of skull and skeleton motifs in Day of the Dead folk art has also influenced perceptions of the typical Mexican view of death. These toys and candies seem to reflect a peculiarly Mexican view of death—an "acceptance of death," as Patricia Fernández-Kelly (1974:535) puts it. Fernández-Kelly sums up the meaning of Day of the Dead folk crafts by stating, "These complex and diversified folkloric traditions—the poetry and songs, the masks and sculpture—inevitably suggest the enormous tenacity and wisdom of a people and a culture whose oppressed situation has not been an obstacle for the expression of a unique and creative philosophy of life and death." For Paul Westheim (1983:9), too, the ubiquitous presence of skulls, skeletons, and the like constitutes a supreme manifestation of the enormous difference between Mexican and Western attitudes toward death. Describing the reaction in Paris during the early 1950s to an exhibit of Mexican art, he says:

> The skull as an artistic motif, a popular fantasy that for millenia has found pleasure in the representation of death . . . this was a tremendous surprise and almost traumatic for visitors to the Exposition of Mexican Art in Paris. They stopped in front of the statue of Coatlicue, goddess of the earth and of death, who wears the mask of death; they contemplated the skull of rock crystal—one of the hardest minerals—carved by an Aztec artist, during innumerable hours of work, with an impressive mastery over his craft; they looked at the engravings of the popular artists, Manilla and Posada, who resorted to skeletons in order to comment on the social and political events of their times. They found out that in Mexico there are parents who on the second of November give their children presents of sugar and chocolate skulls on which are written the children's names in sugar letters, and that these children eat the macabre sweet, as if it were the most natural thing in the world. The popular art, made of very simple materials like cloth, wood, clay, and even chicle, dolls in the form of skeletons . . . common toys loved by the people.

Mexicans, in their popular arts, display an undeniable fascination with skulls, skeletons, and other representations of death, items that elsewhere might cause a sensation of unpleasantness or even dread.

This chapter paints a large canvas, extending from pre-conquest Mexico, through the colonial period and forward to the national and post-revolutionary phase of Mexican history, to explore the nature and origin of death imagery as related to the Day of the Dead. In my reading of the Day of the Dead literature, much of the meaning of skull and skeleton imagery to Mexicans and foreigners alike lies precisely in its presumed uniqueness, a uniqueness which Fernández Kelley and others take to signify a kind of folk wisdom and collective recognition of humanity's inevitable fate. I wish first to ask just how singular these toys and candies really are; then to explore their similarities and differences with related phenomena in ancient Mesoamerica and early modern Europe; and finally to speculate as to why they have assumed such prominence in Mexican art and popular culture.

The literature on death in Mexico, and the Day of the Dead in particular, invariably incorporates a cultural continuity model to explain religious beliefs, practices, and iconography. Consider, for example, Patricia Fernández-Kelly's article "Death in Mexican Folk Culture" (1974), which is structured almost paradigmatically. She begins by talking about the centrality of death to humanity in general and to Mexicans in particular. She proceeds to a lengthy examination of death-related artifacts in pre-Columbian Mexico and what they express about the meaning and importance of death to those people. The author's stated purpose here (ibid.:526) is to point out "the permanence of some traits and in general the sense of continuity of the idea of death within contemporary Mexican folk culture." There follows a brief section on the European conquest (ibid.), which the author summarizes by saying that "The polytheistic religions were replaced by Christianity and the voice of the indigenous Mexican was dimmed forever. Its former power was lost, but a murmur was to remain." Fernández-Kelly fails to identify explicitly the precise nature of that murmur, although it is possibly revealed in her speculative associations concerning the origin of sugar skulls: "When looking at them in the showcases of the sweet shops," she says (ibid.:527), "one cannot help recalling the ancient Aztec *tzompantlis*, special stone structures where the skulls of the men who had died in sacrifice were exhibited." Whatever else that pre-conquest murmur may consist of, it presumably accounts for those aspects of contemporary Mexican funerals and Day of the Dead ceremonies that seem unfamiliar to Westerners. The murmur represents the exotic.

Fernández-Kelly, like the vast majority of scholars who have written on this issue, rightly believes that death in present-day Mexican folk culture is the product of a combination of pre-Hispanic with Spanish beliefs and practices. She states (1974:526): "Without doubt, the Christian tradition has left Mexico a priceless collection of artistic and literary testimonies which document its own interpretation of death. But the fusion of the European cultural patterns with the pre-existing beliefs offers a third and perfectly individualized complex of practices and ideas."

As an overall formulation of Mexican culture today, it would be hard to dispute this fusion model. It is important to note, however, that embedded within the model is a reification of culture. Culture has an existence of its own. It is passed down from generation to generation and blends with alternative, co-existent traditions to create a new cultural product. The role of historical events and socio-economic circumstances in producing particular beliefs and customs is vague at best. Above all, those who express and carry on these traditions—that is, the people themselves—are missing from this type of narrative. The story is essentially Kroeberian in nature. Culture is portrayed as a superorganic entity, undergoing transformation independent of human agency. The actual historical mechanisms through which continuity and change occur are missing from the account.

A similar point of view comes from *The Skeleton at the Feast: The Day of the Dead in Mexico*, a scholarly and beautifully illustrated exhibition catalog written and compiled by Elizabeth Carmichael and Chloë Sayer (1991). The book starts with a detailed description of Day of the Dead activities, especially (befitting a museum catalog) as they incorporate the visual arts. There are reproductions of sugar skulls, papier-mâché skeletons, decorated tombs and home altars, storefronts painted with animate skeletons, and the like. It proceeds to a chapter on "The Pre-Hispanic Background," illustrated with diverse pre-Columbian stone sculptures of deities and humans with skull-like faces; with pages from various codices (Borgia, Laud, Borbonicus) showing skull-like and skeletal-like drawings of supernatural beings; and with the *tzompantli*, or skull-rack, at the Mayan site of Chichén Itzá, among other death-related representations from pre-Hispanic Mesoamerica. The accompanying text focuses on the cosmology, deities of death, beliefs in the afterlife, artistic imagery related to death, and death-related rituals of the ancient Aztecs and related peoples. Carmichael and Sayer make no explicit connection between these phenomena and the Day of the Dead. They avoid committing themselves to a particular point of view: "To what extent these pre-Hispanic festivals and their associated rituals were transmuted into the Christian festivals remains a matter of keen debate" (ibid.:33). Carmichael and Sayer formulate their neutrality with utmost caution. However, the sheer length and detailed elaboration of their textual and artistic presentation related to pre-Hispanic customs, art, and beliefs lead readers to assume that these phenomena are in fact precursors of Day of the Dead arts and crafts.

The next chapter in Carmichael and Sayer, entitled "The Spanish Conquest," tells the story of the imposition of Catholicism in Mesoamerica and briefly describes the Day of the Dead in colonial Mexico. The chapter is illustrated mainly with Mexican death images: an 18th-century painting of a deceased nun, contemporary masked death and devil dancers, an ancient decorated skull, a toy Day of the Dead altar, and the 19th-century artist José Guadalupe Posada's image of "The Grand Banquet of Skeletons," among other pictures. There appear no European images, save a reproduction from a 1972 Mexican printing of Fray Joaquín Bolaños's book, *La Portentosa Vida de la Muerte* [The Portentious Life of Death]. As in the chapter on pre-Hispanic background, this exposition avoids explicit analysis of European origins, with one exception (Carmichael and Sayer 1991:42–43): the citation from Foster (1960) of the Castilian custom, transferred to Mexico, whereby a large funeral bier covered with a black cloth is erected in churches during All Saints' and All Souls' days.

The authors also include in the chapter a general statement (ibid.:40–41) about the syncretism that occurred between the religion of the Aztecs and Catholicism during the first century after the conquest. Their example is the classic one— nowadays seriously challenged (Taylor 1987)—of the image of the Virgin of Guadalupe as representing the pre-Columbian goddess Tonantzin and functioning in colonial times as a saint to whom Indians had particular devotion. Although they make no explicit statement of syncretism concerning the Day of the Dead, the authors state that "where there was some possibility of combining an Aztec fiesta with a feast day in the Catholic calendar, this was done" (ibid.:40). The organization of chapters in *The Skeleton at the Feast* implies the authors' belief that syncretism has occurred, although they do not try to identify which elements of the festival were ancient Mesoamerican and which European. Insofar as European origins go, Carmichael and Sayer are, however, willing to state the following of the Day of the Dead: "*Nominally* this is the Christian feast of the All Saints' and All Souls', but it is celebrated in Mexico as nowhere else in the Catholic world" (ibid.:14; italics added).

Scholars find it difficult indeed to minimize the role of the Aztecs in the Day of the Dead or, conversely, to emphasize European origins. Much of the justification for pre-Columbian antecedents comes from the iconography of ancient Mesoamerica, with its undeniable plethora of skulls and skeletons, as well as from the equally prevalent presence of skulls and skeletons during the Day of the Dead today. What is missing from most accounts is an analysis of the context in which skulls and skeletons appear. Hence, the first step in assessing origins is to examine the essence of Day of the Dead skulls and skeletons, that is, their intrinsic characteristics and how these compare with skulls and skeletons incorporated in related religious traditions.

In order to trace the possible origins of Day of the Dead art, we must first identify some of its essential features. As George Kubler long ago pointed out (1969, 1970, 1973), artistic form and function, content and meaning, must be differentiated. For our purposes, this principle indicates that there is no necessary historical connection between two societies in which skulls and skeletons appear as an artistic motif. Despite the prominence of skulls and skeletons in two different contexts, the form and function of representation might well vary from one context to another.

Consider, first, the place of skulls and skeletons in Mexican popular culture (see Figure 3.2). These artistic representations, as they appear during the Day of the Dead, display at least nine intrinsic characteristics:

1. They are *ephemeral* art. *Pan de muerto* ("dead bread"), sugar skulls and coffins, drawings of skulls and skeletons on storefront windows, death images made of straw and cut into colored paper: all of these items are made for momentary consumption. They tend to be constructed from flimsy, non-durable material. For the most part, at the popular level in Mexico, they are not saved for display or enjoyment. They exist to celebrate the moment.

2. They are *seasonal* art. Artistic images are specifically connected to the celebration of All Saints' and Souls' days. Representations of death that appear at this time of year are decidedly not incorporated into funerals or the permanent decoration of family tombs. Wherever these images are sold or displayed during other seasons, they seem geared towards the tourist market. In all cases, the Day of the Dead, rather than funerals or other mortuary rituals, remains the principal referent for these items.

Fig. 3.2 Papier-mâché skulls, Jalisco, October 2000

3. They are *humorous* in content. For the most part, the skulls, skeletons, caskets, and other death-related images that appear during the Day of the Dead manifest a playful, jocular quality. They evoke laughter rather than sadness, enjoyment rather than pain.

4. They are *secular*. The iconography of death holds virtually no sacred meaning either to its producers or its consumers. True, the sugar caskets with little cadavers inserted inside are sometimes decorated with a simple colored sugar cross. Aside from the cross, it would be difficult to discover religious imagery in the Day of the Dead iconography. Skulls and skeletons, be they made of bread or sugar, are generally eaten. Toys made of wood, paper, straw, or clay are designed for play and quickly fall apart unless treated with the utmost care. Little or no sacred significance attaches to the objects themselves, although they are incorporated into the celebration of a sacred holiday.

5. This iconography is *commercial*. It is made by skilled artisans to be purchased and can be found for sale around the time of the Day of the Dead at virtually all marketplaces throughout Mexico. Urban shopkeepers use drawings of skulls and skeletons to decorate their stores and attract customers.

6. Day of the Dead art is *designed for living people*, not for the deceased. True, this art occasionally decorates tombs and home altars. But it is employed in this fashion solely during the Day of the Dead. Never does it accompany funerals, nor are the recently deceased buried alongside any artistic objects related to the Day of the Dead. The objects and artistic representations associated with the Day of the

Dead tend mostly to be purchased by and exchanged among the living, as a way of reinforcing social relationships. They are also used in commercial advertisements as well as political and social satire.

7. Day of the Dead art is *comical*. The toys and candies are often designed for play. They have moving parts. The skeleton marionettes and puppets are fixed with flexible joints that make them come alive when manipulated. The coffins, crafted with plastic windows allowing a view of little cadavers inside, come laced with strings that allow the cadavers to resuscitate. Much of this art, then, is supposed to be handled.

8. Day of the Dead art is *small, light, and transportable*. This art generally fits in your hand. You can lift it and move it. Even the altars are assemblages of numerous small pieces that can be mounted and disassembled easily by a single person.

9. Much of Day of the Dead art is *urban and shared among Mexico's cultural elite*. It is manufactured and created in the city for consumption by city people, although there is a rural artistic tradition associated with this holiday as well.

In examining the origins of Day of the Dead art, all these characteristics should be taken into account. Day of the Dead art is used and integrated into social and cultural life in particular ways. Any discussion of how and why this art exists, and the reasons for its preeminence in contemporary Mexican life, must recognize that function is as important as form. Two images that look alike might differ greatly in the ways they are employed and interpreted, thereby casting doubt on common origins. It is important to bear this point in mind when comparing Day of the Dead art to similar representations in Ancient Mesoamerica and Europe.

In assessing the possible contribution of ancient Mesoamerica to the iconography of the Day of the Dead today, we must recognize the essential fact that the ancient world was diverse, complex, and long lived. We cannot speak of the pre-Columbian world as if it were, artistically and symbolically, a single undifferentiated entity. Even where symbols appear simultaneously in two different locales or time periods, they might have well operated socially according to different principles. Scholars are fond of pointing out that "The image of death is everywhere in the arts of pre-Hispanic central Mexico" (Childs and Altman 1982:6). Along with Gombrich (1972:20–21), what we want to ask about, however, is "the institutional function of images" as well as "to which genre a given work is to be assigned." As for the ancient Maya, who flourished in southeastern Mesoamerica, it has been said that, although they seemed less obsessed with death than the Aztecs, "this is compensated for by a greater presence of death in abstract form, especially in symbols, which appear with high frequency" (Coe 1975:92).

Let us first consider these Mayan symbols of death. Among them are the ubiquitous human skulls and bones, often crossed. At Toniná, for example, located near Palenque in eastern Chiapas, there survives a spectacular stone panel carved with skull bas reliefs. In fact, practically all of ancient art in the Mayan area and in Veracruz shows crossbones and fleshless mandibles (Winning 1987:55).

Human skulls and bones are, of course, nearly universal iconographic representations of death. However, the ancient Maya also employed a unique iconography of decomposing corpses, symbolized by black spots or blotches on the cheeks of the victims or by a sort of division sign—a horizontally-oriented squiggle with a dot above and below—also situated on the cheek of the deceased (ibid.:92–93). At Palenque there is a vase on which death is represented not only by the skeletal state of the victim but also by long, black hanks of hair coiled in the shape of a bow tie, as well as by disembodied eyes affixed to the skulls (Robicsek and Hales 1988:267). Throughout the Mayan region, too, death was represented by the closed eyes and open mouth of the victims (ibid.). Except for the human skulls and bones, none of these Maya death symbols can be found in present-day popular Mexican art, including that associated with the Day of the Dead.

Throughout central Mexico, too, the iconographic representation of death varies markedly from one culture to another. At Teotihuacán, which flourished during the first seven centuries of the present era, skulls and skeletons as a design motif are relatively insignificant (see, e.g., Berrin 1988). Although Winning (1987:58) briefly describes two monuments at Teotihuacán which display skulls, he states that skull representations at that site are "rare" (ibid.:61). Instead, Teotihuacán artists represented death by a simple sign: "they added a pair of perforated disks, or rings, above the eyes on the forehead" (ibid.:60). Cultures that flourished about the same time as Teotihuacán, in the present states of Colima, Jalisco, and Nayarit, also show skeletal representations rarely (Fuente 1974), although the first Mesoamerican skull rack, containing 61 human heads, was erected prior to the Christian era in southern Mexico, at Coyotera, in connection with Zapotec expansionist warfare (Hassig 1992:42).

At the Toltec capital of Tula, however, there exist the first indications in Central Mexico of a real fascination with skulls and skeletons. Tula flourished from the ninth century until the 13th century A.D. The site includes the decimated remains of a *tzompantli*, or skull rack, which once displayed multiple rows of stone carved skulls adorning the sides of a broad platform upon which the actual skulls of sacrificial victims were publicly exhibited (Hassig 1988:206; Hassig 1992:112). The *tzompantli* appeared during the final phases of civilization at Tula, which was destroyed around 1200 A.D. (Davies 1977). Chichén Itzá, almost contemporaneous with the Toltecs and located far to the southeast in the heart of Yucatan, contains a better-preserved *tzompantli*. Says Diehl (1983:149) of this structure, "The platform sides are covered with grisly carved stone panels showing human skulls strung up on upright posts like beads on a necklace. These probably symbolize the real skulls which once covered the platform summit." In the Mayan area, too, Uxmal displays a *tzompantli*, with skulls and crossed bones.

In addition to the *tzompantli*, there is a freestanding wall at Tula known as the *coatepantli*, or Serpent Wall, which formerly enclosed the north side of the pyramid upon which stands tall rigid warrior figures, the famous *atlantes*. This wall, probably associated with the cult of Tlahuizcalpantecuhtli (the supreme god Quetzalcóatl in the form of Venus the Morning Star), is decorated with a series of carved stone panels, which show feathered serpents devouring human skeletons (Diehl 1983:64). The most remarkable feature of these skeletons is their lanky limbs and prominent joints allowing for corporal flexibility; they are in fact large, stone versions of the wooden and clay toy skeletons found in markets all over Mexico around the time of the Day of the Dead. Like small toys today, these stone skeletons appear animate, with their awkwardly crossed legs and outstretched arms. However, their artistic design and execution occurred centuries prior to the Spanish conquest at the beginning of the 16th century. It is thus unlikely that these life-like skeletons, today an isolated archaeological find, would have themselves survived into the colonial and post-colonial eras in Mexico in the form of figurines associated with All Saints' and Souls' days.

Since the Aztecs were the leading power holders at the time of the Spanish conquest, it is reasonable to suppose that their iconography—rather than that of their predecessors—carried over into the art of colonial Mexico and exerted a long-term influence over folk art associated with the Day of the Dead. There are at least three elements of Aztec art that scholars point to repeatedly as demonstrating the indigenous focus on death. First is the well-preserved *tzompantli*, found at the site of the Great Temple at the Aztec capital of Tenochtitlán. On each side of this structure there exist five horizontal rows of sixteen stone skulls, which form a tightly knit design that completely covers the base of the platform. Second are numerous prominent stone sculptures of deities who are represented with skull-like features. Among the most famous is the image of Coatlicue, also known as Ilamatecuhtli, goddess of earth, life, and death, whose face usually appears as a skull. The fleshless face is sometimes itself decorated above the brow and below the neck with a row of smaller skulls (see, e.g., Anonymous 1963–64:209–210; Spranz 1973:83–85). Similarly, stone sculptures representing Mictecacihuatl, goddess of the underworld and of the dead, also show the face in the form of a skull (Matos Moctezuma 1992). One of the most famous artifacts from the Aztec Great Temple is an enormous circular monolith, 3.25 meters in diameter, showing Coyolxauhqui, the moon goddess, decapitated, with limbs spread across the entire stone slab; she bears a skull-shaped back ornament typical of earth deities. Finally, the Aztecs left skull offerings, which were found at the Great Temple (Carrasco 1992:116–117). These are actual human skulls, decorated with shell and pyrite eyes and sacrificial flint knives, which were inserted into the skulls to represent tongues and noses.

If we examine the art associated specifically with pre-Hispanic burials in central Mexico, there is almost no representation of skulls and skeletons anywhere. At Teotihuacán, for example, "a large variety of pottery vessels were made for everyday use and for burial with the dead, but none bear [sic] elaborate imagery" (Pasztory 1988:54). The multitudinous clay funerary offerings found in Western

Mexico, dating from 100 A.D. to 300 A.D., contain no skeletal or skull-like representations whatsoever. They instead include lively sculptures of musicians, warriors, water carriers, people sitting and people drinking (Fuente 1974). At Tula, burial sites occasionally contain a few undecorated pots, but nothing else (Diehl 1983:90). Tenochtitlán shows offerings of skulls and skeletons, although not necessarily funerary offerings. Contreras (1990:407) describes an offering found at the Great Temple which contained three skulls with some perforations above the forehead and with encrustations of shell and of a material similar to red clay placed within the eye sockets. A ceramic funerary urn from Offering 14 at the Great Temple of Tenochtitlán shows a non-skeletal representation of the deity Tezcatlipoca, and no skulls.

Regarding ancient Mayan burial sites, there, too, we find the presence principally of non-figurative art. Although death themes appear among the polychrome vessels associated with elite burials, most mortuary art reflects various categories of human activities in the context of life, not death. Consider two contrasting Late Classic (ca. 600–900 A.D.) burials at the Altar de Sacrificios, Palenque. Burial 128, belonging to a nobleman, shows that the priests placed the deceased in a large clay urn, together with offerings of mantles, mats, gold, silver, food, and charcoal. At Burial 7, that of a poor commoner, "the only offerings were two plain, inverted bowls, one placed over the head and the other near the pelvis" (Coe 1988:223). In no ancient Mayan burial can we find associated skulls or skeletons—except those of the actual deceased. To the contrary, iconic representations tend to symbolize affirmations of life. To Eduardo Matos, the great tomb at Palenque represents an "allegory of life in the vicinity of death" (Matos Moctezuma 1986:15). In the case of another funerary artifact, the famous polychrome vase at the Altar de Sacrificios, Palenque, iconographic representations include animals, dancers, canoes, flowers, and serpents, with no skulls or skeletons at all (Schele 1988).

What are some general points that might be derived from this brief survey of skull and skeletal art in ancient Mesoamerica? First, however extensive this art might have been, it was unevenly distributed through time and space. Teotihuacán and Western Mexico seem to have incorporated this kind of iconography sparingly if at all, whereas the Maya, Toltec, and Aztec civilizations made important use of it. The Aztecs show representations of skulls, but no full-length skeletons. Their predecessors in central Mexico, the Toltecs, fashioned both. As a rule, skull and skeletal iconography in Mesoamerica is not associated with mortuary ritual as such. It is also stiff, stylized and serious. There are two notable exceptions: the skeleton tablets at Tula, described above, and a ceramic codex fragment from Palenque, known as the Sacrifice of Xbalanque (Robicsek and Hales 1988), in which there appear death figures represented in animated skeletal state.

The archaeological remains that seem closest in feeling and spirit to contemporary Day of the Dead skulls and skeletons are the stone bas-reliefs at Tula and the representations of death on the ceramic codex from the Palenque Sacrifice of Xbalanque. And yet these two artifacts are far removed in space, time, and function both from one another and from the Spanish colonial regime. These remains also display strikingly different styles. It would be difficult to make a case for continuity of iconographic representation dating from these pieces to the present. At Tenochtitlán, on the other hand, we have an abundance of skulls and skeletons, both real and representational, which might very well have exerted a direct influence on church and folk art in colonial and post-colonial Mexico. However, skull iconography at Tenochtitlán displays a kind of stylized rigidity and seriousness that diverges enormously from art associated with the Day of the Dead. These archaeological remains incorporate nothing of the playfulness and humor so essential to contemporary Mexican skull and skeletal representations.

And how could they? Consider Hassig's graphic description (1988:121) of Aztec *tzompantli*:

> Captors did not kill their captives but brought them as offerings to the priests, who carried out the sacrifices, dragging them to the sacrificial stone if they faltered, and sacrificing them to Huitzilopochtli. After they were killed, the bodies were laid by the skull rack, and each warrior identified the one that he had captured. Then the body was taken to the captor's home, where it was eaten; the bones were hung in the house as a sign of prestige. The heads of those who were sacrificed were skinned, the flesh was dried, and the skulls were placed on the skull rack, the *tzompantli* . . .

Contextually, the use of skulls among the Aztecs could not be further removed from that among Mexicans in today's Day of the Dead celebration.

Given the diversity and complexity of skull and skeletal representations in ancient Mesoamerica, it is impossible to discount their cumulative impact on colonial and post-colonial art. Nor can we state that any one culture or civilization contributed to contemporary skull and skeleton representations more than any other. At the same time, it is impossible to draw clearly defined lines of stylistic and thematic influence from ancient times to the present day. Mesoamerican cultures were varied and, each in its own way, showed a concern with death. But that was true, too, of Europe at the time of the Spanish conquest.

Recall, finally, that skulls and skeletons were only a few of the means by which the peoples of ancient Mesoamerica represented death. The archaeological record in this part of the world, as everywhere, is discontinuous and incomplete. Hence, it is impossible to say whether skulls and skeletons were the most common symbols of death or, if not the most abundant, whether they were the most powerful and symbolically salient. It is all too easy to read back into the historical record that which seems to display the most evident continuity.

Similar doubts arise when we turn our attention to Europe at the time of the Spanish conquest and after. José Moreno Villa's essay on "The Death Theme in Spanish and Mexican Arts" (1986:113–137) offers a survey of the topic from the 15th century through the 20th century, with an emphasis on Spain. Nothing from these countries, whether in the form of text or artistic representation, bears the least resemblance to skulls or skeletons. There exist plenty of stone sarcaphagi of well-dressed nobles and clerics; paintings of delicate toga-clad damsels collapsing in the arms of muscular protectors; and, of course, sculpted and painted figures of the deceased Christ hanging on the cross, cradled in the arms of his Mother, laying prone in his casket. From Moreno Villa's vision of Spanish and Mexican representations of death, it would seem that the skull and skeleton are negligible images at best. In the words of another author (Bialostocki 1985:15), it was rather "the cruel death on the cruciform gallows" that dominated Christian thought and its artistic imagination: "From the Early Medieval times down to the Late Baroque sculpture and to the naturalistic painting of XIXth century the image of the dying God in the shape of a suffering man constitutes the main subject of Christian art" (ibid.).

This does not mean that European artists confined themselves to the motif of the dying Christ. Skulls and skeletons were, in fact, an important feature of their iconography during colonial times and after. Bialostocki (1985:28) points out that "The great period of the skull and skeleton ornamentation is the period of the Baroque"—that is, a period coinciding with much of the Spanish colonial era—"which introduces an inflation of these elements." Consider, for example, the no-longer extant tomb of the Good King René of Anjou, which shows the deceased monarch as "a wobbly skeleton, sitting on his throne, his crowned head powerlessly inclined and his scepter and royal globe having slipped from his hand to the ground" (ibid.:28). This description is reminiscent of the holy image of San Pascual, King, a saint venerated throughout Latin America, especially Guatemala (Luján Muñoz 1987). The cult of San Pascual emerged during the middle of the 17th century. He almost always wears a crown on his fleshless skull. Sometimes he is represented as a full skeleton, holding a scythe, with scepter and other accoutrements of his office lying at his feet; occasionally he is clothed in cape and gown. In folk art, he is a full-bodied skeleton wearing no clothing and carrying no identifying objects whatsoever, with the exception of a crown. Though principally a Guatemalan image, portraits of San Pascual can be found for sale outside churches all over Mexico as well. San Pascual and the Good King René of Anjou are not isolated cases. Death heads, sometimes combined with the hourglass, sometimes with bat wings, became a popular design motif. Gianlorenzo Bernini carved skeletons upon two of his most famous papal tombs. That of Pope Urban VIII shows a skeleton emerging from beneath the sarcophagus; the skeleton is portrayed as inscribing on the tablet the name of the deceased.

In 18th-century New Spain, as throughout Europe of the time, allegorical portrayals of the ages of man often included a skeleton as the image of death. Life was represented typically as a two-sided staircase, ascending on the left side and descending on the right. Upon each stair was drawn a human figure representative of a particular age, starting at the lower left-hand side with a picture of a baby representing infancy, and ending at the bottom right-hand side with a skeletal figure symbolizing death (e.g., Museo Nacional de Arte 1994:254–255). Another common 18th-century motif was the "arbol vano" [Tree of Vanity] or "arbol del pecador" [Sinner's Tree] generally portraying a young man, the sinner, reclining or seated at the base of a tree, completely spent from sensual excesses (ibid.:256–263). Invariably, there are supernatural figures surrounding the sinner, often a devil, occasionally an angel, but always a menacing skeleton, wielding an axe or a scythe. The Tree of Vanity in New Spain seems to derive from the engravings of the 16th-century Flemish artist Hieronymus Wierix, who directly influenced artists working in the New World during the Baroque era (ibid.:256).

In 18th-century New Spain, too, elaborately decorated funeral catafalques portrayed animated skeletal figures (Museo Nacional de Arte 1994:271–288). Two of the most elaborate can be observed today in the Museo de Bellas Artes in Toluca (see Figure 3.3) and the Museo de Arte Virreinal in Taxco. The catafalque of El Carmen, displayed in the museum at Toluca, shows multiple scenes of the skeletal death figure. In one panel the skeleton fires a cannon at a fortress; in

Fig. 3.3 "Death runs hand in hand with time"; 18th-century catafalque, Museo de Bellas Artes, Toluca

another the figure helps a nun to card wool, in a third it rides a fancy carriage. Other panels portray the skeleton walking hunched over with a cane, writing while seated at a small table, and of course wielding a scythe. Several of these figures show the skeleton wearing one or another article of clothing; most of them, too, portray the skeleton talking, an act that is symbolized through white banners, strung with Latin words, streaming from the skeleton's mouth (Museo Nacional de Arte 1994:272–276). The catafalque of Santa Prisca, housed in the museum at Taxco, displays equally animated skeletons. One is seated on a tree stump in contemplative mode, legs crossed and head resting on a hand. A scythe and bow and arrow are at the skeleton's feet. Another panel shows the skeleton actually shooting the bow and arrow, another walking by a lakeside holding an hourglass, another toppling a castle, and so forth (ibid.:277–280). Death is as alive in these figures as it is in Day of the Dead iconography today.

Even in the pre-Baroque era, it is clear that skulls and skeletons were characteristic features of European art. The cloister at the Augustinian monastery in Malinalco, dating from 1540, contains an alcove dominated by a friar and skeleton with scythe standing next to one another (Peterson 1993; see Plate 3.1). Consider, too, the open-air chapel at Tlalmanalco, on the road to Amecameca east of Mexico City, constructed by Franciscans in 1550–60. The chapel portrays literally dozens of skulls lining the upper part of its graceful arches, all of them alternating with diverse plants. On each of the central columns there are human figures, dressed in Renaissance garb and holding hands. According to Curiel Méndez (1987), the entire ornamentation at Tlalmanalco is designed to demonstrate "the Triumph of Death over humanity" (ibid.:156). The figures on the open-air chapel suggest different states of decomposition; in the words of Curiel, "there are skeletons, skulls with remains of flesh and in tact heads, all with distinct expressions of horror before the inevitable triumph of death" (ibid.:156–157). Curiel interprets the figures on the open-air chapel at Tlalmanalco as a version of the Dance of Death, an artistic theme which was extremely popular in Europe at the time. His main evidence (ibid.:156) is that some of the carvings represent people holding hands, as is the case with the Dance of Death. This feature, together with alternating skulls and plants, is highly reminiscent of the Dance of Death (see Figure 3.4).

The Dance of Death was popular in Europe for several centuries from the second quarter of the 15th century onward. It even had important reverberations in the 19th century (Goodwin 1988) and possibly up to the present time in the form of Day of the Dead iconography. Most frequently, the Dance of Death appeared as both literature and drawing. In searching for origins, art historian James Clark (1950:90) maintains that, "Whether our starting point is in England, France, Germany, Switzerland, Denmark, Italy or Spain, we find all the signposts pointing in the same direction," that is, to the Cemetery of the Innocents, located in Paris and dated 1424. For others, the Dance of Death motif is much older, in

Fig. 3.4   Sixteenth-century open-air chapel, Tlalmanalco, State of Mexico

that it is a textual and artistic elaboration of old Germanic mythology (American Art Association 1922: Prefatory Note).

There exist innumerable versions of the Dance of Death; collector Susan Minns amassed over 700 separate items, dating from the 15th century through the 19th century, all of them European (American Art Association 1922). The first printed edition was published by Guy (or Guyot) Marchant at Paris in 1485 (Chaney 1945:6). Oddly, the Spanish versions, from the early 15th century onward, contain text alone with no pictorial art (Clark 1950:41–50; Whyte 1931). Probably the most famous rendition of the textual and pictorial Dance of Death is the 41 woodcuts published in Lyons in 1538 by Hans Holbein the Younger (1971). Literary and artistic versions of the Dance of Death vary enormously. However, it is possible to describe a prototypical Dance. Robert Wark (1966:8–9) offers a succinct description:

> Normally the pictorial side of the work consists of a series of human figures each accompanied by a skeleton or cadaver that came to symbolize Death. The figure of Death is frequently represented as if in a grotesque dance to which he is leading his human companion. The human figures are drawn from the various strata of society in more or less descending order: Pope, Emperor, Cardinal, King, Bishop, Duke, and so on, down to the Parish Priest and the Laborer. The order and number of figures vary a great deal from one rendition to another, but the general theme of

Death leading away members of the various ranks of society remains the same. The pictures usually are accompanied by a text that takes the form of a series of brief conversations between the human figures and Death. The meaning behind the presentation is clear enough: Death visits all ranks and conditions of men; he is the great leveler before whom all worldly distinctions crumble.

As in the funeral catafalques of 18th-century New Spain, Dance of Death pictography during the late Middle Ages and the Renaissance portrays highly animated skeletal figures. The most interesting versions of the Dance, from a social and artistic point of view, invest the skeletal figures with a wide range of human emotions: hostility, glee, insolence, furtiveness, haste, and the like. These skeletons symbolize the deceased and yet interact with the living and occupy their world.

Art historians agree that the Dance of Death was above all didactic. As James Clark (1950:105) puts it, "the equality of all in death is the theme, with the further conclusion that man must repent before it is too late." Death was, of course, a daily presence for Europeans in the late Middle Ages and Renaissance. The Black Plague was within collective memory and people lived in daily contact with death. "The mortality rate was high," Werner Gundersheimer (1971:xiii) reminds us, "and the infant mortality rate was such that a family might well confer the same Christian name on several successive children. Funerals were frequent and public, and . . . executions were performed in public places." The Dance of Death, in addition to portraying the inevitable, and demonstrating death as the great leveler of society, was a manner of "realizing graphically, and thereby perhaps of somewhat domesticating, the dreadful fatality that hovered over even the most sheltered lives" (ibid.).

Christian art at the time of the conquest was replete with skeletal representations of death in the abstract. Both in Europe and New Spain, drawings of both the Trees of Vanity and the allegories of the stages of life regularly incorporated skeletal figures as representations of death. James Clark (1950:108–111) concludes that the Dance of Death was not designed to portray individual deceased people in skeletal form. Rather, he says (ibid.:111), "The dance is a symbol of death, nothing more. Poet and artist alike intended to portray in allegorical form the inevitability of death, and the equality of all men in death . . . The motive was at first didactic. John Lydgate put it in a nutshell: 'To shew this world is but a pilgrimage.'"

The Dance of Death is the one prominent antecedent of Day of the Dead art that contains an element of humor, although it is hardly the whimsical, spontaneously generated humor of the sugar skulls and toy skeletons that we find being sold in Mexican markets during the month of October and the first days of November. The most famous version of the Dance of Death, that by Hans Holbein the Younger, published in 1538, includes 41 woodcuts. In most of them "the skeleton mocks the living person while summoning him to die" (Gundersheimer

1971:xii). Since Holbein's woodcuts were published during the first generation after the conquest, they might easily have influenced popular art in early colonial New Spain.

And, yet, there is much to argue against any sort of direct influence, at least in the first two centuries following the conquest. For one thing, the earliest example of what is possibly the Dance of Death in New Spain is the sculptural ensemble at the open-air chapel of Tlalmanalco. Certainly, there is nothing humorous in this ensemble nor, as sculpture, is it executed in the media through which the European Dance of Death appeared. Second, it is by no means definite that the chapel at Tlalmanalco represents the Dance of Death at all. In fact, there is much to argue against it: the portrayal of skulls at Tlalmanalco in lieu of the usual skeletons; the stone in lieu of paint or print; and plants, rather than humans, in sequential alternation with the death figures. Added to this evidence is the complete absence of graphic versions of the Day of the Dead from Spain, the country that of course provided the most immediate influence on Mesoamerica for generations after the conquest.

Further, Day of the Dead skeletons vary notably from Dance of Death skeletons in one critical fashion: in the case of the Day of the Dead representation, skeletons do not interact with live humans. In toys and quotidian scenes, all the Day of the Dead figurines are skeletons—dressed as humans, but entirely fleshless nonetheless. In the Dance of Death, the skeletons almost invariably interact with portrayals of actual live humans. They interrupt their daily activities to carry them off; they tug at the humans, poke them to get their attention, pull them away to their inevitable demise. Death figures in the Dance of Death do assume a mocking expression; but they clearly ridicule the living victims who are about to die, frequently members of the social elite, such as clergy and nobility.

In the case of Day of the Dead figures, death itself is mocked, not any specific human victims. At the countless cemeteries where day or nighttime vigils are held in honor of relatives during the Day of the Dead, humorous iconography is scarce or entirely absent. Mexicans do not mock the real death of their loved ones. And, apart from Day of the Dead vigils, Mexican tombstones rarely if ever display representations of skulls or skeletons. The humor about death emerges most prevalently in anonymous contexts, such as stands and markets where death figures and colorful paper cutouts (Sandstrom and Sandstrom 1986) are sold, as well as in newspapers where the weaknesses of live public figures, portrayed in skeletal form, are exposed publicly. Artistic humor comes out, too, in the labeling of sugar skulls with the names of living persons, never the names of people who are actually deceased. In Mexico, the funerals of very young children—those classified as *angelitos* ("little angels") because they are said to pass directly to heaven after death, without having to go through Purgatory—are often lively affairs, accompanied by music. But there is no special humorous iconography associated with these funerals, as there is for the public celebration of the Day of the Dead. Mexicans, like people virtually everywhere, take the death of friends and relatives seriously. Humorous iconography is a product of and appropriate to a single celebratory moment, the Day of the Dead. For this reason, most of this iconography can be classified under the rubric ephemeral art. It is art that need not last beyond that one occasion.

It is fair to say that in no other predominantly Catholic country in the world are All Saints' and All Souls' days celebrated with the kind of artistic exuberance and humor as they are in Mexico. Certainly, in Spain, which brought this holiday to the Americas, this celebration is thoroughly somber. In New Spain, at some still indeterminate date, All Saints' and All Souls' days began to assume a humorous cast. However, we can be quite certain that it was sometime during the first two centuries after the conquest. By the mid-18th century, the holiday already had acquired its unique Mexican name, the Day of the Dead. By that time, too, humorous figurines had already appeared. We may thus assume that the Day of the Dead at this time acquired its present-day flavor, at least in the Valley of Mexico.

Contrary to the findings in one report that sugar figurines are documented "only to the 1840s" (Green 1980:71), Chapter 2 presents documentation, in the form of testimony from the Capuchin friar Francisco de Ajofrín, that they appeared a full century earlier. However, there is no doubt that the most explicit and abundant evidence of humorous popular art during the Day of the Dead comes from the last half of the 19th century. It was then, too, that broadsides, known as *calaveras* ("skulls") began appearing in significant numbers (see Chapter 5). Childs and Altman (1982:54) view this development as a consequence of the freedom of the press that arrived with Mexico's independence from Spain in 1821. Technical advances in newspaper printing and the emergence of illustrated newspapers were also partly responsible. The first illustrated newspaper in Mexico was called *El Calavera*, which began publication in January 1847. Through drawings, verse, and essays, *El Calavera* specialized in satirizing political currents of the day and particularly poking fun at the new nation's leaders. After 31 issues, it was suppressed by the government and its leaders were imprisoned for trying to incite rebellion (ibid.). And yet the long-term impact of this newspaper was considerable.

Shortly thereafter, journalist Antonio Vanegas Arroyo hired artist José Guadalupe Posada (1852–1913) to illustrate his topical ballads, which he hawked around streets and fairs, pilgrimages and public gatherings (Wollen 1989:14). By the late 19th and early 20th centuries, Posada was creating powerful *calavera* images each year on the occasion of the Day of the Dead. These images portrayed "vivid and lively skeletons and skulls with grinning teeth, dancing, cycling, playing the guitar, plying their trades, drinking, masquerading," and in dozens of other comical manifestations (ibid.:14–15). Childs and Altman (1982:56) observe that "everyone and everything was a likely subject of his illustrations. There are *calaveras* of leaders of the 1910 revolution, such as Francisco Madero who is depicted as a drunken peon and another of Vanegas Arroyo, Posada's publisher. There are grand ladies and gentlemen of the aristocracy and coquettish barmaids all in skeletal form. There are also scenes drawn directly from Días de los Muertos celebrations, such as the one depicting a cemetery picnic and another a seller of sugar skulls." Probably the most famous of Posada's images is that of the *catrina*, the female dandy, portrayed as a fleshless skull, topped with a fancy, wide-brimmed hat which is replete with large, billowing feathers and other decorations (see Plate 3.2). Posada's influence on Mexican art and culture is incalculable. Largely ignored by artists of his day, he was discovered and popularized through the zealous efforts of artists and writers, many of them non-Mexican. Peter Wollen (1989:14) recounts the birth of Posada as a recognized genius:

> The painter Dr Atl, the most persistent early pioneer of modernism in Mexico, and the young French immigrant, Jean Charlot, one of the group of muralists around Diego Rivera, were the first to notice Posada's work in the new artistic context of the post-revolutionary years. Charlot, who first saw Posada prints in 1920, followed up his discovery, showed prints to other painters and wrote the first biographical and critical essays on Posada's work, in the early twenties. In time, other artists— including Rivera, José Clemente Orozco and David Alfaro Siqueiros—took up Posada's cause, often in hyperbolic terms, and acknowledged their debt, direct or indirect, to the humble popular print-maker. The legend was born.

Folklorist Frances Toor promoted Posada's reputation when in 1930 she published *Posada: Grabador Mexicano* (Posada: Mexican Engraver). Diego Rivera, in an introduction to a book portraying 406 of Posada's engravings, called him "an engraver of genius" and "the greatest artist" among those Mexicans who have produced popular art (quoted in Macazaga and Macazaga 1979:21). In his famous mural, "A Sunday Afternoon in Alameda Park," Rivera reproduced Posada's *catrina*, placing both this figure, dressed in a parody of full bourgeois costume, and a portrait of Posada himself in the center of the huge painting, where they flank Rivera himself.

Posada was neither the first nor only great satirical engraver of his day. In fact, Manuel Manilla, among others, preceded him. And these Mexicans were themselves part of an international artistic movement. As Peter Wollen states (1989:19), Posada is part of the more general phenomenon of broadside artist, part of "the whole repertoire of nineteenth century urban popular art—catchpenny prints, peep-shows, panoramas, Punch and Judy, melodrama and fairground attractions." Like the rest of this art, Posada's illustrations addressed themselves to particular historical circumstances in the national arena in which he found himself. This arena was that of a new country with an unstable political framework in which the normal democratic means of criticism were highly restricted. Posada needed to make a living; his art had to sell. He found his market among an enormous restless urban populace, dissatisfied with their political leaders and needy of an outlet for public criticism. Posada's art became just one of numerous forms of popular resistance (Beezley, Martin, and French 1994) expressed throughout Mexican history. As William Beezley (1987:98) puts it, the rhymed, illustrated obituaries "offered the common people the opportunity, without fear of censure or reprisal, to express their dissatisfaction with political and social leaders and to define their grievances, real or imagined."

Posada became nationally and internationally famous through the promotional efforts of famous artists and writers within and outside Mexico. Hence for a second time, Posada's art became popularized, this time not by struggling journalists but rather by the country's artistic elite, who read into his imagery the meaning of Mexico itself. Wollen (1989:16) summarizes Posada's legacy thus:

> [I]t is wrong to see Posada simply as an "influence". His name and legend were constitutive in the establishment of the Mexican renaissance; they symbolized both an alternative tradition and, crucially, a chain of succession. This particular role assigned to Posada was important both in relation to Mexicanism and in relation to Modernism. It gave credibility to claims to be part of an authentically Mexican artistic tradition, crossing both the class gap and the historic divide of the Revolution itself and, at the same time, guaranteed the modernity of the tradition by aligning it with the revival of popular imagery among the European avant-garde. It was a way of solving the classic dilemma of evolutionary nationalism—how to be popular, authentic, traditional *and* modernizing, all at the same time.

By the 1930s, Posada and his *calaveras* became symbolic of Mexico. For their irreverence, the *calaveras* suited the revolutionary ideology of Mexico; and yet the international art community had virtually declared these satirical skulls and skeletons to constitute a kind of high art. In the terms analyzed by Liza Bakewell, Posada's work satisfied the needs of a "cultural nationalism" (1995:31) that started with the Mexican Revolution and persists to this day.

It is important to recall at this point that even though Posada's art has long been widely disseminated, reproduced, transformed and mimicked in non-ritual contexts, he himself used the Day of the Dead as a creative stimulus and, one supposes, commercial opportunity. The Day of the Dead, by Posada's time, was a well-entrenched Mexican tradition. Artistically, as well, the sugar candies in the form of dead people and caskets and related mortuary imagery—all of it humorous—had been a part of the popular celebration of the Day of the Dead for generations. It is not surprising, then, that Posada's satirical imagery, itself the immediate product of crucial developments in Mexico's political history and in the evolution of printing, should have been enthusiastically received in its day.

Both his thematic material and humorous tone coincided with already-established artistic patterns in the celebration of this holiday. It also responded to the desires of Mexican artists, who were in "full revolt against a tradition of dependence on European, especially Spanish, academic art. They wanted to replace it with an art whose genealogy would go back before the conquest, which would be original to Mexico, popular and authentic" (Wollen 1989:15).

As Childs and Altman have pointed out (1982:58), the sugar skulls and skeleton toys that predominate in rural areas of Mexico during the Day of the Dead represent one artistic tradition. The origins of this tradition are explored in the previous chapter, which includes discussion of the artistic and religious legacy of Aztecs and Spaniards at the time of the conquest, as well as demographic circumstances during the colonial regime that might have led to Day of the Dead mortuary figurines. There is a second artistic tradition related to the Day of the Dead that was initiated with broadside illustrations by José Guadalupe Posada during the late 19th century and the early 20th century. This second tradition, as we have seen, had a more overtly political and social mission than the first. It consisted mainly of satirical artistic commentaries, which could flourish because of the humorous license provided by the Day of the Dead.

Posada's art and its offshoots provided what I have called elsewhere (Brandes 1977) a type of "peaceful protest." Members of all social strata came under Posada's mocking eye, but there was an especially biting quality to the humorous portrayal of political leaders and other public figures, who could not ordinarily be ridiculed in public. There is an enormous anthropological literature, skillfully synthesized and summarized by Mahadev Apte (1985), which demonstrates the opportunities provided by religious ritual for the humorous commentary on otherwise forbidden themes, as well as for the mockery of social and political elites. This is essentially the theoretical mode in which Posada's art, and the literary and artistic offshoots of his art, must be understood. Posada could employ *calaveras*—skulls, skeletons and other mortuary imagery—in part because a well-established artistic tradition in Mexican popular art stimulated this thematic emphasis. His *calaveras*, too, were appropriate to the occasion for which they were produced. The Day of the Dead in essence provided Posada a uniquely propitious artistic opportunity. However, the purpose and impact of his art were different from that of the sugar candies that emerged during the colonial era.

Posada's calaveras, through their popularization by famous artists who took up his cause, have influenced Mexican street and gallery art profoundly. Childs and Altman (1982:58–59) provide several apt examples:

> The wire and plaster skeleton figures of the Mexico City artist, Saúl Moreno, are on the surface not very different from toys made in Oaxaca. But Moreno's work is not produced for friends and neighbors, but is made for and consumed by art collectors. A skeleton sculpture by Moreno is more likely to be found in a Berlin art

collection than on a villager's altar in Tepoztlán. Another Mexico City artist, Pedro Linares, works in papier-maché and has created Días de los Muertos objects which have no real counterpart in observances of the festival. He makes large skeleton figures which compare to the Judas figures commonly made for Holy Week. But whereas the Judas figures are made to be burned in a village fiesta, the Linares papier-maché skeletons and skulls . . . have no such function and are intended for a national and in fact international art market.

Political and social commentaries that follow the Posada tradition continue to appear in newspapers throughout Mexico around the time of the Day of the Dead. But the art that his work has spawned, through its validation by world-famous Mexican artists, now transcends Posada's immediate goals. It has become an important commercial enterprise and for this reason—in a nutshell, for the profit motive—has acquired a life of its own. Mexican skulls and skeletons sell well to the international community of tourists and collectors. Judging from the Posada look-alikes drawn annually on store windows and supermarket displays, skulls and skeletons also stimulate business among Mexican consumers (see Figure 3.5).

Fig. 3.5   Cuernavaca bakery window, October 1995

These two separate, albeit related, traditions of mortuary art—the first stemming from the religious and demographic imperatives of colonial times, the second from the political and journalistic developments of a new nation— are now generally perceived by Mexicans and outsiders as one undifferentiated syndrome. They have become virtually emblematic of Mexico itself. As indicated earlier in this paper, scholars interpret the skulls and skeletons that appear during the Day of the Dead as evidence of a peculiarly Mexican view of death. To the contrary, no special Mexican view of death, no uniquely morbid Mexican national character, has produced this mortuary art. Rather, specific demographic and political circumstances originally gave rise to it and commercial interests have allowed it to flourish in the 20th century. It is above all the enormous proliferation of Day of the Dead art that has produced the all-too-familiar stereotype of the death-obsessed Mexican.

PART 3

CONTEMPORARY TRANSFORMATIONS

4

TOURISM AND THE STATE

Tourism is arguably among the most potent forces for all sorts of social change today, including ritual change. Nonetheless, anthropologists, folklorists, and other students of religious behavior have largely overlooked the impact of tourism on ritual. I suspect that this oversight derives largely from the fact that tourism is perceived, whether rightly or wrongly, as a threat to cultural diversity. Tourists are a potentially destructive force, disturbing the presumed purity, harmony, and spontaneity of ceremonial conduct. To many scholars, religious ritual is sacred in more than the obvious sense. It is the repository of cultural exotica, rare, anachronistic treasures that are inherently valuable because they are unfamiliar. When confronted with the possibility that such unique expressions of human diversity might disappear under the weight of mass tourism, many investigators likely ignore the very phenomenon potentially responsible for that change. For obvious reasons, it is impossible to estimate the frequency with which tourists have been screened out of field accounts so that the impression of an unspoiled, wholly traditional ritual might be imparted. But we can be certain that this kind of impression management occurs often, and with the best scientific intentions (see Plate 4.1).

Fortunately, there are notable exceptions to this pattern, among them several dealing with the Spanish-speaking world. Luis Díaz, for example, has analyzed the transformations that tourism has brought to traditional celebrations on the Day of San Juan (June 24) in San Pedro Manrique, a small village in Castile. In this town, where the famous fire-walking ritual almost disappeared due to the paucity of local participants, tourism apparently revived interest in the event and is largely credited with its continuance—albeit, as the author states, in "degraded" form (Díaz Viana 1981). Similarly, Davydd Greenwood, in an analysis of the Alarde of Fuenterrabía, describes how tourism affected the intrinsic meaning of the event. Instead of being a performance which townspeople put on for themselves, and which reinforced their sense of common history, equality, and destiny, the ritual became a performance for money, an attraction that enabled Fuenterrabía to compete for the influx of tourist wealth (Greenwood 1977). In the one case, tourism is held responsible for salvaging a ritual occasion; in the other, the mass influx of outsiders is said to have produced a "commoditization of culture," which "in effect robs people of the very meanings by which they organize their lives" (Greenwood 1977:137). Both cases, however, demonstrate that tourism, far from automatically eliminating local ritual performances, might actually contribute to their perpetuation.

This chapter considers a dramatic confirmation of the same type of development. It examines Tzintzuntzan, in the west-central state of Michoacán, where the Night of the Dead was traditionally celebrated in relatively unelaborated form. Mass tourism, promoted by government agencies, has been responsible for radical changes in the event. Not only do many more local people participate than before, but also the variety of activities associated with the ritual has expanded enormously. In fact, the transformations have been so far-reaching that it might even be said that tourism has actually added a major ritual occasion to the town's annual religious cycle. Far from destroying Tzintzuntzan's Night of the Dead, tourism is virtually the source of its contemporary embellished celebration.

Tzintzuntzan provides an unusually fine study site for the study of ritual. The village, which in pre-conquest times served as capital of the Tarascan Empire (often termed the Purépecha Empire), is located on the shores of Lake Pátzcuaro, west of Mexico City, at an elevation of 6,700 feet. The 16th-century *Relación de Michoacán* (Corona Núñez 1977) documents the elaborate ceremonial life of the city—which chroniclers of the time estimated at some 40,000 inhabitants—prior to the arrival of the Spanish in 1525. Five impressive *yácatas* or circular pyramids, where religious rites were carried out, still dominate one of the hills overlooking the town and lake, and bear contemporary witness to Tzintzuntzan's long history as an important ritual center. The enormous rectangular atrium, or churchyard, too, displays abundant evidence of the village's central religious role. It contains not only two large churches—the parish church, dating from the 16th century, and the church of La Soledad, constructed in the 17th century—but also an impressive two-story convent and a large open-air chapel, both built during the colonial era. Despite a precipitous population decline as well as formal reduction in politico-religious rank during the first century after the conquest, the community has retained a rich calendar of ritual activities over the past five centuries. In terms of ceremonial life, Tzintzuntzan at the turn of the 21st century occupies an importance in the region far out of proportion to its contemporary population of some 3,000 artisans, farmers, and merchants.

For as long as we have had detailed documentation, that is, since George and Mary LeCron Foster began intensive ethnographic research in Tzintzuntzan in 1945 (Foster and Ospina 1948; Foster 1967), certain events on the ritual calendar have clearly stood out as having a major impact on the community. Certainly Holy Week and Corpus Christi in the spring and the four-day festival in honor of the Señor del Rescate, or Lord of Redemption, in February have retained their importance throughout nearly half a century of detailed observation. By contrast, the Christmas *posadas* around which nine days of elaborate celebration are now organized was introduced into Tzintzuntzan only since the 1970s, while Carnival seems to be celebrated on sporadic, unpredictable occasions, and with varying formats and community participation. Anyone who examines the Tzintzuntzan fiesta cycle in detail is bound to come away impressed more by change than continuity. Not only the events that are singled out for special celebration, but also the manner in which ritual activities are carried out and the personnel responsible for them, have demonstrated considerable variation over the years.

Elsewhere I have discussed some of the factors most responsible for these changes, including, among other things, increasing national identity and pride (Brandes 1988), economic development and diversification (Brandes 1983a), and individual innovation (Brandes 1981). The Day of the Dead reveals yet another source of ritual modification: mass tourism, as promoted by state intervention. Overall, the role of outsiders in determining Tzintzuntzan's contemporary ritual cycle has been minimal. During the Fiesta of the Señor del Rescate, thousands of people from surrounding communities and other parts of the state of Michoacán swell the ranks of celebrants. But, on the whole, these people are attracted to Tzintzuntzan in order to worship and venerate the miraculous Señor. They do not mold the shape of ritual activities but rather participate in them. Holy Week, Corpus Christi, and the Christmas *posadas*, despite fabulously picturesque and elaborate ceremony, draw only the merest indication of an outside presence—perhaps several dozen people, if that, not counting outsiders who live within walking distance of town.

There is every indication that minimal presence of outsiders characterized the Night of the Dead in Tzintzuntzan as well, at least until 1971. In that year, a governmental plan was instituted to promote large-scale tourism in Tzintzuntzan and other communities in the area of Lake Pátzcuaro. The impact has been to convert a relatively minor ritual event, in which a small proportion of the town participated and virtually no outsiders showed much interest, into one in which thousands of city people clog the streets with traffic, television cameramen flood the cemetery with glaring lights, and the town becomes more or less a great stage prop for a ritual drama. In this drama native townspeople participate as actors but outsiders run the show.

The Night of the Dead—in Spanish *la Noche de Muertos*—is the term nowadays used throughout the state of Michoacán to refer to the evening of November 1 and 2. Although this terminology may be unique (I have encountered no other reference to it either in Europe or Latin America), the occasion it represents certainly is not. After all, the Night of the Dead is the local celebration of All Saints' and All Souls' days. November 1, according to the Roman Catholic calendar, is All Saints' Day, known throughout the Spanish-speaking world as *el Día de Todos Santos*, while November 2 is All Souls' Day, called variously *el Día de Muertos* (The Day of the Dead), *El Día de los Fieles Difuntos* (The Day of the Faithful Deceased), or *el Día de Ánimas* (The Day of the Souls). By using the term Night of the Dead, the people of Tzintzuntzan, and Michoacán generally, implicitly emphasize the ritual importance of the evening activities in comparison with those of the daytime. It is really only at dusk on November 1 that this festival comes alive in Tzintzuntzan. From that hour until dawn the following morning the town is transformed materially and spiritually in the way that only the most extraordinary community celebrations seem to be able to do.

When discussing fiesta change, or culture change of most types for that matter, it is usual to establish an ethnographic baseline, which is taken to represent the presumed traditional circumstances. In the case of Tzintzuntzan's Night of the Dead this procedure is difficult to follow because informants themselves disagree about the absence or presence of certain fundamental features of the ritual. Unfortunately, prior to 1945 there are no written accounts to clarify the inconsistencies. The most prudent course is simply to set forth the probable course of events along with the possible alternatives.

We are concerned with the Night of the Dead prior to 1971. During this "traditional" period, which itself undoubtedly reflected changes from one decade to another, there prevailed certain outstanding features of the celebration that might be commented upon individually.

(1) *Mass.* The official celebration, as dictated by Rome and developed since early modern tines, requires that parish priests recite special Masses on November 1 in honor of all the saints, and on November 2 in honor of all the deceased. These Masses, of course, have always been celebrated in Tzintzuntzan, with the attendance of those villagers who are moved to participate. Universally in the Roman Catholic world, three Masses are said on November 2. In Tzintzuntzan the first of these takes place at dawn in the open air at the village cemetery. The special Masses on November 1 and 2 (or on November 3, should November 2 fall on a Sunday) are the only rituals required by Rome. However, as Cornides, writing for the New Catholic Encyclopedia states, these dates have always been associated with "many different folkloric and popular customs and practices, especially various forms of food offerings . . . Among religious traditions, the parish procession to the cemetery, visiting the graves of relatives and friends, and leaving flowers and lights on the graves have remained almost universal" (Cornides 1967:319). These informal, or rather unofficial, ritual practices constitute the bulk of Tzintzuntzan's celebration.

(2) *Home altars.* Traditionally, most households have set up home altars in honor of their deceased relatives. Altars may be erected on October 31, especially

in cases where the deceased is an *angelito*—usually a child, but actually anyone who is known to have died in sexual innocence. November 1 is, according to local belief, the day particularly devoted to such departed souls, which is why October 31 is occasionally referred to as La Víspera de los Angelitos, or Angelitos' Eve. In those cases where the deceased relatives include no *angelitos*, the altars are constructed on November 1. Dismantling of all altars takes place at about noon on November 2. In contrast to Mexico, by the way, in Spain there has never been a special celebration for deceased children on one day and a second day devoted to adults (Lomnitz 2005:117).

Although home altars vary widely according to the expense and effort that each family is willing to expend, they share at least two common elements: candles and marigold petals, the latter known locally as *cempasuchil*, a local variant of the Nahuatl *cempoaxochitl* (Foster and Ospina 1948:219). Most home altars additionally bear food, a practice common throughout Spain as well (see, e.g., Behar 1986:172–173; Freeman 1979:109; Gabriel Llompart 1965:96–102; Hoyos Saínz 1944:3053; Violant y Simorra 1956:300–359). Mexican altars commonly incorporate bread, oranges, bananas, and squash among their offerings. Pictures of the deceased relatives who are being honored are often situated on or above the altar, together with trinkets or other small items that the deceased is known to have liked. Villagers feel strongly about the proper components of a home altar, although, with the exception of candles and marigold petals, they rarely coincide precisely in their opinions. Some families make do with several candle-sticks at the foot of their bed, adorned with marigold petals sprinkled in the form of a cross. Others have considerably more elaborate altars erected on a complex of tables and shelves, and filled with a great variety of breads, fruits, vegetables, and colorful ornaments.

(3) *Candlelight vigil.* This event, known locally as *la velación* or the candle-light vigil, traditionally occurred at the town cemetery in the early hours of November 2. Foster and Ospina describe the *velación* of 1945 as follows:

> About 4 o'clock in the morning family groups begin to wend their way to the cemetery, carrying arcos [explained below] and other offerings of food, to take up their vigil by the graves of departed relatives. Again yellow marigold flowers are scattered over all graves, and candles are lighted. Toward dawn perhaps 40 tombs are thus arranged, and the twinkling of several hundred candles in the dark sug-gests will-of-the-wisps run riot. The night is cold, and the mourners crouch, wrapped in serapes, occasionally saying a few words, but for the most part guarding silence. After daylight other persons come, to talk with friends keeping vigil, to eat a little, and to see what is happening. By 11 o'clock most people have gone home and the graveyard is again deserted. The explanation that the vigil is at night rather than during the day—so that the heat of the sun will not melt the candles—appears to be rationalization of ancient custom rather than based on fact (Foster and Ospina 1948:220).

In 1961, when Foster witnessed the event again at four o'clock in the morning, he reported the presence of about 100 family groups at the cemetery.

Had there been a dramatic increase in village attendance at the vigil? Clearly, there was somewhat of an increase, though perhaps not as much as the figures would immediately suggest. In 1945, Tzintzuntzan's population was 1,231; by 1960, it had climbed to 1,840. Given this development, we might expect that simply as a function of population growth 50 percent more families would attend the vigil in 1961 than had attended in 1945, yielding an anticipated attendance of some 60 families. In fact, we have a recorded estimate of about 100. The increased attendance at the vigil can be explained only in part through a consideration of population size. Most of the increase, in fact, must be attributed to the destruction of gravesites when a highway was constructed directly over the cemetery in 1939, thereby bisecting it into two small triangular patches. Many graves were simply covered with asphalt. To this we must add that the cemetery itself was relatively new. In 1930, when Lázaro Cárdenas (the future President of the Republic) was governor of the state of Michoacán, he declared Tzintzuntzan an autonomous *municipio*. At the same time, he ordered that Tzintzuntzan's atrium, which was the traditional graveyard, no longer be used for burials. It was cleared of tombstones and other identifying markers, and the new cemetery was established at its present location just southeast of town. During the 1930s, then, two cemeteries had in effect been destroyed, one by governmental decree, the other through the requirements of modernized transportation. In 1945, there were simply not many identifiable gravesites over which the villagers could maintain vigil. Sixteen years later, with the rapid appearance of numerous new recognizable graves, people had a reason and place to go during the Night of the Dead. This development, as much as simple population increase, accounts for the rise in the number of participants at the *velación* between 1945 and 1961. It is impossible to state with any accuracy what the situation might have been prior to 1945.

(4) *Offerings.* A variety of food offerings, known as *ofrendas*, has been an important feature of the Night of the Dead in Tzintzuntzan for as far back as we have information. Perhaps the most dramatic of the offerings, from a visual point of view, is the *arco*—an elaborately decorated latticework structure perhaps two meters square. The *arco* may be shaped in the form of a large eagle, or angel, or other recognizable being, and is hung with a plethora of fruit, breads, and sugar candies, all nestled within a field of marigolds (see Plate 4.2). *Arcos*—literally "arches"—are built with a stick frame and cross supports that enable the structures to be mounted free-standing on the ground. So-called *ofrendas nuevas* or "new offerings," have been traditionally celebrated with the expensive, time-consuming construction of *arcos*. The first year following the death of a child (or, theoretically anybody who might be considered an *angelito*), the baptismal godparents are responsible for preparing an *arco* in the deceased's memory. On the evening of October 31, the baptismal godparents carry the *arco* to the home

of the deceased's parents, who provide the godparents a *pozole* supper (a hominy-like feast dish) in return. The following day, the parents transport the *arco* to the cemetery, where it may remain until the afternoon of November 1 or all the way through until mid-day on November 2. People differ in opinion on this particular. It is also unclear whether this is simply a Tarascan practice, or whether it has also been a part of the mestizo tradition in Tzintzuntzan.

Most offerings are less elaborate than *arcos*. The term *ofrenda* covers a wide variety of food items and candies, all displayed in honor of the deceased. The fruit, squash, candles, and other objects that adorn home altars are certainly considered *ofrendas*, as are the same array of goods that are placed around and on top of gravesites. Some families take account of the individual tastes of the deceased in deciding the kinds of food to use as offerings. One informant put it this way: "The custom here is to take to the deceased that which they enjoyed a lot in life . . . , fruit and such things . . . *corundas* (a local variant of tamales), tortillas, beans, pork, a duck, if the deceased liked, fish, whatever, whatever the deceased liked the most. . . ." These foods remain on the home altars and gravesites until the end of the celebration, on the morning of November 2. Even as long ago as 1945, it was clear that nobody in Tzintzuntzan actually believed that the deceased relatives descend to earth to partake of these offerings. Rather, the offerings have always been placed out in honor of the deceased, whose spirits may be present and thereby take note of the efforts and concern of the living on their behalf. With the termination of the Night of the Dead, implicitly marked by Mass at the cemetery in the early morning of November 2, families gather up their offerings and take them home, where they are distributed to neighbors, friends, and compadres, and where the families themselves may also consume them.

(5) *El doble*. The *doble*, which has no precise English translation, refers in Tzintzuntzan to a complex of practices associated with institutionalized begging and the tolling of church bells during the Night of the Dead. Traditionally, the young men of the village were accorded certain rights and duties on this occasion. Their main responsibility was to ring the church bells throughout the night of November 1–2 in the characteristic rhythm indicating death, a common practice in rural Spain (see, e.g., Foster 1960:201–203). The Spanish verb *doblar* refers in part to this lugubrious tolling of bells on the occasion of any death, not only during the Night of the Dead; the term *doble* probably derives from that usage. In return for tolling the bells—a chore clearly conceptualized as community service—the young men were given the right to beg from house to house, *pidiendo el doble*, "asking for the *doble*." (In central Spain, too, youth get together on All Saints' Day to cook food for one another; an example is provided by (Brandes 1975:135).) In this sense, the term *doble* denotes foodstuffs and other items, such as firewood, which were family donations to the youth. They would then take these items and cook them in the atrium over an open fire. The *doble* might also take the form of money which, when pooled, could be used to purchase liquor.

The young men organized themselves for this activity, and selected among themselves a *presidente* to lead the group. Some of the youth would be assigned to bell ringing, others to cooking, and yet others to begging. They would period- ically relieve one another of these activities by switching places at regular intervals throughout the night. The *presidente* was in charge of maintaining order and towards this end was entrusted with the keys to the town jail. Apparently disorderly conduct was enough of an ongoing concern that such measures had to be institutionalized.

Apart from the bell ringing and begging of male youth, the term *doble* refers to a type of institutionalized charity that would take place at the cemetery. Needy members of the community would walk from grave to grave, saying a prayer in honor of the deceased at each tomb and collecting from the family members an item or two from among the food offerings. The items, given partly as charity and partly in exchange for the prayers over the dead, were known as *el doble*. The same term was used to refer to the institutionalized act of begging itself on this occasion.

These, then, are the major elements of the traditional celebration of the Night of the Dead in Tzintzuntzan: special masses, home altars, candlelight vigil at the cemetery, offerings of food, flowers, and candles, and institutionalized bell ring- ing and begging. Despite minor changes in the ritualized celebration of the event in the generation prior to 1971, as well as some informant disagreements over ceremonial practices, this complex of beliefs and behaviors may be taken as an ethnographic baseline against which we can measure subsequent transforma- tions. For if anything is certain about the pre-1971 celebration of the Night of the Dead it is this: tourism and state intervention played no significant role whatever.

It is difficult, if not impossible, to reconstruct exactly what the meaning of the event was to the people of Tzintzuntzan at that time. Clearly, as a community celebration it was relatively insignificant, at least in comparison with other events on the town's fiesta calendar, such as Holy Week and Corpus Christi. The Night of the Dead was primarily a family fiesta. Probably the vast majority of village households erected home altars. By best estimates, a small minority attended Mass and participated in the *velación*, although the latter event, in particular, stands out in people's memories because it represented a publicly marked break from ordinary daily routine. It is impossible to guess what proportion of the male youth participated in *el doble*, but it may be presumed that this was a pretty popular affair that included not only unmarried men in their teens, but also recently married men who were still unburdened with the responsibility of supporting children.

What accounts for the absence of tourists during this period? To begin, the pre-1971 infrastructure was unsuitable. The Night of the Dead occurs at an inconvenient time to attract foreigners, while the Mexican oil boom that swelled the ranks of the country's middle class and led to a notable increase in domestic tourism had still not taken effect. And then, too, there was the proximity of

Janitzio, a small picturesque island on Lake Pátzcuaro, where the Tarascan inhabitants had become famous for essentially the same practices as were being carried out in Tzintzuntzan at the time. Foster and Ospina in 1948 declared that All Souls' Day in Janitzio "has become one of the most famous spectacles of Mexican indigenous life" (Foster and Ospina 1948:220). The outsiders who did come to the region to witness traditional celebrations therefore were attracted to Janitzio; Tzintzuntzan and other villages were relegated little or no importance. Indeed, there was much more reason to visit Janitzio's cemetery than Tzintzuntzan's. Probably stimulated by the influx of tourists, the people of Janitzio would spend all night at the graveyard, rather than arriving in the early hours of the morning, as was the case in Tzintzuntzan. As Foster and Ospina put it, "All night long boats arrive from Pátzcuaro with the curious, and from the water the island stands out sharply illuminated for many kilometers around, in contrast to the rest of the year when, with great difficulty, one can pick out a light or two from the mainland" (ibid.:221). During this period and for several decades subsequently there was really no competition for tourists in the Lake region. Janitzio had stolen the show.

Anybody who goes to Morelia, the beautiful capital of the state of Michoacán, is likely to encounter large posters during the month of October announcing Day of the Dead celebrations in nearby communities. A typical poster displays a dark blue field representing the night sky, on which are stenciled bold white letters reading: NOCHE DE MUERTOS EN MICHOACAN (Night of the Dead in Michoacán). The bulk of the poster is taken up by a drawing of a Tarascan Indian woman, wrapped in a *rebozo*, and seated aside *ofrendas* of tall candles, fruit, and *corundas*. Against her chest is blocked a "Programa de Eventos Durante la Celebración de Noche de Muertos en Michoacán," that is, a long list of sightseeing events throughout the state associated with the Night of the Dead. Tzintzuntzan figures among 14 towns and villages. We read that on November 1 in Tzintzuntzan we can see a performance of the mid-19th century Spanish drama "Don Juan Tenorio" by José Zorilla, as well as attend a "Festival de Danzas y Pirekuas." On November 1–2, according to the poster, Tzintzuntzan offers us "Tianguis Artesanal y Comida Típica," in addition to the *"Velación"* that is portrayed on the announcement itself. The second poster, in red, is devoted entirely to information about the play "Don Juan Tenorio"—the seven towns where it can be viewed, including Tzintzuntzan, with corresponding dates and times, and names of the sponsoring theater company, major production technicians, and starring performers. The posters implicitly indicate that Tzintzuntzan is part of a large, coordinated drama, organized by some central authority and involving a variety of settlements throughout the state.

This impression is, in fact, correct. The radical change in Tzintzuntzan's program of activities during the Night of the Dead can be traced precisely to 1971. In this year, three interrelated governmental entities coordinated their efforts to make this event a major tourist attraction well beyond the confines of

Janitzio, where it had achieved national fame on its own. The goal was to draw visitors throughout the state of Michoacán. A considerable amount of money would be invested. Since funds were limited, however, only the most propitious locales would be targeted for development. Tzintzuntzan, with its ancient heritage and colonial monuments, was a perfect candidate. The governmental agencies responsible for tourist promotion could not have overlooked Tzintzuntzan's national reputation and tourist potential. However, they did bypass Janitzio, which figures in none of the official announcements and posters. Presumably this island community, with a well-established tourist industry of its own, could maintain its success without state funds or promotional schemes.

The governmental agencies responsible for attracting tourism during the Night of the Dead were the Casa de Artesanías, the Casa de la Cultura, and the Ministry of Tourism of the state of Michoacán. These agencies, although independent entities, are all branches of the state government, and thereby coordinate their efforts into one virtually indistinguishable campaign. Their collective impact was to institute what people in Tzintzuntzan term *La Feria*. The *Feria*—literally, fair— refers to a broad complex of commercial activities and recreational events that coincide in place and time with the actual religious celebration. By the time that I witnessed the Night of the Dead in Tzintzuntzan in 1980 and 1984, the *Feria* had in many respects overtaken in importance the sacred fiesta activities. One middle-aged informant, herself not particularly devout by Tzintzuntzan standards, offered her opinion of the changes that had occurred by stating, "The event has become shameful. People hardly talk about the Night of the Dead anymore. Rather, they say *Feria*, or *Vamos a la Feria de los Muertos* [Let's go to the Fair of the Deceased!]! It's practically scandalous."

What exactly had changed as a result of state intervention? To begin, there was the introduction of cultural performances. Throughout the 1970s and up to the present, the theatrical company of the Casa de la Cultura in Michoacán has come to Tzintzuntzan to put on "Don Juan Tenorio", a classical Spanish drama. The play is given in a spectacular outdoor setting: the seventeenth-century open-air chapel that is one of the town's most important colonial monuments. Performed at 11:00 p.m. on the night of November 1, "Don Juan Tenorio" draws an audience of more than one thousand. Perhaps unfortunately, this group includes only a handful of villagers. The vast majority of people, though proud that the play is so popular with the visiting public, balk at the thought of paying an entry fee equivalent to about one to three days' income. "We don't tend to like things like that," one informant proclaimed, "That's mostly for city people, for people who've studied a lot and understand what's going on." In my experience, the people of Tzintzuntzan willingly lay out large sums for fiesta activities that they value. The performance of "Don Juan Tenorio" is obviously not among these.

Then, too, the Ministry of Tourism introduced a *Festival Folklórico*, as they term it. In 1980, on the first occasion I witnessed it, the Folklore Festival consisted of regional dances from all over Mexico, not just Michoacán. A large platform had been erected for the purpose near the Presidencia. For several hours just prior to the "Don Juan Tenorio" performance (these activities are obviously timed so that tourists can observe them all), dancers and musicians entertained an audience of perhaps five or six hundred of which, again, only a handful were from the village of Tzintzuntzan itself. Television cameras were on hand, flooding the scene with their glaring lights, and middle-class visitors, many of them dressed in urban versions of peasant costume, flashed their cameras at the colorful scene. Despite the fact that there was no entry fee for this event, however, townspeople showed little or no interest.

By 1984, on the second occasion I visited, the event had both grown and changed character. It was now being held on a raised platform in front of the *yácatas*, the circular ancient Tarascan pyramids. The event was now termed *Festival de Danzas y Pirekuas*, *pirekuas* being traditional Tarascan songs and music. In fact, the entire 1984 Festival was devoted to so-called folk performances from the region; representatives from other parts of Mexico were eliminated. There was a new entry fee of 100 pesos, an amount which would not have deterred villagers had they been interested. Nonetheless, among the thousands of onlookers, seated on folding chairs for the open air performance, the only local people I could identify were small groups of boys, teenaged and younger, who had climbed up the hillside by a back route and surreptitiously entered without paying. The audience was composed almost exclusively of middle-class Mexicans, fully urban in appearance and demeanor, many of whom had arrived for the occasion in tour buses from as far away as Mexico City. There were a number of large senior citizen's groups, made up of retirees who were bused from one locale to another in order to catch highlights from the Night of the Dead proceedings at three or four different places. One such group arrived, paid their entry fee, and stayed only a half hour or so before rushing off to nearby Ihuatzio; they were to conclude that night at the island of Janitzio, the grand finale to their tour.

The *Festival de Danzas y Pirekuas* was performed by young dancers and musicians from outside Tzintzuntzan, people who might well have been Tarascan, but nonetheless resided elsewhere in Michoacán. The female performers were dressed in a stylized, simplified version of Tarascan women's costume; the men, donning white pants and shirts, and adorned by bandanas and old-fashioned straw hats, looked nothing like the contemporary local Indian population. Most of the dances and songs were Tarascan style. One, however, was said to represent a "reconstruction" of a pre-Columbian Tarascan dance. The Instituto Nacional Indigenista—a national agency for promoting and protecting Indian culture—was announced as having sponsored the research and preparation that went into the dance. As far as was evident, nobody seemed to question the authenticity of this performance, which of necessity had to have been invented practically anew. Periodically, the announcer would fall into speaking Tarascan.

At several points in the show, in fact, he used Tarascan for a full five minutes or more, despite the obvious inability of the urban, middle class audience to understand a word that he said. Nonetheless, this linguistic detail, combined with the floodlit *yácatas*, and the folk music and costumes, added immeasurably to the impression that here, indeed, we were in the heart of Tarascan country. To assure that this event would be a success, it seemed irrelevant that fewer than 5 percent of the population of Tzintzuntzan speaks or even understands Tarascan. It was the image, not the reality, of indigenous culture that the Ministry of Tourism aimed to convey.

Insofar as the performative aspect of the *Feria* was concerned, the people of Tzintzuntzan were really incidental to the proceedings. At least on the two occasions that I observed, they participated directly neither as performers nor onlookers. In only one way did they really seem to exert influence, and that was in the seemingly trivial but actually very telling matter of how the *yácatas* were to be lit. Traditionally, on the Night of the Dead the *yácatas* remained as dark as they did during the rest of the year. With the suggestion and at the expense of the Ministry of Tourism, the municipal government of Tzintzuntzan situated *torchas*—diesel-fueled flares mounted in large tin cans—on the road leading up to the *yácatas*, as well as along the pyramids themselves, so as to outline the ancient structures when viewed from the town and highway below. During the celebration of 1983, a year prior to my second field stint, the municipal government had decided to substitute electric floodlights for the fuel lamps. Townspeople complained about the noxious smell of the diesel oil, and the fumes from the lamps blackened the surface of the *yacatas*, thus requiring a costly, time-consuming clean-up job afterwards. By 1984 the fuel lamps had returned. Stated one town official by way of explanation, *"No les gustó"*—"[The people] didn't like it." At first, I interpreted his remarks to mean that the villagers themselves objected. But, no, it turned out that he was referring to the tourists, who clearly preferred the oil lamps, which were presumably much more evocative of ancient times than was electricity. As a compromise, however, and to facilitate the dance and song festival, floodlights were retained for several of the *yácatas*. The others were once again lined with oil lamps, as was the road leading up to the Festival. With the collaboration of its own town government, Tzintzuntzan had been converted into a great, open-air theater, its ancient and colonial monuments serving as dramatic stage props.

Aside from theatrical and folk performances, the state agencies introduced two additional components to the *Feria*: a crafts competition and open-air market. From the very initiation of the *Feria* in 1971, the Casa de Artesanías in Morelia established an annual crafts competition in Tzintzuntzan to coincide with the Night of the Dead. With backing from an organ of the central Mexican government known by the acronym FONART (Fondo Nacional de Artesanías), the Casa de Artesanías offered prizes for the best craftsmanship in three categories:

(1) pottery, (2) *arcos*, and (3) all other crafts. First-place winners in each category received 3,000 pesos, second-place winners 2,000 pesos, and third-place winners 1,000 pesos, substantial sums that stimulated high-quality production efforts. Prestige clearly accrued to those who came out on top, for, during periodic visits to Tzintzuntzan at various times of year, friends and informants rarely failed to mention the success of one or the other craftsman, potters in particular. The open-air market devolved naturally from the crafts competition. The competition drew attention to artisan specialization in the village, and tourists and townspeople alike were drawn by curiosity to the crafts displays. Moreover, there was a financial incentive for crafts displays, since the Casa de Artesanías had agreed to purchase everything that remained unsold at the end of the *Feria*. Under these conditions, the Tzintzuntzan town government could charge substantial rents for space where artisans and food vendors set up temporary stands. For a number of years the market flourished. State subsidies assured profits for everybody— craftsmen and local government alike—and the presence of a bustling market added to Tzintzuntzan's appeal to visitors from Mexican cities and abroad. That appeal, and the tourist pesos it would bring, were obviously the ultimate aim of the Casa de Artesanías and associated agencies.

This highly favorable situation changed in the early 1980s. In 1981, and as a result of a variety of circumstances, the Casa de Artesanías ceased to sponsor the annual crafts competition. The most likely reason is that high rates of inflation had by then severely limited the government's willingness to invest in relatively expensive luxuries, such as paying artisans for their unsold wares. The Casa de Artesanías, and its mother agency FONART, were no doubt in a worse financial state in 1981 than they had been ten years earlier. At the same time, the so-called *tianguis* or free market, had been established in Pátzcuaro, only a half hour away. The Pátzcuaro town government permitted the artisans free use of space. As a large market town, with a well-established tourist infrastructure, Pátzcuaro naturally attracted a considerably larger buying public than Tzintzuntzan ever could. So, freed from expensive rental overhead and assured of a large affluent clientele, Tzintzuntzan artisans began to display their crafts in Pátzcuaro during November 1 and 2, rather than in their home town. Added to these developments was an unfortunate political murder that occurred in Tzintzuntzan during the Night of the Dead in 1977 and that received a good deal of sensationalistic publicity throughout the state of Michoacán. Villagers themselves claim that the Casa de Artesanías lost interest in supporting Tzintzuntzan after that traumatic event. For whatever reason, the result was a serious decline in the number of temporary stands erected during the *Feria*, although there were still about a dozen evident in November 1984.

Food stands, however, profited and grew in number. Mexicans like to snack under any circumstances, and an event such as the *Feria* is precisely what stimulates this tendency. The entire street on which the Presidencia is located is filled with dozens of temporary stalls selling everything from tacos, buñuelos, atole, corundas, and other cooked items, prepared on the spot, to bottled soft drinks and packaged candy. Several hot chocolate stands cater to tourists and villagers who crave this traditional breakfast delicacy in the early morning hours of November 2, following the cemetery vigil. There is also plenty of *ponche*, the typical alcoholic beverage of the occasion. Food vendors do very well during the Night of the Dead. The proximity of the plaza where they are located to the cemetery, and at the base of the hill leading up to the *yácatas*, makes the stands readily accessible to the thousands of tourists who visit Tzintzuntzan on this occasion. This market represents the most obviously successful commercial offshoot of state intervention since 1971.

The introduction of the *Feria*, with its theatrical and commercial dimensions, constitutes the most direct, immediate impact of state intervention on Tzintzuntzan's Night of the Dead. The indirect impact, however, has been equally notable, if not more so. The transformation of traditional aspects of the fiesta has manifested itself mainly in two areas: the *velación* and the *doble*.

In principle, the cemetery vigil, including the display of offerings and the graveside accompaniment of the deceased, is basically the same as always. The changes have mostly come in the scale of the event, as well as in the atmosphere it conveys. It includes many more participants and lasts much longer than ever before. The cemetery, flanking both sides of the highway leading into town, is now packed with decorated tombs and family members watching over them. Tombs may be left unattended for brief periods throughout the night, making an exact count of families impossible. Nonetheless, it would be safe to say that there are two to three hundred decorated gravesites, adorned with literally thousands of candles and food and flower offerings. Instead of arriving early on the morning of November 2, which was the traditional practice, villagers nowadays remain at the graves of their departed relatives throughout the late evening of November 1. Shortly after dark, people have already cleaned and decorated the tombs and begun their vigil. Except for brief periods of absence—and even that among the minority of participants—people stay at the cemetery throughout most of the night, many of them remaining to celebrate sunrise Mass at the cemetery itself.

The overall atmosphere at the *velación* is far from what Foster and Ospina witnessed in 1945, with "the twinkling of several hundred candles in the dark," suggesting "will-of-the-wisps run riot" (1948: 220). Occasionally, with assistance from the imagination, the onlooker can perceive the kind of magical quality to the occasion that the tourist brochures and announcements promise, and that Foster and Ospina experienced. For the most part, however, what we encounter today is unexpectedly carnavalesque. In the center of the lower, larger half of the cemetery, television cameras are situated to record the event for later broadcast. A huge, noisy electric generator is employed to provide energy for the floodlights that brightly illuminate a great portion of the cemetery. Meanwhile, hundreds of tourists, many of them listening to portable radios, stalk from grave to grave, commenting openly on the quality of the offerings, and on the picturesque costume and posture of the mourners. As they jostle past one another, they jockey to position themselves to best photographic advantage. The flash of cameras competes with the graveside candles in lighting up the dark evening sky, though neither source is very successful when compared with the glaring beams that emanate from the television outpost.

Since the cemetery is located right on the highway—bisected by it, in fact—the automobile traffic automatically contributes to the atmosphere. Enough cars enter Tzintzuntzan during the Night of the Dead so that traffic jams have become a regular feature of the event. Police from Pátzcuaro and Morelia are on hand to direct cars to parking spots. The highway bordering on the cemetery is lined on both sides with parked cars, many of which are used almost like temporary campsites. A Red Cross team is on hand to care for tourists who suddenly fall ill. With car doors open and stereos blaring, families gather round their automobiles to eat picnic dinners and exchange impressions. The commotion naturally reaches the gravesites just a few yards away.

The second major traditional feature of the Night of the Dead that has changed radically is the *doble*. In 1980, on the occasion that I first witnessed this fiesta, the *doble* had ceased to be the event that Tzintzuntzan had known for generations. In that year, according to the parish priest, *"Se prohibió"*—"It was prohibited." By using the vague passive tense, the priest undoubtedly was attempting to disguise his responsibility for this largely unpopular move. Indeed, responsibility cannot be imputed with certainty, although the priest clearly favored the change and contributed to its implementation. He continued: "The authorities perceived a certain disorder to the custom, that sometimes reached the point of drunkenness. It's one thing for individuals to drink, but when it's done by an organized group the drinking creates a certain disorder." And disorder there surely was, if town legends are to be believed. It is said that on one occasion, the boys entered the sacristy, clothed themselves in the priest's garments, and staged a fake Mass in the parish church. One member of the group, angered by the misbehavior of his companions, called the police, who punished these youth with a day in jail.

On another occasion, one young man stole all the bread that his companions had collected from door-to-door begging and tried to make off with it. When they discovered what he had done, they chased him wildly through the streets, producing a minor town scandal. Even today, when describing what the event was like, many informants casually assert the observation that it was, as they somewhat indelicately put it, *una borrachera*—a drunken orgy. And nonetheless, the bells got tolled as they were supposed to. In the end, the boys fulfilled their obligation to church and townspeople.

Then why was the *doble*, such as it was known, suspended? I suspect that there was a convergence of reasons, all stemming back to mass tourism. For one thing, in order to assure the tourist influx, town officials, together with the priest, had to make sure that order and harmony were preserved throughout the Night of the Dead. With so many outsiders passing through, there was already considerable concern about the potential for chaos and disruption. The presence of Pátzcuaro police, borrowed for the occasion, together with a Red Cross emergency medical unit, bore sufficient witness to the extraordinary nature of the event. It was no doubt thought that the youth in charge of the *doble* could only add to the difficulties. Then, too, there was apparently a loss of interest among the youth themselves. Begging from door to door, tolling the church bells, eating and drinking around a bonfire—these were all forms of diversion, which had been rendered more or less obsolete. Now the tourists themselves provided enough of an entertaining spectacle, not to mention the food and drink and carnival atmosphere as a whole. Besides, as several informants pointed out, the young men who would have participated in the *doble* were now occupied in manning the temporary stalls, helping their families take full advantage of the financial opportunities presented by tourism. They could hardly afford to waste time on the *doble*, which had become, under the circumstances, little more than a form of leisure.

And yet the bells had to be tolled. To substitute for the original youth group, one of the main Tzintzuntzan religious brotherhoods (Brandes 1981), the Cargueros de la Soledad, was recruited to perform the job. From 1980, these 12 men and their spouses have divided the responsibility for the bell ringing among themselves. The door-to-door begging has entirely disappeared. Besides, with the large influx of tourists, there are several thefts each year, and villagers, understandably frightened by this development, barricade their houses against the outside world. Begging, under these conditions, is hardly a feasible option. Instead, the Cargueros de la Soledad take turns walking from gravesite to gravesite, reciting prayers for the dead, and requesting *"el doble"* in return. As in the past, when the unorganized poor were recipients of donations, the mourners respond by placing an offering on the *cargueros'* tray—a banana, a chayote, a piece of sweet bread, or whatever. In 1984, when I witnessed this little ritualized exchange of prayer for offering, one *carguero* stopped between graves and turned to a mourner below, stating, "We're ashamed to go begging like this, but the priest gave us permission." Traditionally, only undisciplined children or the desperately poor would go begging. Here were fully adult, competent men carrying out the same role. The sense of embarrassment could not escape them, although they, like everybody else, could recognize the structural appropriateness of what they were doing: receiving material compensation for praying and tolling the church bells. The commodities being exchanged were traditional; the actors involved were not. As a result, the *doble* is now a radically different institution from what it was prior to 1971.

Of course, certain components of the Night of the Dead have remained virtually unchanged from what they were prior to 1971. The order and number of Masses, as dictated by Rome, is of course the same. Nor can any significant differences be detected either in home altars or in the types and abundance of *ofrendas*, with the exception of *arcos*, which seem to be less numerous than they were in 1945. Foster had noted a precipitous decline in 1961, and apparently the prizes offered by the Casa de Artesanías did nothing to stimulate production. It is time consuming and expensive to produce an *arco*, and the only justification would seem to be religious: to commemorate the death of an *angelito*. With fewer and fewer children dying, due to antibiotics and the near total acceptance of modern medical practice, the decline in *arcos* is understandable. Foster noted only one in 1961; there were two in 1984. It is likely, then, that the number of *arcos* would have declined even without tourism and state intervention.

As for the rest—the theatrical performance, the bustling commerce, the altered *velación* and the *doble*—the Night of the Dead bears slight resemblance to its former self. It is now an immense event of national significance, which people all over the Republic can observe on television. Of equal importance, the changes have affected the symbolic meaning of the occasion to the people of Tzintzuntzan, and perhaps even modified the way they perceive themselves.

One of the first accounts of the impact of tourism on the Day of the Dead is a marvelously detailed ethnography by Jesús Angel Ochoa Zazueta (1974). In Mizquic, the town near Mexico City (and today nearly engulfed by that city) described by Ochoa, tourism seems to be an older, more institutionalized presence than is the case with Tzintzuntzan. According to Ochoa, after 12 p.m. on the night of November 1, tourists are encouraged to make the rounds of home altars (Ochoa 1974:99–100). In his words (ibid.), this visit:

> is the only form . . . in which the bothersome visitors are permitted and attended to with kindness. The children, proud, run through the streets fighting for the groups of tourists and passersby in order to take them to their houses to admire the *ofrenda*. On each altar a small, discrete receptacle is placed for the donations that visitors wish to make towards the expense of the celebration. With the value of each visitor's donation in mind, household heads distribute tamales, atole, a shot of tequila or pulque and occasionally even mole and tortillas, insisting—if the donation was respectable—that the visitor return to see the altar the following year.

The Day of the Dead in Mizquic also includes an exposition of local archaeological artifacts, displayed in an old Augustinian convent, to which tourists are charged an entry fee. Visitors, too, are required to pay in order to see the cemetery vigil. As Ochoa says, "The visitors on this date pay for everything" (ibid.:100). How have the people of Mizquic reacted to tourism on the Day of the Dead? According to Ochoa, the tourists "are somewhat bothersome" (ibid.:108). In the end, however, they "benefit the village, a village which, taking everything into account, puts up with them because the *almas* [souls of the departed] are pleased by the visitors" (ibid.). Ochoa's informants told him that the departed souls "like fiestas," that they "don't like to see sad faces," and that "they are very happy when their living relatives have a lot of friends who remember them and who participate in the celebration" (ibid.). Hence, the tourist presence in Mizquic would seem to be consonant with traditional beliefs and values; it has neither challenged nor destroyed them.

In Tzintzuntzan, too, belief systems do not seem to have been disrupted by the introduction of massive tourism. Nowadays people laugh at the notion that the spirits actually descend to consume the offerings laid out on their behalf. Foster and Ospina provide evidence that even in 1945 no such belief existed (1948:221). However, it is clear that the villagers did and still do believe that the deceased are somehow present, watching; the *ánimas* take note of the proceedings without directly intervening. A village woman compared the event to a vacation for industrial urban workers; on the Night of the Dead, she says, "Our Lord gives the souls a much-needed change from what is apparently a very dull heaven" (Foster 1981:129). Nobody in Tzintzuntzan ever mentioned to me that the souls actually like having tourists around, which is what Mizquic informants claim. However, Tzintzuntzeños surely enjoy the fiesta nowadays more than they did prior to state intervention in 1971. "It used to be so sad," lamented one old man, as if this emotion were somehow inappropriate to the Night of the Dead.

Of course a sense of animation and play have always been present in the Tzintzuntzan Night of the Dead, particularly in the *doble*, but also in the fanciful creation of *arcos* and offerings, which are frequently shaped to resemble cheerful ghosts, skeletons, and the like. The main incompatibility between the traditional situation and that of today lies more in the meaning of events than in the substance of the events themselves. The Night of the Dead was previously a fiesta that the people of Tzintzuntzan put on for themselves. For most villagers it was a family celebration, commemorated by erecting home altars and paying short visits to ancestral graves. The festival has now become a community affair, which relates the town of Tzintzuntzan as a unit to the outside world. It is this new dimension of the Night of the Dead, the fact that it has become practically a theatrical performance, which is the source of deepest transformation. Dean MacCannell, whose innovative book, *The Tourist* (1976), was almost single-handedly responsible for the promotion of tourist studies, long ago suggested that a major impulse behind tourism is the search for authenticity. He recognized, as well, that supposedly authentic cultural events are often intentionally staged for the sake of tourist patronage. Tzintzuntzan's Day of the Dead provides support for this general observation.

For one thing, there can be no doubt that the Tzintzuntzan cultural landscape becomes transformed literally into a stage prop for performances, such as the classical drama "Don Juan Tenorio" and the Festival of Danzas and Pirekuas.

Food stands are erected nearby with the explicit purpose of tourist sales. But even more significant is the symbolic conversion of the town cemetery into a stage set. By comparison with the celebration in Mizquic, the people of Tzintzuntzan have not yet succeeded in converting their cemetery vigil into a paid performance. But there is sufficient evidence to suggest that this process is well underway. For example, while attending the vigil in 1984, I expressed my reluctance to take pictures. From my point of view this act would constitute an intrusion into the private, contemplative world of the mourners. "Go ahead," encouraged a village friend, "Nobody minds. We do this [the vigil] for the tourists." And, indeed, not one villager expressed annoyance or displeasure of any kind at being photographed, at listening to blaring radios, at having gravesites trampled. These deeds, which I considered inherently disrespectful, were all perceived as intrinsic to the tourist presence. Most townspeople expressed a great deal of pride in the attention that they and their community were to receive during the Day of the Dead. Surely Tzintzuntzan greets more people on this occasion than on any other. The influx of visitors is flattering, as are the attention and resources lavished on the town by state governmental agencies.

Above all, the Day of the Dead provides a financial bonanza to villagers. Most community fiestas throughout the yearly cycle require donations, usually in the form of mandatory quotas used to support the festival, but also the expenditure of considerable amounts of time and money, extracted from individuals largely by the force of public opinion (Brandes 1988:59–87). The Night of the Dead is perhaps the only exception in that it requires no financial outlay to some central town or church authority. The cost of the fiesta is borne by state agencies and individual households. It is the one time of year that households can decide on their own expenditures, mainly in the form of altar and cemetery *ofrendas*. Outside agencies support the remainder of the festival activities.

Villagers can also earn money on this occasion. The Night of the Dead is profitable for vendors who set up food stands. It is a perceived source of income from as yet untapped sources, as well. Consider the following incident. A few days prior to the Night of the Dead, in 1984, one of my village friends had told me a story about a tourist couple visiting the island of Janitzio. The couple was approached by some islanders, who asked if they wanted to come inside to see their home altar. "Yes, thank you," replied the tourists; but when they reached the altar they were appalled at the sign attached to it, reading: "CONTRIBUCION 100 PESOS." The story was recounted in order to signal the difference between Tzintzuntzan and Janitzio. It was a way of saying, "Yes, we have our tourists. But our celebration is authentic; we do it for ourselves—not, like the people of Janitzio, to make money."

At about 2:00 a.m. on November 2, 1984, just a few days after listening to this tale, I lingered in the upper cemetery, camera in hand. I spotted three women guarding vigil over a beautiful *arco*. I had taken very few pictures, because of my own reticence, but decided this would make a good one. Awkwardly, I asked permission. The women stared at me blankly for a few moments. Then, the eyes of one lit up. She consulted her companions quietly, after which the decision was rendered: the picture would cost me 100 pesos! To my knowledge, this event provides the first evidence that a traditional feature of the Night of the Dead is becoming commercialized, that villagers realize that they can turn their sacred religious practices to profit. Afterwards, when I told what had occurred to me, a village friend expressed his disgust; *"Es abusivo"*—"It's abusive," he declared in my defense. This small incident is a harbinger of much more widespread transformations that ultimately will leave Tzintzuntzan in the same position as Janitzio, Mizquic, and other towns and villages that acquired fame for authenticity.

For the most part, and despite the dismay of my village defender, villagers appreciate the changes that have come to the Night of the Dead. They like the liveliness, the outside attention, the influx of money, the governmental support and exposure. Not once, and in spite of some discreet hints on my part, did I ever encounter a complaint about tourist noise, impoliteness, or sacrilege. There is some deserved concern about theft. Each year, at least one or two stores are robbed, which has given rise to a heightened feeling of insecurity. But nobody has suggested that the Day of the Dead be suspended. To the contrary, Tzintzuntzeños think only of changing the town infrastructure to accommodate even more tourists, for example by converting the atrium into a parking lot!

Townspeople are aware that there is such a traffic jam that many drivers turn away from the village out of frustration, without even bothering to park. They are now attempting to solve this problem. For the priest, however, the event has gotten out of hand. "I don't wish to seem immodest," he told me in the mid-1980s, "but it was I who was the main impulse behind the Night of the Dead." "The event occurred," he continued, "fourteen years ago [i.e. 1971]. I had a certain amount of experience with folk dance concerts and thought that this sort of thing would attract tourists." So, relying on his influence in Morelia, the priest lobbied in favor of governmental support for Tzintzuntzan's Night of the Dead, and his efforts succeeded. "I wanted to promote the economy of the community, attracting people through an artisan contest." This, too, came to pass. His fear, however, is that "the fiesta should lose its spirit, lose its indigenous flavor." He now regrets, he movingly confessed, "the problem of so many people who visit us." In short, the priest seems to have lost control over the very event that he had successfully orchestrated.

Anthropologists, adopting a holistic perspective, recognize what the priest himself had overlooked, that is, that all parts of a cultural system are intimately interrelated. It is impossible to change one item without inducing far-reaching, often unpredictable alterations in other aspects of the society and culture. By inviting state intervention into Tzintzuntzan's Night of the Dead, the priest had begun a chain of events that were to transform the way the villagers perceived themselves. They were no longer actors in a ritual drama played out, as Geertz would have it (1973:448), by and for themselves. They would now be performers, acting out ancient rites for the benefit and amusement of others. The state had already converted the material dimension of their village into a stage set, with outsider dancers, actors, and musicians playing the role of Tzintzuntzeños. It only remained now for the actual people of Tzintzuntzan to adopt the theatrical role prescribed for them by the state. With or without the priest's approval, the people in 1984 did not seem reluctant to adopt this new stance. They were fast on the road to becoming part of the great performance that the Ministry of Tourism had produced and directed.

Far from waning over time, the state's intervention in the Day of the Dead on a national level has only increased since the 1980s. One of the most dramatic examples of this trend comes from the town of Huaquechula, located just southwest of the state capital of Puebla. There, according to Morales and Mysyk (2004), governmental promotion of the Day of the Dead began in earnest in 1988 "and has proceeded at an accelerated rate since then. . . ." According to these scholars, two events stand out in people's minds as creating the necessary conditions for the Day of the Dead to become a tourist attraction: first, a visit to the town in 1988 by then-President Carlos Salinas de Gortari, who explained the potential benefits of NAFTA—the North American Free Trade Agreement which came into effect several years thereafter—and announced the paving of a road leading into town; and, second, an agreement with the Program of Development of the Tourism Sector, secured by the town's president in the late 1990s and assuring that Huaquechula would be included on the state's tourist circuit.

With specific regard to the Day of the Dead, the State of Puebla established a state-wide competition for the authenticity of altars for the dead. Morales and Mysyk declare that, "the competition provided the impetus for change from the smaller, less elaborate, and more somber altars of less than a generation ago . . . to the bright and highly ornate altars . . . that attract recreational tourists today" (Morales and Mysyk 2004). In 1997, the State of Puebla named "Altar Offerings of Huaquechula" to be part of the cultural patrimony of Puebla. "By declaring Day of the Dead in Huaquechula to be a certified part of Puebla's cultural patrimony," state Morales and Mysyk (ibid.), "the state, in its role as marketer of cultural meanings, is attempting to capitalize on the national ideology of *indigenismo* . . . With the stroke of a pen, the decree excised the influence of 500 years of Catholicism on pre-Hispanic ritual and glorified the mystique and exoticism of the Aztec world view."

In Huaquechula, as in Tzintzuntzan, cultural tourism has become an economic development strategy, with similar positive and negative consequences to those in Tzintzuntzan. With the introduction of numerous outsiders into the town, thefts have occurred. But family altars are a minor source of income, at least for those households that place trays in front of their altars to encourage donations. Householders also seem to take pride in the tourist presence. Said one villager, "Tourists join us and the town becomes famous. Our economic status increases and we are no longer so poor" (ibid.). But no one could actually explain to observers precisely the form of this economic benefit. Indeed, costs of mounting elaborate altars have become so high that, in the words of one villager, "It will not be long before we will be unable to celebrate Day of the Dead because we have to spend so much money." From the tourist point of view, there is increasing disappointment at having to travel so far to view essentially the same altars that are on display in the state capital (ibid.). Tourists also balked at the crowds, the inaccessibility of homes in which altars are set up, and the restricted viewing hours.

Tourist development has been expensive in much more than monetary terms, however. On November 3, 2004, there appeared a news report in the country's most respected paper, *La Jornada*, which describes the Night of the Dead as celebrated only a few days before in Tzintzuntzan. The report is, frankly, shocking.

> Streets filled with garbage, empty liquor bottles, beer cans, scraps of food, garbage, and tens of youth still wandering through the streets affected by drink. The Purépecha ruins known as Yácatas served to house hundreds of people who set up their camping tents. And for the first time, in the face of the number of outsiders, in the *atrio* of the Franciscan church, where ancient olive trees still stand, tents were also set up. When the performance of "Don Juan Tenorio" ended at three in the morning, you could still find youth arguing and drinking outside their tents. The street was transformed into the largest cantina in Michoacán . . . In the lower part of the Yácatas, the cemetery lit by thousands of candles, while in the streets the hamburgers, noisy cars, drinks, trinkets, *pozole*, *tamales*, and spiked punch, showed the mixture of customs into which this tradition has evolved.

Apparently, the problem of disorderly conduct extends to other parts of the Republic as well. Kristin Norget reports that in Oaxaca "official regulations continue to pivot around concerns about hygiene and safety in the cemetery— above all in relation to consumption of food there. And some people I interviewed, for example, turned their noses in distgust at the idea of eating in the graveyard or deplored the drunkenness and 'debauched' behavior of certain individuals, who, in their view, contributed to 'bringing the community down'" (see Figure 4.1) (Norget 2005:254).

In the end, the economic and emotional price of tourist development might prove intolerable for residents of Tzintzuntzan and other well-known meccas of so-called traditional life. Promotion of cultural attractions like the Day of

Fig. 4.1 Oaxaca hotel lobby poster, October–November 1996

the Dead has transformed ritual practice almost beyond recognition. For the moment, however, the federal government and local authorities, in their quest for economic development, continue to define the Day of the Dead, for Mexicans and foreigners alike, as a supreme example of pre-Columbian ritual.

5

THE POETICS
OF DEATH

In *The Act of Creation*, Arthur Koestler (1964:52) states that humor "must contain one ingredient whose presence is indispensable: an impulse, however faint, of aggression or apprehension." This assertion, controversial in its time, provides a condensed reformulation of insights presented earlier by Freud (1974), Wolfenstein (1954), and other psychoanalytic thinkers. Subsequent analyses of humor (e.g., Dundes (1971); Legman (1968, 1975)) have confirmed the veracity of Koestler's formulation. There can be no doubt that humor derives at least some of its impact from its aggressive character. Teasing, for example, provides an outlet for personal criticism. As a genre, teasing is a form of "permitted disrespect," an ingredient essential to what anthropologists know as the joking relationship (Apte 1985:29–66). Almost half a century ago, Radcliffe-Brown (1965:90) defined this relationship as "a relation between two persons in which one is by custom permitted, and in some instances required, to tease or make fun of the other, who in turn is required to take no offense." Keith Basso has shown (1979) that the person who teases walks a delicate tightrope. To remain on good terms with the victim, the speaker must know well his or her target. This means assessing which personality traits are safe subjects for ridicule and which not. It also means understanding the conditions and context under which ridicule can take place, without creating offense. Similarly, ethnic humor (e.g., Apte 1985:108–148; Brandes 1980:53–73; Brandes 1983b), sexual humor (e.g., Fine 1976; Legman 1968, 1975), and political humor (e.g., Brandes 1977) all have prominent deprecatory themes. All types of jokes—that is, verbal narratives with a humorous punch line—invariably include aggressive content. They may be either self-effacing or, alternatively, function to comment negatively on some despised outside group. In either case, the narrator must select theme and audience carefully, in order for the joke to be perceived as humorous and listeners' feelings remain unscathed.

Rituals, religious or secular, are among the most prominent occasions for the release of aggression through humor. The ritual itself provides a safe frame by dictating the specific form of humorous expression and occasions on which it can emerge. Aggressors and victims are stipulated in advance, so that everyone—actors and audience alike—knows more or less what will transpire and when. To be sure, effective humor always contains an element of surprise. Teasing or joke telling falls flat without it. Clown figures, among the most common bearers of humor in religious ritual, need to innovate and improvise in order to produce laughter (Bouissac 1976; Brandes 1979). Gestures, actions, and words are only funny if they are perceived to be spontaneous. And yet, in the context of ritual, spontaneity is always contained by predetermined rules as to form, content, and timing. These rules provide safe boundaries, which assure that aggressive sentiments will be contained and not seriously threaten the social and political order. Occasionally, however, as with *Carnival in Romans* (LeRoy Ladurie 1979), the action breaks through invisible barriers and produces rebellion, or, at the very least, enhanced awareness of prevailing injustices (Davis 1975).

Mortuary rituals, on the face of it, would seem inappropriate occasions for the expression of humor. However, anthropologists and folklorists have long been aware of what we might call counter-intuitive instances, in which jocular inversions are intrinsic to the proceedings (Narvaez 2003). Jacobson-Widding reminds us, for example, that throughout sub-Saharan Africa a "funeral is a complete inversion of prescribed and normal social behavior. The hierarchical order, controlled behavior, and the prudish etiquette of normal social life are transformed at funerals into the chaos of people shouting, embracing one another, rolling on the ground, tearing their clothes off, performing ritual jokes, and excelling in obscenities" (Jacobson-Widding 1990:63). In Madagascar, we are told (Metcalf and Huntington 1992:112), that the "most striking aspect of Malagasy funerals is the bawdy and drunken revelry enjoined on the guests. Malagasy participants state that these lively events are necessary because the deceased is in transition. He or she is isolated and lonely and needs to be amused and entertained." Europe provides comparable examples. Quigley (1996:64) states that, in traditional Scandinavia, a wake "was often an opportunity for courtship. In medieval Europe, most notably Ireland, mourners engaged in drinking, smoking, storytelling, song and dance, and mockery." Although Quigley's reference to smoking —a practice introduced into Europe only after the Spanish conquest—seems suspect, it is probable that during centuries, and up to the middle of the 20th century, in fact, Irish wakes were major occasions for jocularity and amusement (Ó'Súilleabháin 1967). They regularly included the perpetration of practical jokes involving the animation of corpses (Harlow 1997).

In Mexico, particularly rural Mexico, ritual humor is a well-known feature of annual celebrations involving the veneration of patron saints (e.g., Brandes 1988;

Bricker 1973). Much less has been written about humor in Mexican mortuary ritual, with the exception of one notable event: the Day of the Dead. Around this time of year, political cartoons—since the 19th century, ever-present in the Mexican press—begin to proliferate and use death and dying as a metaphor for political commentary. Consider, for example, a cartoon published one November 2 that portrays an image of the Monument to the Revolution—a major Mexico City landmark. The Monument is drawn as a gigantic, freshly decorated gravestone, a clear symbol of mourning for the Mexican Revolution. Cartoonist Ahumada indicates with a few brushstrokes the demise of the Revolution and its ideals, both victims of the neoliberalism and privatization that were rampant during the 1990s, when the cartoon appeared (see Figure 5.1).

A major expression of humor during the Day of the Dead, as we saw in Chapter 3, takes the form of the small, whimsical skulls and skeletons made of plastic, papiêr-maché, candy, and wood. Ordinary citizens and merchants draw

Fig. 5.1   Cartoon, *La Jornada*, November 2, 1995

upon artistic *calaveras* such as these to decorate home altars, family grave sites, and storefront windows. When made of sugar paste (*alfeñique*), chocolate, or amaranth seed dough (*tzoalli*), they are also eaten. The word *calaveras*, or "skull," refers first of all to these toy skulls sold ubiquitously in Mexican shops, markets, and street stands. Increasingly, they are easy to find in shops north of the border as well. *Calaveras* are often customized by being inscribed on the forehead with the name of a friend or relative. As indicated in Chapter 3, this type of *calavera* is presented as a gift to the person whose name appears on the skull—a simple, graphic representation of combined humor and aggression.

An equally prominent type of *calavera*, less famous outside Mexico and rare even during the Day of the Dead season in the United States, is the poetic epitaph. This is a literary genre, a mock memorial in verse dedicated to the memory of a living personage. At least one author (Norget 2005:207) speculates that the term *calavera* as applied to these epitaphs comes from the skull drawings that, in pre-revolutionary Mexico, decorated the broadsides bearing these verses. Without documentation, however, there can be no certainty about its origin. The literary *calavera* is almost always rhymed and often organized into quatrains. Though *calaveras* nowadays are generally short—four to twelve lines at most— they can vary from simple couplets to minor epics stretching several pages in length. A good example of a two-liner comes from the Veracruz newspaper, *La Opinión*. On November 3, 1912, the editor published a *calavera* in honor of a long-forgotten political figure, Don Angel C. Colina: *"Dicen que se ha muerto entero/ Por defender a Madero"*—"They say that he died whole because he defended Madero" (i.e., Francisco Madero, President of Mexico during the early stages of the Mexican Revolution (1910–20)).

Although *calaveras* are sometimes complimentary, they are usually bitingly satirical and mock the victim's weaknesses through humorous teasing. In this respect, they bear close resemblance to the baroque literary form known as *túmulos*, literally caskets or funeral verses. Satirical epitaphs, known to scholars as *túmulos burlescos*, were common during Golden Age Spain (Arellano and Roncero 2002). Among the most famous were two mocking epitaphs—equivalent to a public "roast"—that Francisco de Quevedo dedicated to Luis de Góngora while the latter was alive. Miguel de Cervantes, Alonso Jerónimo de Salas Barbadillo, Juan del Valle Caviedes, and many other Golden Age literary luminaries wrote satirical epitaphs, which ridicule not only weaknesses of character (e.g., "Epitaph to a man who is friend of eating and letting another pay," by Jacinto Alonso Maluenda) but also the foibles of particular occupational groups (e.g., "About Antímaco, astrologer," by Lope de Vega).

It is impossible at this point to infer a direct historical connection between these Spanish Golden Age verses and the Mexican *calaveras* of modern times. The most one can say, without further investigation, is that the two genres pertain to a common literary tradition. In addition, by virtue of the fact that *túmulos burlescos* flourished during the first two centuries of Spanish colonial rule, there is a good chance that satirical epitaphs were transmitted during that period from Spain to Mexico. In Mexico they might well have remained within the domain of high literary tradition until broadsides eventually converted them into a popular poetic form. An alternative theory, proposed by Rafael Jesús González (2005:24), is that Mexican *calaveras* derive from *pasquines*, or "mocking verses scrawled on walls to which passing readers added their own lines and comments" (ibid.). *Pasquines*, characteristic of the early colonial period, became disseminated through broadsides, which were posted on walls for all to read. Eventually the *pasquín* developed into what we know as the literary *calavera* (ibid.) of contemporary times.

In Mexico today, friends and relatives occasionally present *calaveras* to one another during the Day of the Dead. The *calavera* author normally dedicates his or her verse by making the victim's name the title of the epitaph. However aggressive they might seem, short verses of this sort almost always operate to reinforce friendships and other social ties. They are an expression of ongoing joking relationships. By presenting a *calavera* to a friend or relative, the poet implies that there exists such a strong bond between the two that not even a mocking jab at the victim's weaknesses will threaten the relationship. In turn, by accepting the *calavera* with good humor, the victim states in essence that he or she feels so close to the poet that the bond can well withstand an innocent personal jab.

The principal form of *calavera* is the published *calavera*, which appears at the end of October and beginning of November in newspapers and periodicals throughout the Republic. Ever since the late 19th century and early 20th century (Wollen 1989), enterprising writers and artists have taken the opportunity of the Day of the Dead to produce broadsides and small magazines exclusively devoted to the dissemination of these sometimes clever, sometimes corny epitaphs. The authors of *calaveras* are generally anonymous. Anonymity, which is surely an intentional editorial decision, is a literary device that assures that authors as individuals fade into the background so that their verses lose any semblance of prejudicial feelings. Anonymity enhances the impression that *calaveras* express opinions held by the masses, that they convey popular judgments, that they are the voice of the people.

One recent innovation is the *calavera* contest, sponsored by newspapers through-out the Republic. (These are in fact the literary counterpart of recently introduced altar contests, sponsored by municipal governments and discussed in Chapter 4.) Each year at the beginning of October, newspaper editors solicit poems from readers. The winning entries are published, in this case under a byline. One successful contribution to the nationally distributed newspaper *Reforma* (November 1, 2000:16) is a *calavera* dedicated "to *las calaveras*." It gives an excellent overview of the nature and meaning of these whimsical epitaphs.

A las calaveras
Noviembre siempre es el mes
ya conocido y notorio
cuando se habla a la vez
de calacas y el tenorio.

Pues son nuestras tradiciones
el escribir calaveras
donde hay muertos de a montones
mas nadie muere de veras.

Rescatar nuestras costumbres
esto cumple esos fines
hablar de cielo y de lumbres
y déjense de "jalogüines".

Es broma, lector, lectora,
no hay agravios encubiertos
y no le carguen los muertos
a quien escribe ahora.

Si acaso en esta ocasión
con tus huesos aquí asomas
has de disculpar las bromas:
¡Calaveras, bromas son!

  To the Calaveras
November is always the month
already known and notorious
when skeletons and *el tenorio*
are spoken of simultaneously.

Well, it's our tradition
to write *calaveras*
in which there are mountains of dead people
but no one really dies.

Rescuing our customs
satisfies those goals
of speaking of heaven and fire
and leaving behind "Halloweens".

It's a joke, readers,
there are no hidden insults
and let the deceased not denounce
the present writer.

> For it's the case that on this occasion
> with your bones showing
> you have to forgive the jokes:
> *Calaveras*, they are jokes!
>   (Maestra Hortensia Galindo Garrido
>   Colonia Lindavista (México, DF))

The reference to *"el tenorio"* at the end of the first stanza refers, of course, to "Don Juan Tenorio," the Spanish classical drama by José Zorilla, which, as discussed in Chapter 3, is widely performed throughout Mexico during Day of the Dead season. A large part of the play takes place in a cemetery, which makes the work particularly relevant on this occasion. When the author speaks of leaving behind Halloweens, she alludes to the symbolic competition between Halloween and the Day of the Dead that forms the substance of Chapter 6.

Calaveras directed at the reading public occasionally express unqualified praise and admiration. Consider, for example, a *calavera* dedicated to beloved writer, Elena Poniatowska (*El Metiche*, November 1, 1995):

> *La pelona aunque con reuma*
> *para leer no se hace rosca*
> *nos dejó sin la ágil pluma*
> *de Elenita Poniatowska.*

> The hairless one (i.e., Death), although with rheumatism
> is still able to read,
> [she] left us without the agile pen
> of Elenita Poniatowska.

Use of the diminutive Elenita is a public, and widely used sign of affection, which adds to the generally positive message of this *calavera*.

Historian Miguel León Portilla, widely acclaimed for his mastery of pre-Columbian life and thought, also receives praiseworthy treatment in the press (*Calaveras Encanijadas* 1995:4):

> *El ínclito historiador*
> *tras de ser galardonado*
> *en un foro del Estado*
> *habló con mucho valor;*
> *a la medalla hizo honor*
> *como quedó allí patente*
> *y hasta el mismo Presidente*
> *la festejó su entereza.*
> *Descansa en paz, de una pieza,*
> *muere la gente valiente.*

The illustrious historian
after receiving an award
in a State forum
spoke with great worthiness;
he did honor to the medal
as was obvious there
and even the very President [of the Republic]
celebrated his integrity.
Rest in peace, people of valor
Die whole.

Highly accomplished intellectuals and people in the arts, such as Miguel León Portilla and Elena Poniatowska, are subjects most likely to receive epitaphs with a clearly positive message.

Occasionally, people of lesser renown are also rewarded with affectionate *calaveras*. From Ciudad Juárez, bordering on the state of New Mexico, comes the following poem in honor of a local citizen (*El Mexicano* (Ciudad Juárez, Chihuahua)), November 2, 1933:

Pedro Rodríguez
Siempre vivió silencioso
y silencioso murió
este amigo generoso
que Pedrito se llamó.

He always lived silently
and silently he died
this generous friend
called Pedrito.

As with the Elena Poniatowska's *calavera*, this verse incorporates the diminutive form of the subject's name, indicating a kind of tender respect for the subject.

On the whole, however, *calaveras* are designed to ridicule well-known figures from the world of politics, sports, the arts, and other high-profile professions. Poets use mocking *calaveras* to draw attention to negative aspects of the victims' public record. In the case of political calaveras in particular, the verses are a form of what I have elsewhere (Brandes 1977) called "peaceful protest." They not only make fun of known foibles and weaknesses of their leaders but also express cynicism about politics itself at both the local and the national levels.

In this respect, political *calaveras* help to create a shared political community. *Calaveras* directed at elected officials in Oaxaca, in the south of Mexico, might well mean nothing to a Mexican from the state of Coahuila, located on the northern frontier. Some *calaveras* are aimed at extremely local readerships, such as members of particular professions in small towns and cities. These *calaveras* inherently assume the character of in-group humor. Consider, for example, a *calavera* published in a local supplement of the national newspaper, *La Jornada*. The *calavera* bears the title, "The Photographer and the Skull".

El fotógrafo y la calaca
Estaba Enrique Agatón
frotando su camarita
en eso que sale la bella genio
y le hace una preguntita:
¿Qué quieres hacer tú
con ese aparatito?
Quiero sacar lindas fotos
Y chance tu retratito.
Ese deseo te concederé
espérate un ratito
Pero si no salen bien
me hago el muertito.

The Photographer and Death
Enrique Agatón was
stroking his camera
when with this the beautiful genius (i.e., Death) appears
and asks him:
What do you want to do with that apparatus?
I want to take fine photographs
and attempt your portrait.
This wish I will grant you
wait a minute
But if they don't turn out well
I'll fall dead.

This *calavera* concerns a photographer little known outside his home town, Cuernavaca, capital of the small state of Morelos. Published in a newspaper supplement with restricted distribution (*La Jornada Morelos*, November 5, 2000), the *calavera* addresses the photographic community in Cuernavaca, where Enrique Agatón lives and works. By contrast, verses that mock the President of the Republic and the national political process are directed to Mexicans and followers of Mexican politics everywhere.

Election year 2000 provided particularly fertile ground for *calavera* poets, given that on July 2 of that year the PRI (Partido Revolucionario Institucional, or Institutional Revolutionary Party), which had ruled Mexico for 76 years, finally lost both presidential and congressional elections. The winners were members of rival right-leaning party, PAN (Partido de Acción Nacional, or National Action

Party), headed by presidential candidate Vicente Fox Quesada. Recognition of corruption on the part of PRI leaders and officials, together with the self-imposed exile of former President Carlos Salinas de Gortari (1988–94); the lengthy imprisonment of Salinas' brother, Raúl Salinas de Gortari, in Almoloya de Juárez, the country's most famous high-security prison; and almost daily revelations of illegal accumulation of wealth on the part of government authorities—these were among the immediate factors that finally caused the downfall of the PRI. During the Day of the Dead season 2000, anonymous poets and the reading public expressed anger and criticism at the PRI through the biting medium of *calaveras*.

It seemed that virtually every Mexican periodical saw fit to print epitaphs dedicated to the PRI itself. A writer contributed the following *calavera* to the newspaper *Nacional* (November 2, 2000):

PRI

El PRI estaba preparado,
se gastó un dineral.
Sin embargo el dos de julio,
acudió su funeral.

Su cadáver deshicieron,
fue un desmembramiento "atrox".
Y sus huesos se los dieron,
A los amigos de Fox.

Dicen que murió de viejo,
o que un cáncer lo mató.
O que por un mal reflejo,
una bota lo aplastó.

PRI

The PRI was prepared,
It spent a fortune.
Nevertheless on the second of July
It attended its funeral.

They took apart its cadaver,
It was an atrocious dismembering.
And they gave its bones,
To the friends of Fox.

They say it died of old age,
Or that a cancer killed it.
Or that because of a bad reflex,
A boot crushed it.

The word *atrox* in the second stanza derives from the word *atroz*, standard Spanish for "atrocious." *Atrox* is meant to rhyme with Fox, the name of the presidential winner that appears two lines below. This kind of poetic license appears frequently in *calaveras* and is in fact a humorous device. There are elements of this *calavera* that speak to a knowing public alone. The reference to cancer in the last stanza alludes to the popular belief that the PRI fell because it was rotten and eaten up from inside its ranks, just as cancer destroys its victim from within. And the boot in the last line refers to the dress code maintained by Vicente Fox, the presidential winner from the opposing party. Fox comes from the ranching state of Guanajuato and never wears standard shoes, only cowboy boots. He is so insistent on wearing cowboy boots, in fact, that during his inaugural ball on December 1, 2000, the normal practice of wearing tuxedos was suspended. It was deemed unacceptable to combine a tuxedo with riding boots. Since Fox himself would not dress in a tuxedo, male guests were instructed to wear dark colored suits instead.

From the *Unión de Morelos* (November 2, 2000) came another epitaph for the PRI:

> El PRI
> *Ahora sí se murió,*
> *Estiró toda la pata*
> *Déjole a los suyos*
> *Puras dudas, nada mas.*
>
> *Era el gran partidazo*
> *Pero el cambio no aguantó*
> *El merito dos de julio*
> *La parca se lo llevó.*
>
> *The PRI*
> Now, yes, it died,
> It lay down flat (lit. "extended its entire leg")
> Leaving to its members
> Only debts, nothing more.
>
> It was the great important party
> But it couldn't take change
> On the very second of July
> It was taken away by death.

Calaveras published in November 2000 commented on every sort of short-coming manifested by the PRI and its leaders. In the preceding *calavera*, the party's rigidity and financial imprudence are main targets of criticism. Still other poems

emphasize the intrigue and insider profiteering which were demonstrable
practices of the PRI (*Milenio*, November 1, 2000).

> *En panteón semidesierto*
> *un gran hoyo se ha cavado*
> *pa' que quepa junto al muerto*
> *tanto secreto del Estado.*
>
> *Y la Muerte ya ha ordenado:*
> *"Escarban más por aquí,*
> *hay que dejar reservado*
> *un huequito para el PRI."*

> In a semi-deserted graveyard
> a large hole has been dug
> in order to fit next to the deceased
> so many state secrets.
>
> And Death has ordered:
> "Dig further over here,
> we have to reserve
> a little empty space for the PRI.

Calaveras, ever adapted to changing circumstances, most often comment on
the most current political news. In October 2000, the papers were filled with
reports of a recorded conversation between Raúl Salinas, imprisoned elder brother
of former President Carlos Salinas de Gortari (1988–94), and Raúl's wife, Adriana.
Segments of the conversation (the veracity of which was later confirmed
by scientific analysis) convey Raúl's open condemnation of his brother Carlos's
conduct. The scandalous episode is inscribed in the following *calavera*:

> Raúl Salinas
> *Según una información*
> *fueron varias las catrinas*
> *que llevaron al panteón*
> *al mayor de los Salinas.*
> *Quedó en sepulcro enrejado*
> *sin abogado y sin lana,*
> *pero bien comunicado*
> *con el sepulcro de Adriana.*

> According to some information
> there were several female dandies
> who carried the eldest Salinas [i.e., Raúl]
> to the graveyard.

He remained behind bars in his tomb
without lawyer or money
but in good communication
with Adriana's tomb.

The reference to female dandies in the epitaph's second line evokes the image of José Guadalupe Posada's famous graphic image of an elaborately dressed female skeleton (see Chapter 3), replete with feathered hat and all manner of fineries. This highfalutin bourgeois lady—today one of the most famous symbols of Mexico itself—is not only represented as dead, but in the *calavera* above also becomes transformed into a pallbearer to one of the most ill-reputed citizens of Mexico. In Posada's image, she, like the deceased in the verse above, is cut down to size.

According to longstanding, but now obsolete, Mexican political tradition, the outgoing president would handpick his successor, who automatically became the PRI electoral candidate. The designated candidate was certain of winning. In 2000, however, President Ernesto Zedillo proved incapable of delivering the majority vote to the PRI candidate and the outcome was specifically perceived as the result of his ineffectiveness. For this, he came under bitter attack by members of his own party, who accused him, in somewhat contradictory fashion, of intentionally losing the election. (After all, if he were ineffective, how would he have been able to succeed in his attempt to lose the election?) *Calaveras* all over the country were quick to mock his self-destructive behavior. Consider the following epitaph, published in the national daily, *Reforma* (November 1, 2000).

> Al Presidente Zedillo
> *A Zedillo llevaron a enterrar*
> *a un camposanto lugar.*
> *Cansado de tanto luchar*
> *dicen que se dejó ganar.*

> *To President Zedillo*
> They carried off Zedillo to be buried
> in holy ground.
> Tired of so much struggling
> they say that he stopped himself from winning.

In the view of some citizens, Zedillo was too good for the PRI. Presidential elections under his leadership were, in popular opinion, the most democratic that Mexico had experienced in three generations. Hence, the following concluding stanza from a lengthy *calavera* (*Reforma*, November 1, 2000):

Al Presidente Ernesto Zedillo
Se llevó a Zedillo la calavera,
se lo llevó muy lejos de aquí,
buena persona que era,
ni parecía del PRI.

   To President Ernesto Zedillo
[Death] carried off the skeleton Zedillo,
carried him far from here,
good person that he was,
he didn't seem to belong to the PRI.

That which some citizens interpreted as goodness, however, others condemned as weakness and cowardliness. By Mexican standards, politicians who manifest these characteristics, defined nationally as feminine, deserve only scorn and disdain. Another calavera (*México Hoy*, November 2, 2000) targets the outgoing president thus:

Ernesto Zedillo
Entre brujas y vampirios
demonios y mil horrores
la muerte arrastra unos huesos
entre cantos y vítores.

El pervertió su suerte
pues nunca quiso entender
que el poder que había usurpado
lo era para ejercer.

Prefirió el poder castrante
del que no sabe qué hacer
incongruencias y temores
sin talento y sin saber.

   Ernesto Zedillo
Among witches and vampires
Demons and a thousand horrors
Death drags some bones
Among songs and cheers.

He perverted his luck
Well, he never wanted to understand
that the power that he had usurped
was there to be used.

> He preferred a castrated power
> of the one who doesn't know how to use it
> incongruousness and fears
> without talent and know-how.

At the turn of the millennium, PRI leaders were for the most part hated for their corruption, hypocrisy, and authoritarianism. At the same time, many Mexicans are attracted to political strongmen for their leadership, decisiveness, and ability to effectively wield power. Politicians, such as Zedillo, who demonstrate an inability to exploit their power to full personal advantage, are pitied for their impotence. And the term impotence inscribes the meaning perfectly. By incorporating the phrase *poder castrante* ("castrated power"), the *calavera* emphasizes the association between political and sexual power. Mexican politicians enjoy no escape from criticism: either they are too weak to rule effectively or too authoritarian for the common good.

During the Day of the Dead season, power holders of all ranks have long come under attack by critics with literary flair. Consider the following *calavera*, dating from the 1940s and dedicated to the Tijuana police commander (*El Condor*, Tijuana, November 1, 1943):

COMANDANTE DE POLICIA

Este pobre "chaparrito"
y su corte celestial
en el infierno está frito
porque todo lo hizo mal.

Persiguiendo a las mujeres
por orden de su patrón,
abusaba de su puesto
pa' tener un galardón

Mas todo tiene su fin
y la parca lo cogió
en tan triste situación
que hoy exclama el pobrecito:
sácame de aquí, patrón.

POLICE COMMANDER

This poor "shorty"
and his heavenly court
fry in hell
because of all they did wrong.

Pursuing women
by order of their boss

who abused his office
to get a large reward.

But everything must end
and Death caught him
in such a sad situation
that today the poor guy exclaims:
get me out of here, boss.

Abuse of power—power over women, power to obtain wealth illegally—is among the most prominent *calavera* themes.

This theme emerges, as well, in critiques of the clergy. From *El Chivo* (November 2, 1996), an Oaxaca periodical, comes the following humorous epitaph. Its victim is Archbishop Héctor González Martínez.

Dicen que este santo cura
en su vida fue capaz,
que dentro de su locura
con el diablo, hizo la paz . . .

Este vivió de limosna
que le dimos los humanos
por eso con mucha sorna
fue botana de gusanos.

Luchó contra la maldad
ilustrísimo prelado
más nunca dió caridad
como lo hubo pregonado.

Así su ríspida lengua
quedó tieza, de una tira,
este no tuvo mengua
en predicar la mentira . . .

Bartolomé lo enterró
cuando adoraba el dinero,
boca abajo lo enterró
allá por el basurero.

Así con toda la calma
a la eternidad fue en pos,
este que no tuvo alma
y ni fue al reino de Dios.

They say that this holy priest
while alive was capable,
given his craziness,
of making peace with the Devil.

He lived from the alms
that humans gave him,
for this reason with much scorn
became an appetizer for worms.

He fought against evil
this illustrious prelate
but never gave charity
as he advocated.

Thus his harsh tongue
became rigid all at once,
this one never let up
preaching lies.

Bartolomé buried him
when he idolized money,
he was buried face down
there by the garbage pit.

There with great calm
He went for eternity
This one who had no soul
And didn't even go to the Kingdom of God.

It might seem paradoxical, even perverse, that a sacred occasion such as the Day of the Dead should give rise to anti-clerical sentiment. However, literary *calaveras*, such as the one reproduced above, constitute part of a Bakhtinian, carnivalesque anti-rite. They are just one of many manifestations of the profane which emerge as counterpoint to sacred actions and belief. The Day of the Dead awakens contradictory emotions and allows them to flourish simultaneously.

Clearly, too, the Day of the Dead, though fundamentally a religious occasion, has long been imbued with a commercial dimension. Literary *calaveras* derive from the mid to late 19th century, during which José Guadalupe Posada (1852–1913)—a figure discussed more fully in Chapter 3—"became the master of the *Calavera*. Personalities and professions of the time were portrayed as skeletons and accompanied by humorous verses" (Sayer 1993:26). Posada's *calaveras* were printed on broadsides and reproduced in the popular press. In fact, throughout the last half of the 19th century in Mexico, broadsides were known generically as *calaveras*. The first illustrated newspaper in Mexico was even called *El Calavera*. From the time of its founding in January 1847, until it was suppressed by the government 31 issues later, *El Calavera* specialized in satirizing political currents of the day, and particularly poked fun at the nation's leaders through drawings, verse, and essays (Childs and Altman 1982:54).

A generation ago, Edward Tinker (1961:25) remarked that during the Day of the Dead:

> *calaveras* appear to add their sardonic flavor to the gaiety of the occasion. Printed on colored paper, adorned with the grisly insignia of death, they carry verses satirizing people in the public eye, speaking of them as though they were dead, and often ending with burlesque epitaphs. They are peddled on the streets and read in cafés with many a chuckle. The newspapers, too, take this opportunity to run caricatures and caustic verses in *calavera* vein, about politicians and government officials against whom they have some grudge. No one illustrated these better than Posada, for his grotesque improvisations, fertility of imagination, and the human quality he imparted to his grinning, dancing cadavers, made him the supreme master of this kind of work. Another talent he possessed was for depicting the life and types of his countrymen—a genius he used to arouse the public conscience to realization of the wrongs of the down-trodden.

What commentators often overlook, or at least de-emphasize, is that *calaveras* were and still are profitable items. Whether as broadsides or as newspaper features, *calaveras* are a predictable feature of the Day of the Dead. The Mexican public demands and expects them at this time of year and is willing to spend money to read them. They are also used effectively to advertise store merchandise (see Plate 5.1) Hard to determine though such matters may be, it is fair to say that Mexicans, now an overwhelmingly literate people, demonstrate as great a craving for literary, satiric verse as for visual caricature. Although literary and artistic *calaveras* often accompany one another, the drawings popularly known as *calaveras* are often printed very small when compared with ample text.

This formatting represents a significant change from the situation a century ago. It is true that, in Posada's day, text and drawing sometimes occupied equal space on the broadside page. For the most part, however, drawings most often overshadowed satirical verse, probably in response to market demand from a non-reading public. In published media today, at least during the season of the Day of the Dead, the written word, in the form of literary *calaveras*, has replaced *calavera* drawings in prominence.

Literary and visual *calaveras* seem to occupy distinctive, if overlapping, niches as popular artistic genres. Childs and Altman (1982:54) believe that literary *calaveras*, published mainly on broadsides, emerged in the mid-19th century mainly in response to the freedom of the press that came with Mexico's independence from Spain in 1821. Technical advances in printing were also partly responsible for this development. Over the course of time, *calavera* verse, which had been a year round phenomenon, became increasingly restricted to the Day of the Dead. Certainly from the mid-20th century to the present, the rhymed, satirical epitaphs known as *calaveras* have flourished mainly during late October and early November, a seasonality that does not pertain to *calavera* drawings.

William Beezley (1987:98) states wisely that *calavera* verse "offered the common people the opportunity, without fear of censure or reprisal, to express their dissatisfaction with political and social leaders and to define their grievances, real or imagined." To this extent, published *calaveras* exert a social and political leveling effect. Through ridicule and satire, they denigrate and chastise, thereby symbolically toppling power holders from their self-constructed pedestals. Literary *calaveras* assert the very egalitarian principle that Mexicans attribute to death itself. From the press of Posada's printer, Antonio Vanegas Arroyo, comes the following *calavera*, published in a pamphlet dated 1905. Only a fragment of this exceptionally long verse is reproduced here. There exists no better description of the common fate that awaits all humanity.

> Gran Baile de las Calaveras
> *Allí irán los abogados*
> *Con toda su vanidad;*
> *Allí irá la Facultad*
> *Y los Doctores borlados.*
>
> *En revuelta confusión*
> *Estarán las calaveras,*
> *Y las meras petateras*
> *Disfrutarán la ocasión.*
>
> *Será una gran igualdad*
> *Que nivele grande y chico*
> *No habrá ni un pobre (ni) rico*
> *En aquella sociedad.*
>
> *De este mundo en extensión*
> *El oro a todos pervierte*
> *Pero después de la muerte*
> *No hay clases ni condición . . .*
>
> Great Dance of the Skulls
> There will go the lawyers
> With all their vanity;
> There will go the [university] Faculty
> And the certified Doctors.

In mixed-up confusion
Will be the skulls,
And even the straw mat makers
Will enjoy the occasion.

It will be a great equality
That levels big and small
There will be neither poor nor rich
In that society.

In this widening world
Gold perverts everyone
But after death
There are neither classes nor rank.

The same message comes across in a moving *calavera* published nearly a century later in *El Imparcial* (October 31, 1996), an Oaxaca newspaper:

*Toditos los que hoy están
en este apretado osario
ya vivieron su calvario;
iguales ahora serán
el lego y el sacristán
el sardo y el comandante
el reportero y el director
todos en este instante
llegaron a su panteón
con las patas por delante,
calaveras del montón.*

*No importa que fuera ministro
magistrado o presidente
todos pelaron el diente
y llegaron a lo mismo:
el que vivió con cinismo
o en una cueva de fieras,
señoritas o rameras
dieron el azotón
y ahora son calaveras,
calaveras del montón.*

All those who today are
in this crowded ossuary
already lived their calvary;
will now be equal.

> The layman and the sacristan
> the guardsman and the commander
> the reporter and the director
> all at this moment
> will arrive at the cemetery
> with their feet stretched out in front
> piled-up skulls.
>
> It doesn't matter if he were minister
> judge or president
> All smiled fawningly
> and arrived in the same place:
> he who lived with cynicism
> or in a cave of wild beasts,
> young maids or whores
> fell over dead
> and now they are skulls
> piled-up skulls.

By advertising the personal weaknesses of the rich and powerful, *calavera* verse symbolically situates these public figures on the level of the common man. Through poetry, the satirical epitaphs in effect bring about the equality that death will seal once and for all.

Although printed *calaveras* generally emphasize the common human condition, they occasionally highlight social inequality, including a portrayal of the Day of the Dead as an occasion for ostentatious display. The dead might all be equal, and all men and women share eventual mortality. But the living must endure an unequal distribution of rank and privilege. The best example of this message comes from *La Opinion* (November 4, 1913), a Veracruz newspaper printed in the early years of the Revolution (1910–20).

NO VOY

¿Ir al Cementerio? ¿a qué?
necedad en mí sería
ir a ver tanta viuda
enlutada y compungida,
frente a otros tantos sepulcros
donde moran sus fosillos
adornándolos con flores . . .
poniéndoles siemprevivas,
moco de pavo, gardenias,
flor de muerto y margaritas
Compradas Dios sabe cómo
y qué clase de pastilla,

para mirarla después,
riéndose a toda mandíbula
con quienes, de aquellos muertos,
son suplentes en caricias.
¿Ir al cementerio? ¿a qué?
¿a ver tanta hipocresía?
No soy afecto de observar
ese llanto de mentira,
no quiero ver el dolor
sin consuelo de la hija,
que ante la tumba del padre
manifiesta en este día,
para al poco rato verla,
por las calles y avenidas,
prostituyendo aquel nombre
que guarda esa tumba fría.
¿Ir al Cementerio? ¿a qué?
¿a ver ciertas damitas
luciendo vistosos trajes
cuando a ese lugar debían
asistir, si nó de luto,
porque no se vean bonitas,
al menos no haciendo alarde
de que los valen cerilla
el respeto a los difuntos
y el ídem a sus familias?
No, marchantes, no estoy loco,
si para desgracia mía
y desgracia de otros muchos
que vivimos en la invieta,
la ciudad es un panteón,
desde por las hortalizas
hasta cerca de Vergara,
en el que duermen sin vida
los timbres de muchos nombres
matados en estos días.

I am Not Going

Go to the cemetery? For what?
it would be foolishness for me
to go to see so many widows
in mourning and remorseful,
in front of so many other tombs
where their little fossils rest
adorning them with flowers,

placing down immortelle,
cockscomb, gardenias,
orchids and daisies
Purchased God-knows-how
and with what kind of money [*pastilla*],
[only] to watch them afterwards,
laughing wide-mouthed
together with those people, who are substitutes for the
deceased in caresses.
Go to the cemetery? For what?
to see so much hypocrisy?
I am not fond of observing
that false weeping,
I don't want to see the daughter's pain
without consolation,
which before the father's tomb
is manifested on this day,
only a little later to see her
on the streets and avenues,
prostituting that name which
watches over that cold tomb.
Go to the cemetery? For what?
to see certain ladies showing off
flashy suits
when in this place, which they have to
attend, if not dressed in mourning,
because they won't be seen as beautiful,
at least not showing off
that respect for the deceased and
their families is of little importance to them.
No, customers, I am not crazy,
if through my misfortune and the
misfortune of many others
we live in the *invieta*,
the city is a cemetery,
from the vegetable gardens
to near Vergara,
where the imprints [*timbres*] of many names killed on
these days sleep without life.

As portrayed in this *calavera*, the Day of the Dead proceeds against a backdrop of revolutionary violence and killing. Under such circumstances, death takes on a special meaning, which makes humor and satire more difficult.

Nonetheless, the *calavera* is true to its genre in its display of irreverent sentiments. It provides a scathing critique of hypocrisy, the kind of social pretense that is carried out under the guise of traditional religious observance. If most *calaveras* serve to level humanity, this one comments on the *calavera* genre. It not only demonstrates the sensitivity of *calaveras* to historical circumstances and to the mood of the times, but also shows that nothing—not even the *calavera* itself—is above judgment. The *calavera* is poetry as protest, made all the more effective by its jocular guise.

Plate 1.1   Cemetery in Tlayacapan, Morelos, November 2, 2000

Plate 1.2 Serenading the dead at the Panteón Jardín, Mexico City, November 2, 1995

Plate 1.3 Multicultural stairwell altar dedicated to Chicano leader, César Chávez, San Francisco, California, November 2, 2005

Plate 2.1 *Huesos de santo* displayed in a bakery window, Madrid, 2003

Plate 3.1 Sixteenth-century fresco, Augustinian chapel at Malinalco, State of Mexico

Plate 3.2 Multimedia *catrina*, after Posada, for sale in a Jalisco tourist shop, October 2000

Plate 4.1   Tourists visit a Day of the Dead altar at the Oakland Museum, November 23, 2005

Plate 4.2   *Arco*, Tzintzuntzan, Michoacán, November 2, 1977

Plate 5.1 Literary and pictorial *calavera* at La Jaiva Bakery, Cuernavaca, October 1995

Plate 6.1   Begging for *"jalöüín"* in the Panteón Jardín, Mexico City, November 2, 1995

Plate 6.2   Halloween school parade, Oaxaca, October 31, 1996

Plate 6.3 Night of the Dead vigil with jack o'lanterns, Ihuatzio, Michoacán, November 2005. Photo courtesy of Cristina García Rodero

Plate 6.4 "[Day of the] Dead Sale" sign, photographic studio window, Oaxaca, November 1996

Plate 7.1 Elmhurst school altar, Fruitvale Festival, Oakland, October 30, 2005

Plate 8.1   Oakland Museum entrance, Days of the Dead Community Celebration, October 23, 2005

Plate 8.2 A *conchero* prepares his altar at the Fruitvale Festival, October 30, 2005

Plate 8.3 Revelers protesting junk food at the San Francisco Mission Day of the Dead parade, November 2, 1989. Photograph courtesy of Janet Delaney.

Plate 9.1 Day of the Dead grave, Ihuatzio, Michoacán, November 2005. Photograph courtesy of Cristina García Rodero

6

THE DAY OF THE DEAD
AND HALLOWEEN

The Day of the Dead, from colonial times to the present day, has been first and foremost a religious holiday. Whether you believe that the Day of the Dead derives principally from Roman Catholic roots, or that it expresses a syncretic combination of Spanish and pre-Columbian elements, it is impossible to overlook its sacred essence. It is this quality that Mexicans cite above all to distinguish their holiday from that to which it is often compared—American Halloween—which they perceive as fundamentally secular and commercial. And yet, as David Kertzer points out, any ritual—including religious ritual—provides "an important means for structuring our political perceptions and leading us to interpret our experiences in certain ways" (Kertzer 1988:85). The close relationship between religion and politics in any part of the world, and at any time throughout history, is incontrovertible. The Day of the Dead provides a dramatic instance of the ways in which religious ritual and political ideology reinforce one another.

The Day of the Dead promotes an interpretation of the world in which Mexico is unique, culturally discrete, and above all culturally distinct from the two powers that have dominated the country throughout its long existence: Spain and the United States. Citizens on both sides of the Rio Grande have come to perceive Halloween and the Day of the Dead as two completely separate observances. The rapid penetration of Halloween symbols into Mexico since the mid-1990s increasingly evokes Mexican nationalistic sentiments, which express themselves ever more assertively in a campaign to preserve the country from what is perceived as U.S. cultural imperialism. Increasingly, the Day of the Dead has come to symbolize Mexico, and Halloween has come to symbolize the United States. To many journalists, politicians, and members of the intellectual elite, the presence of Halloween candies and costumes within Mexico represents nothing less than an act of imperialist aggression. As interpreted by these vocal elements of Mexican society, Halloween threatens the very existence of Mexico as a unique and identifiable nation. They believe above all that Halloween will eventually obliterate the Day of the Dead and that the fate of these two holidays is symptomatic of the unequal power relations between the two countries. The incursion of Halloween into Mexican national territory, and the incorporation of Halloween symbols into Day of the Dead celebrations, have become rallying points for nation-builders, eager to preserve a unique Mexican national identity.

Mexican national identity is no easy subject for discussion. It has long been the object of scholarly deliberation and passionate public debate of a philosophical, historical, and psychological nature. Literary and social scientific reflections on Mexican national character include penetrating and influential portraits by Samuel Ramos (1962), Octavio Paz (1961), and, more recently, Roger Bartra (1987), among others. The topic has received sensitive treatment in the writings of Matthew Gutmann (1993), who demonstrates that ideas about alleged Mexican distinctiveness undergo transformation from generation to generation in the face of the country's marked cultural diversity. States Gutmann:

> Analysts of a would-be uniform "national character" (or culture) of Mexico often resort to origin myths, downplaying class, gender and ethnic divisions within the geographic boundaries of the nation state, and also discount the fact that new and significant cultural features have emerged since the Revolution and Independence. (1993:56)

More recently, Claudio Lomnitz's magisterial historical tome, *Death and the Idea of Mexico* (2005), advances the provocative thesis that colonial and post-colonial states in Mexico seized upon the control over death-related activities and ideology as a means of wielding power and, ultimately, consolidating the nation. "If death has been a looming presence in Mexican political discourse," he says (Lomnitz 2005:483), "it is because political control over dying, the dead, and the representation of the dead and the afterlife has been key to the formation of the modern state, images of popular culture, and a properly national modernity."

The Mexican state is like many other states in that it has had to forge a national consciousness and unity among a multitude of diverse regions and ethnic groups. A major strategy in achieving this goal has been to create a sense of national distinctiveness by promoting the contrast between Mexico, on the one hand, and the two great powers to which it has been subject for over five centuries—Spain and the United States—on the other hand. With respect to Spain, Mexico suffers particular difficulty in creating a sense of discreteness. Most analysts would agree, after all, that two of the most salient features uniting any people are language and religion. Mexicans, who overwhelmingly speak Spanish and practice Roman Catholicism, can claim neither of these features as a source of difference from the imperial conqueror. Insofar as Mexican relations with the United States are concerned, the dominant language and religion in each country differ. They therefore provide potential rallying points around which to build separate national identities.

More important, however, is Mexican victimization at the hands of the economically and militarily powerful neighbor to the north. From 1848, when the newly independent Mexico lost half of its territory to the United States, to the present day, which is characterized by overwhelming disparities in national wealth and the increasing presence of U.S. financial and manufacturing institutions within Mexico, Mexicans have had to struggle against unfavorable odds in order to maintain a sense of autonomy and equality. From one vantage point, Mexican dependency upon and domination by Spain and the United States have impeded the emergence of a fully autonomous nation. From another, however, Mexicans have been able to use these countries as ideological foils against which to emphasize their own undeniable uniqueness.

In its quest for a unique identity, Mexico has benefited from one major resource: the Indian, past and present. It is Mexico's Indian heritage, as demonstrated through archaeological and ethnographic evidence, which clearly separates the country from both Spain and the United States. And it is the Indian heritage that the Mexican state has chosen for symbolic elevation. One common way to further a distinct sense of national identity is through art and museum displays (see Karp and Lavine 1991), and this is the route that the Mexican state has taken. The National Museum of Anthropology in Mexico City is, among other things, a glorious monument to Mexican uniqueness and authenticity. Its two main floors are designed to show, first, the archaeological record, as displayed chronologically on the ground level; and, second, the contemporary indigenous presence, as exhibited throughout rooms devoted to Indian communities representative of distinct ethno-linguistic groups, on the top level. Taken as a whole, the National Museum of Anthropology strives to display, whether to nationals or to foreigners, an official view of authentic Mexico, which is to say of indigenous Mexico—of a Mexico unaffected by contaminating outside influences.

As indicated in Chapter 4, the Day of the Dead has become just this sort of museum, albeit a living and breathing museum, an installation of gigantic proportions which is dedicated to Mexican uniqueness. It is not surprising that, in the quest for national identity, the Indian should be elevated to a prominent position in the official presentation of this holiday to the Mexican and foreign public. Nor should it come as a revelation that the Day of the Dead, associated as it has become with indigenous Mexico, should be transformed into a major symbol of Mexican national identity. Government officials, tourist agencies, journalists, scholars, and public intellectuals have successfully promoted the Day of the Dead as a unique national treasure and a vibrant expression of Mexico's distinctiveness. It is to preserve this national treasure, more than for any other reason, that many of the most vocal Mexicans object vehemently to the growing presence within their country of Halloween costumes and customs.

Fig. 6.1   Halloween masks for sale at the Oaxaca municipal market, October 1996

Any observer of Day of the Dead ceremonies since the 1990s would be impressed by the presence of Halloween symbolism. Prefabricated children's costumes—mainly witch, devil, and ghost costumes, all prominently displayed in markets and store windows—are sold in shops small and large throughout the country. Ubiquitous items for sale, too, are diverse plastic and rubber masks, everything from satirical images of Mexican and U.S. political leaders to red-faced satanic figures, apes, and a plethora of unidentifiable beasts (see Figure 6.1). Orange-colored plastic jack-o'-lanterns in every imaginable size can also be found. These items are generally mixed indiscriminately among the usual Day of the Dead ware, including special seasonal sweet breads, brightly decorated sugar and chocolate skulls and caskets, wooden and papier-maché skeletons with movable joints, as well as long-stemmed orange marigolds and tall white candles, which are regular components of the *ofrenda* at most burial sites and home altars.

On the face of it, the presence of Halloween symbolism should cause no surprise. For one thing, Halloween, which occurs on All Saints' Eve, has for centuries shared a close resemblance to the Day of the Dead. Jack Santino traces Halloween to the ancient Celtic (including Breton, Irish, Scottish, Welsh) festival of Samhain, the New Year's Day of the Celts, celebrated on November 1. This pre-Christian holiday, says Santino (1994:xv), "was also a day of the dead, a time when it was believed that the souls of those who had died during the year were allowed access to the land of the living. It was a time when spirits were believed to be wandering." Many of the beliefs and practices that were characteristic of Samhain survived to the Christian era. These include the belief that October 31 was a time of the wandering dead as well as the practice of providing food and drink to masked and costumed revelers on this night. This night as such was known to Christians as the Eve of All Saints' or Hallows Even, a term yielding the familiar contraction *Hallowe'en* (ibid.:xvi). Santino can trace how symbols of the dead—including skeletons, ghosts, and malevolent creatures such as witches and the devil—became incorporated into All Saints' Eve. These symbols, he believes, were the transmuted pre-Christian gods and goddesses, whom the early Christians used as a syncretic means to spread their new religion. "Because of these events," concludes Santino, "Halloween is associated with All Saints' Day and, by extension, with the church calendar" (ibid.).

Santino calls the Day of the Dead a "cognate" (ibid.:xviii) or, one might say, a functional equivalent, of Halloween. Indeed, the historical origins of the two holidays, if not identical, are nonetheless closely intermeshed. For centuries, too, they have displayed an array of shared symbols of death, a kind of playing with death, including humorous replicas of skulls, skeletons, and souls. During Halloween, the souls take the form of ghosts; during the Day of the Dead, they become inanimate but ever-present spirits. Special sweets are an important part of Halloween, with its characteristic black and orange candies, and the Day of the Dead, with its *pan de muertos* ("dead bread"), and sugar and chocolate replicas of skulls and skeletons. Ritualized begging is a significant part of the two holidays as well (see Plate 6.1). During All Saints' and All Souls' days in Mexico, as much as in Europe, bands of young men wander from house to house asking for food and drink. I have observed this custom, for example, in Tzintzuntzan, Mexico (Brandes 1988:94–95), and Becedas, Spain (Brandes 1975:135), although institutionalized begging and the offering of charity have been traditional throughout the Roman Catholic world on this day (see Aguirre Soronda 1989; Brandes 1997; Espinosa 1918; Llabrés Quintana 1925; Parsons 1917). Halloween practices, of course, include a particularly aggressive form of begging, known as "trick or treat" (Tuleja 1994).

These common origins and shared symbols by no means erase major differences between Halloween, on the one hand, and All Saints' and All Souls' days, on the other. Perhaps the single major difference is that All Saints' and All Souls' days remain a part of the Roman Catholic liturgy, while Halloween has long assumed a completely secular cast. Despite possible readings to the contrary, we might also say that All Saints' and Souls' days are fundamentally occasions for adult ritual performance. Halloween, however, is largely a children's holiday—or at least has been so until the turn of the 21st century, at which point it seems to be embraced by older and older age cohorts. And there is at least one more significant difference: in Mexico, the Day of the Dead has come to symbolize Mexican identity and autonomy, while Halloween, at least as perceived by Mexicans, has become representative of the United States and its cultural imperialistic designs. The actual origins and meaning of ritual beliefs and practices during Halloween and the Day of the Dead have proven more or less irrelevant to the ever more salient significance of these holidays for national identity.

As an example, consider the testimony of Juanita Garciagodoy (1998:28), one of the most serious Mexican scholars of the Day of the Dead:

> I cannot count how many informants have answered my questions as to the meaning of Días de Muertos for them, their reasons for performing this or that aspect of it, their reason(s), for that matter, to celebrate it at all by saying, *"Es muy mexicano,"* "It's very Mexican," or, *"Porque somos mexicanos,"* "Because we're Mexican."

Speaking for herself as a Mexican national, the author continues:

> Many of us feel more patriotic during this celebration and because of it. This is partly because we think our way of relating to death and the dead—and by implication to life—is unique in the world, setting us apart from (and at least a little above) everyone else. We are *más machos*, braver, and we have *más corazón*, more heart, than other cultures. (ibid.)

As an international scholar, Garciagodoy understands well how the Day of the Dead contributes to Mexican national identity. But as a Mexican, she cannot help but experience herself the nationalistic sentiments that have become an inherent part of the holiday. In fact, at one point in her discussion she includes herself among a group of "nationalistic Mexican scholars," as she calls them (ibid.:163). Nationalism leads Garciagodoy, like so many other Mexican intellectuals, not only to reaffirm the Day of the Dead as a symbol of Mexican national identity but at the same time to reject Halloween. In fact, she entitles one of her chapters "Hallowe'en as a Threat to National Tradition and Identity."

Garciagodoy is hardly alone in her assessment. Consider the statement of Mexican pathologist and writer Frank Gonzalez-Crussi (1993:36) that there are disquieting signs within Mexico of Halloween's ascent. During a recent trip to Mexico City on the Day of the Dead, Gonzalez-Crussi found that:

> The stores are stocked with objects intended for use at Halloween, many imported from the United States. In shop windows, hollowed-out pumpkins, mostly made out of plastic, with cutout holes that figure eyes, nose, and mouth, beam their ghostly smiles, abetted by the flickering light within. Groups of children come out of schools or private homes disguised as monsters, werewolves, vampires, and extraterrestrial beings. Have we come this far to see an imitation, in third-world gear, of the North American Halloween?

Exactly how has Halloween entered into the celebration of the Day of the Dead? Garciagodoy correctly identifies two main classes of Mexicans who nowadays celebrate the Day of the Dead by drawing on symbols and customs more usually associated with Halloween. First are the urban middle-class Mexicans, many of whom dress their children in store-bought, Halloween-style costumes. Judging from the costumes I have seen on sale at middle-class malls, as well as from my observations of the way the children themselves dress on Halloween, I would say that there is considerably less variety in Halloween gear in Mexico than there is in the United States. In Mexico, the costumes tend to play on one of five basic themes: witches, ghosts, skeletons, vampires, and devils. Unlike in the United States, I have rarely seen a Mexican adult wear a costume—or even a portion of a costume. In 1996, in the city of Oaxaca, I observed a parade of hundreds of costumed schoolchildren, accompanied by dozens of teachers and parents (see Plate 6.2). None of the adults put on so much as a witch's cap, although merchants in Mexico City and environs increasingly wear Halloween garb as a marketing ploy.

The urban, middle-class Halloween manifests itself, too, in disco dances, with advertisements and disco decorations based on icons such as witches, carved pumpkins, ghosts, and the like, usually colored in black and orange. Newspapers throughout Mexico display commercial advertisements aiming at a middle-class audience and incorporating Halloween symbols. Consider a computer store advertisement that appeared on October 31, 1996 in the national daily, *Reforma*. The advertisement appears with black background, white lettering, an orange jack-o'-lantern, and the silhouette of a cloaked skeleton wielding a scythe. "Do our competitor's prices scare you?," reads the text. A Goodyear tire advertisement that appeared in *Reforma* on October 30, 1996 is drawn in white against a black, nighttime scene. Bats fly high above, scraggly cats arch their backs, and jack-o'-lanterns grin at the readers. "Macabre night sale on tires," states the advertisement. Expensive clubs all over Mexico City—Snob, for example, and the Men's Club—use the press to announce Halloween parties and dances at this time of year.

For the working class, the Halloween appeal is somewhat different. For one thing, although some children might put on an inexpensive mask, for the most part they remain in everyday dress. Halloween for these children—and the participants seem to be mainly boys—means a moneymaking opportunity. Carrying any sort of small container that they can find, everything from a battered cardboard box to a miniature plastic jack-o'-lantern with handle (the kind that children in the United States commonly use to collect candy), the boys beg on the streets and in the cemeteries, asking for their "Halloween"—the word used to refer to the donated treat, almost always a small coin or two. The term "Halloween," used in this sense, is even entering the Mexican Spanish lexicon, spelled phonetically *Jaloüin*. Some children ask for money instead by imploring passers to "Give me my *calabaza*." The young beggars use the word *calabaza* here not in the sense of "squash", but instead to mean the specifically Halloween form of squash—that is, pumpkin—or even to refer to "jack-o'-lantern". Other than to solicit money in this form, the working-class Halloween seems limited to the purchase of orange-, white-, and black-colored candy shaped as witches, ghosts, and jack-o'-lanterns. Also, on the Day of the Dead, the occasional carved pumpkin or plastic jack-o'-lantern rests on graves, mixed along with the usual offerings (see Plate 6.3).

Most middle-class Mexicans are well aware that Halloween symbols are part of U.S. culture and probably use Halloween symbols consciously as a means of elevating their status. It is unclear that this can be said of the working classes, for whom Halloween seems to have become seamlessly sewn within the fabric of Day of the Dead proceedings. I asked two migrants from the state of Oaxaca, a Mixtec fruit vendor and his wife, why they decided to sell Halloween candies in their tiny local store. I also inquired whether they had received any complaints for supporting Halloween in this way. The wife responded with laughter, as if the idea were simply absurd. "We Mexicans are *muy fiesteros* [great merry-makers]!," she said. "We like everything that contributes to festivities!" While observing schoolchildren carry out their Halloween march in 1996 in the city of Oaxaca, I asked several teenagers on the street to tell me how many years ago the march was initiated. They answered, "Maybe ten years ago, or fifteen . . . or five." They did not know. However, they added that if I really wanted to learn about "these customs" I should visit one of the surrounding villages, where they have been practiced as long as anyone can remember. From all I can determine, in 1996 rural schoolchildren did not participate in Halloween marches. Nor did they dress as witches, ghosts, devils, and the like. These teenagers simply experienced a cognitive merging of Halloween and the Day of the Dead symbols. For them, as for most Mexicans in central and southern Mexico, there is one major holiday at the end of October and beginning of November. It did not occur to these young men to distinguish between Halloween and Day of the Dead traditions.

In fact, there are Mexican regions in which Day of the Dead celebrations are hardly traditional and where they have in fact arrived rather recently. The northern border states of Chihuahua, Coahuila, and Sonora, for example, are places in which Halloween has enjoyed a long and undisturbed presence. I have met several university professors of middle age who are from these states. As children, they all celebrated Halloween, and Halloween alone. In the 1940s and the 1950s there was simply no widespread commemoration of the Day of the Dead, as we know it today. One friend from Coahuila would visit relatives in Mexico City at the end of October. He recalls that, as a child, he was horrified at the ubiquitous sight of skulls and skeletons and it was because of these objects that he perceived the residents of Mexico City as unusually morbid. Since 1996, however, key clerics in the northern border states actually have prohibited Halloween celebrations on the grounds that this holiday, which they deem secular and commercial, represents a threat to the sanctity and very existence of the Day of the Dead.

Statistically there probably exists only a small percentage of Mexicans who perceive Halloween as posing a threat to their national culture. But those who do are visible and articulate Mexicans, the intellectuals, representatives of church and state, and outspoken members of major cultural institutions such as the press. All over Mexico today there appears evidence of formal and informal resistance to the Halloween invasion from the north. A large mural painted along a wall on the streets of Tepoztlán, in the state of Morelos, shows a soccer player kicking a gringo off his feet. The gringo's head is a gigantic jack-o'-lantern. The accompanying text reads, "No to Halloween. Preserve your cultural traditions" (see Figure 6.2).

On October 29, 1996, the national daily *La Jornada*, famous for its quality photography, showed a picture of a man on a busy city street dressed and masked in skeleton costume. The caption reads "Costumbre foránea," or "Foreign custom." Ironically, the costume is far from being foreign to Mexico. Death figures very similar to the one portrayed in this photo regularly appear in local fiestas, where

Fig. 6.2   Mural, Tepoztlán, Morelos, October–November 1995

they often play the role of clown figures (see, e.g., Brandes 1979:127–145). And, as elsewhere in Mexico, the figure portrayed is clearly a man. Throughout Mexico, only men—never women—disguise themselves as skeletons, devils, and the like. The photograph in *La Jornada* shows a phenomenon that is new, not because of the costume or the person wearing it, but rather for the occasion on which it is worn.

Not only the press, but also municipal governments increasingly show official resistance to Halloween. Numerous cities and towns have begun to mount competitions with prizes for the most beautiful Day of the Dead altar. Among the contest guidelines for the city of Oaxaca is an item that declares, "Altars which present elements foreign to our tradition [*elementos ajenos a nuestra tradición*] will be automatically disqualified." Although the word Halloween is not mentioned in the contest guideline, this holiday certainly contains the core of disqualifying elements, the elements that Oaxaca officials consider the gravest threat to the cultural purity of this, the most Mexican of fiestas. Throughout the Mexican Republic, altar competitions such as that in Oaxaca have become a regular feature of Day of the Dead celebrations. There can be no more dramatic proof of Handler and Linnekin's insightful statement that "one of the major paradoxes of the ideology of tradition is that attempts at cultural preservation inevitably alter, reconstruct, or invent the traditions that they are intended to fix" (1984:288). Among other things, the altar competitions signify a gradual transformation of the Day of the Dead from a primarily family celebration into a community event.

In the city of Oaxaca, as elsewhere in Mexico, not only the municipal government, but also Catholic and even Protestant churches have mounted campaigns to preserve the alleged purity of the Day of the Dead. *El Imparcial*, a newspaper published in Oaxaca, published a feature article (October 31, 1996) entitled "Halloween or no Halloween? A Fearful Dilemma." The term *fearful* was rendered in Spanish as *de miedo*, a clear reference to the scariness of Halloween. Through this clever use of language, the article itself, which questions the validity of Halloween, actually reaffirms the influence of this holiday. The article describes a unified effort on the part of the city's Christian churches to stamp out Halloween. A seven-year old boy is quoted as saying:

> I don't know what to do. In church they told me that it's not good to participate in Halloween because it has to do with evil spirits, and that's why the stores choose witch and vampire costumes to wear in the streets. The bad thing is that my friends already have their costumes and I do want to join them, but I don't want to do anything sinful. (*El Imparcial*, October 31, 1996:1)

The same article also tells about a third grader who heard at Mass that he should not participate in Halloween. In school, however, he was told the opposite, that

Halloween is fine, "as long as he first familiarizes himself with the Mexican traditions of the Day of the Dead" (*El Imparcial*, October 31, 1996).

For many Mexican intellectuals, Halloween represents the worst of the United States. It is reputed to be excessively commercial. Garciagodoy declares that:

> While Días de Muertos is undoubtedly an occasion for extravagant spending, it does not enter the style of consumerism that characterizes U.S. celebrants on Hallowe'en all year round . . . As far as the inculcation of beliefs is concerned, I would speculate that the most important belief the exporters of Hallowe'en wish to inculcate is one in the acceptability of seasonal, disposable merchandise. (Garciagodoy 1998:131)

For Garciagodoy, as for other Mexican intellectuals, Halloween serves political interests as well. She states,

> I do not want to fuel the fires of xenophobia or cultural paranoia, but I would not want to trivialize the cultural impact of the exportation of holiday traditions which, surely inadvertently, serve American interests not only economically, but also by cultivating a strong pro-U.S. element that will continue to insure political and diplomatic harmony between two countries with an extraordinarily long and porous border. It is not impossible that such an effect is consciously desired by a few powerful people on one or both sides of the Río Bravo [Rio Grande]. Still, to me it seems more likely that the cultural impact is a side-effect of the principal objective of economic gain. (ibid.:129)

It would be hard to dispute that Halloween provides a financial boon to business or that the American public, at least at the turn of the 21st century, spends a collective fortune on Halloween paraphernalia. However, economic gain is in fact close to the heart of the traditional Day of the Dead celebrations as well. And, as we have seen (Chapter 2), it has been so since at least the middle of the 18th century, when small sugar figurines were already popular sale items on the streets of Mexico City. Clearly, even in colonial times, the Day of the Dead was largely commercial in character.

Nowadays, toys and figurines in the shape of skulls and skeletons are available not only during Day of the Dead season, but rather year round and wherever tourists congregate throughout Mexico. The Day of the Dead has spawned a thriving artisan craft industry based on skull and skeleton iconography. Although it would be difficult to prove, it is likely that these items appeal more to foreigners than to Mexican nationals themselves. To tourists, Day of the Dead iconography, whenever and wherever it can be purchased, has come to symbolize Mexico. During the holiday season itself, stores all over the country decorate their windows with fanciful Day of the Dead icons. Newspapers are filled with advertisements playing on Day of the Dead themes, including not only pictures, but also text, such as the humorous epitaphs known as *calaveras* (see Chapter 5), which are sometimes geared to increase sales. The Day of the Dead provides an enormous economic opportunity to workers in the flower industry, including farmers, florists, and middlemen. The same is true for artisans throughout Mexico who have for generations supported their families mainly through the production of sugar skulls and figurines. Judging from what I have been told by artisans in Toluca, capital of the State of Mexico and a center of *alfeñique* figurine production, they bear no objection to the introduction of Halloween ghosts, witches, and jack-o'-lanterns, as long as these items sell. Wenceslao Rivas Contreras, an *alfeñique* craftsman in Toluca, states:

> I've often been told to stick to what's Mexican, yet I enjoy trying my hand at different things. Ten years ago I added pumpkins to my range of products. Pumpkins are a feature of Halloween in North America, but I'll make them if I can sell them . . . and witches as well! I want my displays to have variety and my customers to have a choice. In truth, although these different styles all sell, skulls sell best— they belong to us, to Mexico! (quoted in Carmichael and Sayer 1991:115)

Some Toluca artisans specializing in *alfeñique* have told me that they begin crafting skull and skeleton figures as early as February, well over half a year prior to the Day of the Dead season (see Figure 2.2). Only a lively commercial market could support this significant degree of labor input.

Even the liturgical aspects of the Day of the Dead have long borne a commercial cast. The observance of special Masses on November 1–2 in honor of the saints and departed souls originally had an economic component. In colonial Mexico, for example, it was customary to give part of the food offerings to the priest in return for the celebration of these Masses. The ritualized begging that characterizes Day of the Dead practice virtually everywhere (as discussed, e.g., with regard to Tzintzuntzan in Chapter 4) is exemplary in this regard.

Yet this aspect of the festivities, which has grown through time and persists in ever more salient fashion into the present day, remains virtually unacknowledged by Mexican cultural nationalists. Cultural nationalists are comparable to those folklorists who, as Dan Ben-Amos (1984:107) states, identify and seek to purge so-called enemies of that which they themselves consider traditional and authentic. For cultural nationalists in Mexico, Halloween—in contrast to the Day of the Dead—is a grossly commercialized and profane holiday. To cultural nationalists, Halloween also contaminates the Day of the Dead by introducing foreign elements into otherwise ancient, sacred proceedings. In other words, Halloween and the Day of the Dead—holidays that derive largely from a common source and that still exhibit many similar features—have become metaphors for relations between the United States and Mexico. Halloween has become the prime symbol of gringo imperialism.

Given the long-term presence of U.S. communities within Mexico, as well as the lengthy border which the two countries share, it is not surprising that Halloween has made an impact within Mexico over the past several generations. Only recently, however, have the markers of Halloween—particularly costumes and jack-o'-lanterns—become an obvious part of the end-of-October festivities throughout central and southern Mexico. Only since the 1990s, too, has there emerged a vociferous reaction from Mexico's religious and intellectual elite. From these sources, as from the press, there seems to be a well-orchestrated opposition to the incursion of Halloween symbols into Day of the Dead proceedings.

It is now, too, at the turn of the 21st century, that the destinies of Mexico and the United States are closer than ever. The NAFTA, ratified in 1993, has facilitated a much-increased presence of U.S. citizens and products within Mexico. Sanborns, the enormous department store chain distributed throughout Mexico and geared towards the ever-more prosperous middle and upper middle classes, now engages in large-scale marketing of Halloween costumes, candies, and party decorations. As for the working classes, the ever-increasing migrant stream means growing numbers of Mexican returnees, who bring to Mexico an exposure and predilection for select aspects of U.S. popular culture, including Halloween. A good number of these Mexican migrants are children and learn about Halloween in the classroom, if nowhere else. This trend is promoted as well through the ubiquitous presence of U.S. programming on Mexican television, which functions to familiarize the Mexican public with typical U.S. holidays, Halloween among them.

As a result of all these developments, Halloween has indeed become a palpable part of the Day of the Dead season, affecting everything from religious observance to commerce (see Plate 6.4). Mexicans who resent the growing U.S. influence over Mexican economic and cultural affairs respond effectively by focusing on a concrete, neatly defined event such as Halloween. Halloween's success, to these Mexicans, represents their own country's failure. As we shall see in following chapters, Day of the Dead celebrations are becoming an increasingly important part of Halloween within the United States. Turner and Jasper (1994:133) substantiate in vivid detail their assertion that "Mexican-derived Day of the Dead traditions are currently enjoying immense popularity in galleries and museums north of the border." The increasing presence of Day of the Dead symbols and activities to date has caused only minimal concern within the United States, probably because power relations between the two countries clearly favor the preeminence of Anglo-American customs. But, at least within the southwestern United States, a fusion of Halloween and Day of the Dead, especially in public institutions such as schools and museums, is becoming increasingly evident. It is to that story that we turn next.

PART 4

NORTH OF THE BORDER

7

TEACHING THE DAY OF THE DEAD

Holiday celebrations—whether in the United States or Mexico, whether family or community centered—generally involve people representing all segments of society: men and women, young and old. Nonetheless, until recently, one of the major differences between Halloween, as practiced in the United States, and the Day of the Dead, as it functions in Mexico, is that Halloween has been almost exclusively oriented around children. A generation ago, folklorist Catherine Ainsworth (1973:163) declared that, "Halloween appears to be the most child directed and influenced of all our holidays." Psychologists Susan Isaacs and Robert Royeton (1982:67), writing in the same era, believed Halloween to "have deep psychological significance for children and contribute directly to their development." Margaret Mead (1975:202) and scholars investigating the matter even today (Anne Armstrong 1992:13–15) have expressed the same opinion. To be sure, adults have always participated in Halloween festivities, as organizers of school parades, designers of colorful and original costumes, providers of trick-or-treat candy, and the like. But, whatever the latent functions of these activities, all of them, until about the last decade of the 20th century, have focused primarily on promoting the momentary joy of little boys and girls. Over the past decade, older children and full-grown adults—especially lesbians and gays—seem to have claimed Halloween as an occasion for their own enjoyment. There now exist numerous Halloween parades, such as the exuberant Castro district celebration in San Francisco or the Greenwich Village parade in New York City, where adults participate as the principal observers and celebrants. Increasingly, too, adults throughout the United States organize Halloween parties, where guests are proud to display artistic ingenuity through the invention of original costumes.

At the same time, at least within the United States context, Day of the Dead celebrations have become increasingly child centered. This is not to say, of course, that the Mexican Day of the Dead does not involve children. As we have seen

(Chapter 1), October 31 is generally set apart for mourning the death of *angelitos*, children who have died in sexual innocence or before becoming baptized, and who therefore are believed to ascend directly to heaven, without having to pass through purgatory. Mexican children often maintain vigil along with their parents at the tombs of deceased ancestors. They consume sugar candies and sweets that are specially prepared for this holiday. They learn to compose satirical *calaveras* and they play with the cardboard and wooden skulls and skeletons that become ubiquitous during this holiday. Nonetheless, in Mexico, the Day of the Dead is and long has been an occasion where the principal celebrants are adults. So, too, are tourists and other onlookers.

As the Day of the Dead becomes increasingly popular in the United States, children have become ever more prominent participants in its celebration, a circumstance that is working to define this holiday as a ritual counterpart of Halloween. North of the border, children from virtually every ethnic background, including those of Latino heritage, learn about the Day of the Dead through publications, school projects, and museum exhibitions. In fact, teaching about the Day of the Dead has become a vehicle not only for introducing children to life in Mexico, but also for exposing them to the multiculturalism and ethnic diversity that prevail throughout the urban United States. Children's literature devoted to the Day of the Dead has burgeoned and forms part of school and public library collections throughout the country. Given the growing inter-dependence between the United States and Mexico since the mid-1990s, when NAFTA began to take effect, it is no wonder that the vast majority of children's books centering on the Day of the Dead have been published during this period and after.

Pablo Remembers: the Fiesta of the Day of the Dead, by George Ancona, was first published in 1993 and has received wide distribution in schools and the children's sections of public libraries. Replete with informative, colorful, and ethnographically vivid photographs, this book recounts the story of holiday preparations as carried out by a family from Oaxaca: a father, a mother, three daughters and one son, Pablo. This family seems to be a real life family and their story is written as if it were true. The story begins when Pablo and one of his sisters, Shaula, accompany his mother to the Oaxaca market to buy Day of the Dead provisions. The author takes this occasion to introduce readers to a bit of material culture, as well as to Mexican Spanish:

> People everywhere in Mexico are busy preparing for the *fiesta*, the holiday. Bakers are baking the traditional *pan de muertos*, the bread of the dead. Candy makers are making sugar skulls. Children are cutting out cardboard skeletons. Artisans are stamping out tissue-paper decorations called *estampas*. Farmers are harvesting *cempasúchil*, marigolds, the flowers of the dead. (Ancona 1993:11)

What follows is an informal Spanish lesson, as the reader is introduced through word and image to Pablo's family purchases at market. These include both foods familiar to North Americans—for example, as listed in the book, *naranjas* (oranges), *manzanas* (apples), *calabaza* (pumpkin)—as well as exotic items—*chapulines* (fried grasshoppers), *copal* (a resin incense), *cal* (lime), and *caña* (sugarcane)—with which young readers are likely to be unacquainted (Ancona 1993:12–17).

As Pablo and his mother are at market, the sisters at home erect an altar to the "*angelitos*, spirits of dead children, to come back for a visit tonight" (ibid.:21); "They place sugar skulls decorated with their own names on the altar. Pablo lights the copal incense, and its smoke fills the room with its perfume" (ibid.). Ancona provides a detailed description of the festival breakfast and main meal, with foods listed in Spanish and English, as prepared by the Señora Refugio, the mother. Readers learn about the typical *ofrenda* which the family erects on an elaborate home altar, together with "*pan de muertos, frutas* (fruits), *flores* (flowers), cups of *chocolate* and *atole* . . . When the *tamales* are cooked, some will be placed on the *ofrenda* as well" (ibid.:30). "Finally, they place photographs of dead relatives on the altar. 'Now Abuelita can come to visit,' says Shaula" (ibid.:32). Ancona ends the story of Pablo and his family with an account of the home visits and food exchanges that occur among relatives during the Day of the Dead, as well as the cleaning and decoration of family gravestones.

> Then the family sits together, eating, singing, laughing, and keeping their dead relatives company . . . They have spent the last three days celebrating their ancestors. For Pablo, being with Abuelita has been the most special of all. Pablito knows that he will always remember her. And as the years pass, he will celebrate her memory again and again on *el Día de Los Muertos*". (ibid.:41–42)

Pablo Remembers: the Fiesta of the Day of the Dead is a children's book, written in simple English, with Spanish translations for the foods and other material items typical of this holiday. In its emphasis on eating, the book in fact establishes the Day of the Dead as a culinary high point. The book is clearly directed to monolingual English speakers—whether Anglo or Latino—both as an instructional treatise on the Day of the Dead and as an introduction to Mexican language and culture. The book ends, however, with a three-page note from the author, conveying his ideas of the origins of the holiday as a blend of Aztec and Catholic beliefs. The Catholic part, in his estimation, extends back to ancient Egypt—"The ancient Egyptians thought that the spirits of the dead returned in the autumn to visit to world of the living. They welcomed these spirits with food and light. These customs spread to ancient Rome, and when Christianity was born, the remembrance of the dead was adopted" (ibid.:45). Ancona speaks in this note, too, of José Guadalupe Posada's influence on this holiday and mentions the blending of the Day of the Dead with Halloween in the North American context. Everything about this end note—its literary style, its dense text and absence of photographs, its unnumbered pages—sets it apart from the body of the book as a didactic tool. It is clearly directed towards teachers, parents, or others who require information supplementary to Pablo's story.

Children's literature focusing on the Day of the Dead ranges from the most elementary texts, containing eye-catching pictures supplemented by a few simple words, to relatively sophisticated reading material suitable for young adults. *The Festival of Bones/El Festival de las Calaveras*, by Luis San Vicente (1999), is like a number of Mexican holiday books in that it is bilingual. Originally published only in Spanish, it is directed to a very young audience and its pages are filled with whimsical drawings of skeletons dancing, playing the guitar, riding bicycles, and riding paper airplanes through the sky. It's major message is that on the Day of the Dead, skeletons, such as the ones pictured in the book, are to be found everywhere, dressed in silly garb, engaged in everyday activities, and fully enjoying themselves. "These are the dead. How happy they are!," states the author at one point in the narrative. The end of the book has the skeletons "strung out in rows, dancing a wild dance" as they proceed to the cemetery (San Vicente 1999:17–18).

Following the children's story itself, *The Festival of Bones/El Festival de las Calaveras* appends eight densely packed pages of instructional text, clearly directed towards adults. Here the author outlines the origin ("an ancient Aztec celebration of death" (ibid.:19)) of the Day of the Dead and explains that this holiday is commemorative of both life and death. He indicates that although this occasion is essentially Mexican, readers should rest assured that "In other places outside of Mexico, people freely borrow elements of the Day of the Dead to create their own traditions" (ibid.:21). "Just remember, though," states the author (ibid.), "It's a party, not a funeral." The book ends with instructions on how to build an altar, and recipes for making *pan de muerto* and sugar skulls (see Figure 7.1). Along the way, the author interprets the meaning of these items for neophytes, stating, for example, that even though sugar skulls remind us of our mortality, they are "not morbid or sad. Instead it is a reminder to enjoy life while we are here" (ibid.:24). Readers learn about the material culture associated with the Day of the Dead as well as about how they should feel during this holiday.

Whether addressing themselves to children or adults, whether fiction or nonfiction, books on the Day of the Dead provide readers with emotional prompts. They instruct the uninitiated in the feelings that are supposed to accompany this occasion. Hence, in *Maria Molina and the Days of the Dead*, the fictional protagonist, Maria Molina, a little girl of indeterminate age, begins her narration in the following fashion: "When I woke up from my nap, I was in the graveyard. But I was not scared" (Krull and Sánchez 1994:2). At the cemetery vigil, where Maria Molina and her family gathered at the family grave, "Laughing faces loomed all

Fig. 7.1 Altar workshop, Museo del Barrio Family Day, New York City, November 2, 2004

around. People visited, prayed, gossiped—like a big family reunion" (ibid.:15). "I think the children had the most fun," reports Maria Molina (ibid.:16); "Perhaps not as much fun as Halloween in the United States, but we were excited to be up so late, excited just to be out of school during these special days."

The following autumn finds Maria and her family newly settled in the United States. Maria begins to anticipate Halloween with relish: "I began to think of costumes already, and of the mountains of sugary candy. . . ." But after "enjoying my first Halloween," states Maria, "there was something bothering me" (ibid.:24). She began to worry about her deceased grandmother and baby brother, who were honored during the previous year's Day of the Dead celebrations, and who she thought would be saddened without similar recognition in the new family environment. Maria's mother reassures her that, although they are far from their relatives' graves, deceased family members can still be remembered. Maria's mother and father erect an altar with all the familiar accoutrements, the mother bakes *pan de los muertos*, everyone maintains a vigil over the altar, and the proper order of the universe is reestablished. To Maria, "it *was* magic, the most magic thing of all" (ibid.:26). And there the book ends.

One theme that appears over and over in the children's literature is the Day of the Dead as an occasion for satisfying alimentary desires, particularly the craving for sweets. In *The Day of the Dead*, by Tony Johnston and Jeanette Winter (1997), the action takes place in rural Mexico among a typical family. Children awaken to "a soft sound . . . *Slap, slap, slap, slap.*" The sound comes from the kitchen, where the mother is "making *empanadas*, little pastries fat with meat." The children beg for a taste, but their mother implores them to wait. The story continues with the children attempting in vain to sneak tastes of different foods that are being collected for the impending festivities. "*Los tíos*, the uncles, have picked fruit. Bright oranges, red apple, *tejocotes* of gold . . . For days *las tías*, the aunts, have been grinding dry *chiles* to power . . . For days *papá* has been visiting the bakery, bringing back bulging bundles . . . For days *mamá* has baked *pan de muertos*, bread of the dead . . . Today *papa* has cut up long wands of *caña*, sugarcane . . . ," and so on, throughout the book for these and other foods such as *mole* and *tamales*. When the family arrives at the cemetery and fully decorates the gravestone, the children at last are given permission to eat: "*Papá* unwraps his bundles. *Calaveras de azúcar*! Sugar skulls! The children squeal and eat this treat. *Mamá* slices *pan de muertos*" and everyone enjoys this delicacy as well. Their appetites and cravings sated, the children fall asleep and are carried home to bed.

Most Day of the Dead children's books take place either in the United States or in Mexico. *Maria Molina and the Days of the Dead* is unusual in that it is a migration story, in which Maria is first in her native Mexico and then in the United States. The story shows the salience to a young Mexican girl of both the Day of the Dead and Halloween, a holiday about which she is well aware even before arriving the United States. Far from being historically or culturally related, these holidays, to her mind, are distinct from one another. Although they are both enjoyable, she imbues the Day of the Dead with a subtle emotional texture lacking in Halloween. This texture—a mixture of family unity, nostalgia for one's homeland, and longing for the company of deceased loved ones—is conveyed in the story's telling to readers, young and old. The book not only instructs readers about how to celebrate the Day of the Dead but also demonstrates to them the feelings that motivate the faithful to build altars and maintain vigils. Implicit in the author's words is that these are the feelings that ideally should accompany the Day of the Dead.

The Day of the Dead: A Mexican-American Celebration (Hoyt-Goldsmith 1994) brings this fiesta squarely within the North American context. It concerns the actual holiday preparations and activities of Armando Cid and his family, residents of Sacramento, California, who are portrayed in photographs through-out the book. Their story is told through the words of his twin daughters, Azucena and Ximena, who are bilingual but relate their account in English. Proper names and Spanish words throughout the text are followed by phonetic transliterations placed within parentheses, designed to enhance the readers' knowledge of Mexican Spanish. As with the other children's books, this one focuses on creative, artistic endeavors and products, all the more so since Armando Cid is a professional artist. According to an introductory note, he is also co-founder of Day of the Dead observances in Sacramento.

The book begins, as do so many others, with an account of the origins of this holiday. ("So, although the Day of the Dead and Halloween occur at the same time of year, the two holidays come from very different traditions and origins" (Hoyt-Goldsmith 1994:12).) Food preparations and the decoration of an elaborate altar—in part devoted to one of their cousins, Ron Talamantez-Nevarez, who died of AIDS at the age of 32—occupy a good part of the twins' narrative. What is unusual about this book is the long section on masks, which are integral to the Sacramento celebration and which readers learn to construct through attention to the text. Unusual, too, is the community procession to St. Mary's cemetery in Sacramento, where the congregants—some with painted skeleton faces—march in the direction of each of the four cardinal points to celebrate, in order, the elderly deceased (north), the female deceased (west), *los angelitos* or deceased babies (south), and the deceased warriors (east). The last stop is the east, we are told, "because this is where the sun rises each morning. According to Aztec belief, this is also where the spirit first enters the body of the Earth at birth" (Hoyt-Goldsmith 1994:26). Readers learn that "The procession is not a typical parade where people are having fun and showing off . . . The atmosphere is serious and many people cry as they think of those who have died" (ibid.:24).

When the procession ends, the community as a whole erects an altar at the cemetery and a priest arrives on the scene "to perform a Mass in Spanish" (ibid.:29). (This is the only account of formal Roman Catholic ceremony that I have found in the children's literature.) Last, we learn that Azucena and Ximena's mother

has come to the procession dressed in a native costume influenced by several Mexican Indian tribes—the Zapotec (*sa-POH-tec*), Puebla (*PWEB-lah*), and Yaqui (*YAH-kee*) . . . Although our mother's heritage is Yaqui Indian, she grew up speaking Spanish. Wearing a mask that she herself made, our mother joins the dancers in their traditional movements. Whirling, turning, and stamping her feet, she dances without shoes. She balances, sometimes on one foot, sometimes on the other, as she turns and turns and turns. The dancing and the music are an important ending to the procession. The dancers' movements show their unity with the souls of the people who have lived before them and are now a part of the spirit world . . . In life and in death, the Mexican-American community is strong partly because it stays together. Somehow it is comforting to think that we can come back after death, even if only for a short time each year, to visit the people who love and remember us. As we celebrate the Day of the Dead, we are in touch with our ancient ancestors. The Aztec beliefs, though changed by time and history, are still an important part of our lives. (Hoyt-Goldsmith 1994:29–30)

And so ends the twins' account of their Day of the Dead experiences.

The Day of the Dead: A Mexican-American Celebration is of particular interest in part because the ritual preparations and activities it describes vary so much from those found in other accounts of this holiday directed towards children. Readers are exposed to a unique mixture of beliefs and practices, which the twin narrators of the story interpret as having Christian, Aztec, and contemporary Mexican Indian origins. The construction of altars and visit to the cemetery are standard features of the Day of the Dead, wherever celebrated by Mexicans and people of Mexican descent. So, too, is the performance of Mass in the cemetery. Other features of the Sacramento Day of the Dead, however, would probably mystify most Mexicans—face painting and the production of individualized plaster masks, for example (see Figure 7.2). The same is true of the processional route to the

Fig. 7.2 Face painting at the Oakland Museum Days of the Dead Community Celebration, October 23, 2005

four cardinal points, or the barefoot dancing of Azucena and Ximena's mother. A multicultural message, which resonates positively in the contemporary United States, is embedded within the twins' narrative. By referring throughout the book to Native American beliefs and ritual practices, *The Day of the Dead: A Mexican-American Celebration* goes beyond the reference to Spanish and ancient Aztec customs which are predictable in this body of children's literature. The book's dedication—"to all of our *antepasados*, but especially to Joe N. Talamantez, our Yaqui grandfather"—provides a subtle addition to the multicultural message. The timeliness of the Sacramento celebration, and its suitability to contemporary California, is reinforced by reference to their deceased cousin, an Aids victim, who is prominent among those they honor during the Day of the Dead.

What is most unusual about this volume, however, is its explicit discussion of the Roman Catholic Mass, which takes place on November 2 at the cemetery. The book even includes a photograph of a priest at an outdoor altar holding the communion wafer high in the air. The caption reads, "A Catholic priest performs a Mass for all the participants when the procession ends at the ofrenda made by the community" (Hoyt-Goldsmith 1994:29). Moreover, a photograph of the community procession prominently displays a couple, at the head of the large group, holding a large banner of the Virgin of Guadalupe, patron saint of Mexico. Whether situated within the Mexican or Mexican-American context, most children's books dealing with the Day of the Dead incorporate a kind of universalistic spiritual message: we all die, it is possible to confront death directly, death is an extension of life, death can be treated with humor and playfulness, children need not be protected from the sight of death, and the like. By contrast, *The Day of the Dead: A Mexican-American Celebration* clearly associates the holiday with Roman Catholicism. Among all children's books, it is the one that most clearly presents a dual image of the Day of the Dead as both a deeply religious occasion and a creative expression of ethnic pride.

As the Latino population of the United States expands, and with it the number of Mexicans and citizens of Mexican descent, the Day of the Dead has increasingly become an integral part of the school curriculum. This is particularly true in both public and parochial elementary schools, extending from the southwestern states all the way to cities in New England. Children not only learn about the Day of the Dead through the written and spoken word, but they also make crafts associated with this holiday and take field trips to museums and art galleries exhibiting seasonal displays of Day of the Dead art. Children of all ethnic and religious backgrounds, not only Latinos, engage in these school activities. Learning about the Day of the Dead is promoted educationally as a means of gaining appreciation for a new multicultural world.

Merchants collaborate in this endeavor, probably as a means of increasing business. In Pasadena, California, for example, a store called the Folk Tree in the fall of 2003 offered a free teacher's Day of the Dead Workshop, "Designed for

Teachers, Parents and Adults." States the advertising copy, "This class includes slides, lecture, hands-on sugarskull making, skull decorating (take one home!), papel picado cutting, paper flowers and altar building. You will learn the philosophy and history of this multi-cultural holiday" (www.mexicansugarskull.com). The Folk Tree offers a separate Sugar Skull Making Workshop including "slideshow, lecture, sugarskull making and decorating" (ibid.).

On October 15, 1994, the Oakland Museum of California mounted its first Day of the Dead exhibition, consisting mainly of altar installations created by Latino artists, students, and community groups. The exhibition was so successful—with its roster of reserved classroom visits filled, and 80 schools on the waiting list—that the exhibit has been repeated every year thereafter. The program of activities associated with this exhibition has become increasingly elaborate. From October 11 through December 7, 2003, for example, the Museum offered a much-expanded display entitled *Global Elegies: Art and Ofrendas for the Dead*. To orient teachers to the exhibition, and in preparation for student field trips, the Museum mounts a well-publicized instructional open house. The announcement of the event states that, "This program is FREE for teachers and chaperones" (Carrillo Hocker 2003). It provides "a chance to meet altar makers" as well as to "meet other teachers and share ideas" (ibid.). A hefty curriculum packet (Davidman 1993) explains the goals of the exhibition, among them to build "self-esteem and pride in Latino students", to facilitate "cross-cultural programs and experiences that promote harmony in our multi-cultural classrooms and communities", to bring together "families of all ethnic and social economic origins," and to understand "this major Mexican and Mexican American cultural tradition". The stated objectives judiciously combine a mixture of culturally specific (to provide a "broader understanding of Mexican and Central American culture as linkages to Mesoamerica's ancient past") and cross-culturally universalistic ("to emphasize our common experiences such as death, family and the recognition of individuals who have contributed to the betterment of our lives") features.

The booklet instructs teachers as to the origins of the Day of the Dead in both pre-Hispanic and Catholic ritual. It explains the functions ("purpose") of ritual in general, and suggests that teachers query pupils about their experiences with other kinds of rituals. The curriculum packet also describes an altar and the *ofrenda*, with detailed sections about the diverse foods, toys, and decorations that are placed upon it. The booklet expands at length upon Mexican art, provides full-page outline drawings of death-related pre-Hispanic glyphs and sculptures, which pupils are supposed to color. There are also cut-out patterns for skull masks, altar tables, and skeletons with movable parts. Teachers are encouraged to use these cutouts as the basis of Day of the Dead crafts projects. They are also supposed to inspire personal reflection, by asking the pupils to dedicate their imaginary altar to some deceased individual (or to "a special pet who has died"), and to ask themselves "why is this person special to me?"; "what do I want to remember about him/her?"; "what objects should be on the altar to tell people about the person I am honoring?"

The booklet pays special attention to the Chicano celebration of the Day of the Dead and in doing so promotes, once again, the dual vision of this holiday as an expression of ethnic pride as well as reflection of universal experience.

> The transference of *El día de los Muertos* from Mexico to the United States has been of significant value. The Day of the Dead practices in the United States enable Mexican Americans to establish bonds with their historical and cultural roots and generate an understanding and appreciation of Mexican culture in the general community. These traditions also inspire the emergence of ethnic traditions in the United States among other cultural groups. The Day of the Dead celebrations are open and enjoyed by all members of the community and since death and the loss of loved ones is a common human experience, these types of rituals promote feelings of kinship among all participants.

This passage is typical of the curriculum packet as a whole in that it largely obliterates the connection between the Day of the Dead and Roman Catholic religious teaching. Where Roman Catholicism appears in the text, it is only briefly and in passing.

A curriculum packet published by the influential Bay Area Bilingual Education League (BABEL), lists suggestions for classroom activities. Predictably, the list includes nothing that could be interpreted as fundamentally spiritual or religious. Typical suggestions are to "cook *mole* and/or *pan de Muertos*" (see recipe in index) foods which are traditionally eaten on these days; to "draw and cut out a mask"; and to "teach primary children 'El baile de los esqueletos'," which "consists of very loose-boned type of movements, with hopping and miming of skeleton-type movements." There is only one suggested activity which might be construed as religious, depending on the teacher's approach: for students to "do a simple dramatic presentation of a family setting up a commemorative altar and the ghost visiting them to share the food." This curriculum packet, like others, contains background information for teachers who might be unfamiliar with the holiday. There are drawings of Day of the Dead toys, *ofrendas*, candies, and the like for children to color. There is also a section on the satirical verses known as *calaveras* (see Chapter 5), which prepares teachers for instruction to older students.

In a multicultural environment, such as the San Francisco Bay Area, it is obviously necessary for public school teachers in particular to emphasize the cultural meaning of the event—particularly neutral aspects of the holiday, such as food, flowers, and material culture—as well as the possible life lessons it embodies for all humanity, as opposed to doctrinal aspects of any specific religious tradition. In Mexico, of course, where Roman Catholicism overwhelmingly predominates, no blunting of a religious message is necessary. In fact, throughout Mexico the religious and cultural messages overlap one another, whereas in the United States these domains are usually presented to the public as distinct domains. The separation of religious and cultural messages operates to convert the Day of the Dead from its Mexican identity as a definitively Roman Catholic holiday into an ecumenical celebration, attractive to people of all faiths. Above all, by presenting the Day of the Dead devoid of its religious content as much as possible, schools can maintain at least the appearance of a separation of church and state.

Throughout California, teachers who introduce the Day of the Dead into their classes tend to focus on the visual aspects of the holiday. In a brief questionnaire distributed among teachers in several San Francisco Bay Area elementary schools, we asked whether and in what fashion they introduce the Day of the Dead into their classrooms. Although we have no thorough coverage of any single school—much less city or geographic area—typical responses include: "We cut out and color skulls and make a skeleton man"; "We cut and paste a skeleton on orange construction paper & then we name the body parts"; "Make 'skeleton' puppets, calaveras—sing songs"; "We do art work and see slides or movies"; "bake bread shaped like skeletens." A fair number of teachers also construct altars and "set up an 'ofrenda'" in the classroom and explain to students its meaning. This act is, like the others, a visual learning exercise, but one that inescapably borders on the transmission of a religious belief system (see Plate 7.1). When asked why they choose to observe the Day of the Dead, respondents state that although their school districts do not require the observance of multicultural holidays, they "strongly suggest" it.

The questionnaire requests teachers to list holidays other than the Day of the Dead that they celebrate with their students. One teacher answers, "Chinese New Year, St. Patrick's Day, Laotian New Years, Cinco de Mayo, 4th of July, Black History Month, Children's Day." Another says, "Cinco de Mayo, Kwanza, Chinese New Year." The other holidays recognized in the schools include Las Posadas, Christmas, Martin Luther King's Birthday, Earth Day, Native American Day, Thanksgiving, Mexican Independence Day, and, of Japanese origin, Boys and Girls Day. My suggestive, if unscientific, sample of responses indicates that there is no direct relationship between the teacher's ethnicity and the types or number of classroom holiday celebrations. The list seems to be a fusion of national, ethnic, and ecologically based holidays, some of which—such as Thanksgiving, St. Valentine's Day and St. Patrick's Day—originated within a specific religious setting, and others not.

In fact, this list is a much-attenuated compilation of holidays from diverse religious and national traditions, which appear annually on The Oakland Unified School District Office of Bilingual Education Multicultural Calendar. The District distributes this calendar to teachers at the beginning of every school year. In the 1990s the calendar highlighted many holidays other than the ones named above.

These include Jewish Rosh Hashanah and Yom Kippur; Vietnamese Kitchen God Day, Confucius Day, and Tomb-Sweeping Day; and Laotian Mountain Temple Festival Day. Occasions such as these appear on the Multicultural Calendar alongside Botswana Independence Day, United States Labor Day, and the Battle of Wounded Knee. The supposedly sacred and secular holidays receive equal emphasis as they are listed on the Multicultural Calendar. There is nothing to distinguish them one from the other and all are presumably eligible for recognition by classroom teachers.

Many holidays that United States citizens take for granted as national holidays were, at a different place and time, deeply sacred occasions. Saint Valentine's Day, Thanksgiving, Halloween, and, despite its name, St. Patrick's Day have all become transformed through time into largely secular celebrations. In the U.S. context, they are both celebrated and interpreted more as affirmations of national or ethnic identity than of religious conviction. Currently, the Day of the Dead as practiced and taught in the United States, seems to be undergoing a similar transformation.

It is no doubt in part the transitional nature of this holiday that has made it a recent subject of legal controversy. On the one hand, the Day of the Dead—a derivative of the pan-Catholic All Saints' and All Souls' days—is filled with Roman Catholic symbolism and significance. As far as supernatural phenomena are concerned, this holiday incorporates the belief that death is an extension of life and that the souls of the deceased in Purgatory visit their living relatives. Priests chant special, obligatory masses during the Day of the Dead. And the altars and graveside vigils that mark the Mexican celebration of All Saints' and All Souls' days are an integral feature of Roman Catholic liturgy and mortuary ritual. On the other hand, with many of the explicitly religious aspects of the holiday suppressed in the context of the contemporary United States, the Day of the Dead can appear to be as much of a secular family affair as Thanksgiving and as devotional an occasion as the Fourth of July.

The truth is that the Day of the Dead can be what people want and expect it to be. In California schools, and in many other educational systems throughout the country, the holiday is celebrated above all for two reasons: first, as an expression of Mexican American pride and in recognition of the right of Mexican Americans to have their culture represented in their public schools; and, second, as a means of teaching students to appreciate cultural beliefs, practices, and values other than their own. An informal handbook distributed to teachers in San Francisco puts the matter succinctly:

> In our North American Anglo culture we usually squirm and feel uncomfortable at the sight of skeletons, the thought of death, or the passing of a funeral procession. We speak about death in euphemisms to ourselves and to our children . . . Death to us is somber, its color black . . . In contrast, the Mexicans (and many other

cultures) celebrate death in an open and joyous way. Spirits are encouraged to visit
and to stay in touch with family and friends. This is a completely different attitude
toward death that both children and adults can share . . . If children can learn about
different ways of looking at death, they may be more open to and tolerant of other
cultures and be better informed about our complex multicultural society. By participating in the . . . activities of the Day of the Dead, the children and teachers will
directly experience this new concept of death and share a meaningful experience
with each other.

We may suppose that Mexican children and children of Mexican ancestry are
already familiar with the attitudes towards death expressed by the Day of the
Dead. Since these children are forced daily to transcend their own background
through constant exposure to the dominant Anglo culture, it is non-Mexican
youth who presumably benefit the most from learning about and experiencing
the Day of the Dead.

This argument, which is a regular feature of teachers' guides and museum
handouts, completely sidesteps religious aspects of the holiday to take advantage
of its secular aspects, be they artistic, social, or philosophical. Throughout the
state of California, bilingual and other teachers claim that Day of the Dead
celebrations are consonant with official mandates to introduce cross-cultural
experiences into the classroom. Those who advocate Day of the Dead school
celebrations state that to teach about another culture is not to proselytize. Children
can and should learn to transcend their own point of view, these advocates state.
Moreover, they say, America's youth can be exposed to ways of thinking and
acting other than their own, without the risk of sullying, much less abandoning,
their family's particular religious or cultural traditions.

Not all segments of California society agree with this point of view, however.
An increasingly vocal contingent of Anglo parents raise serious objections to Day
of the Dead school activities on the grounds that they violate the constitutional
separation between church and state. Kathy Bricker, parent of a fourth grade
student at McNear Elementary School in Petaluma (a city in Sonoma County,
just north of San Francisco), brought suit against the Petaluma City Schools for
violation of the First Amendment, as well as for discriminatory treatment against
her daughter. Represented by the United States Justice Foundation, a conservative, nonprofit legal foundation based in Escondido, California, Kathy Bricker
filed suit against the Petaluma City Schools. The lengthy petition—filed on
October 29, 2002 in the California Superior Court, Sonoma County—reads in
part as follows:

> "Day of the Dead" is a religious holiday that is recognized by religious adherents in
> Latin America, and in some limited portions of the United States, including, but
> not limited to, San Francisco, California. According to the written handouts being
> provided to PCS [Petaluma City School] parents, the Day of the Dead celebration

can be described as follows: (1) "Ritual event in which the spirit of dead loved ones are invited to visit the living as honored guests"; (2) Reflects the belief that death is a part of life . . . ; (3) Families often set up *ofrendas* or altars, bearing pictures, lighted candles and traditional items including marigolds, bread, fruit, favorite foods of deceased family members . . .

The "Day of the Dead" is a time dedicated to remembering the dead through various forms of religious rituals, sectarian forms of prayer, and worship . . .

PCS children are expected to mimic or actually engage in such practices . . .

The religious practices associated with the "Day of the Dead", as described by Defendents' own video materials (to be presented to the children), are associated with images of crosses, pictures of "Our Lady of Guadalupe", sexual references made about the living and the dead, and testimonies and descriptions of religious beliefs by persons interviewed on the videotape . . .

Attached to the petition is reference to a long list of academic and popular documents designed to prove that "a wide array of universities, private citizens, and even local agencies view Day of the Dead as essentially religious in nature." As such, public school celebration of this holiday, claims the suit, violates the Establishment Clause of the First Amendment, assuring the separation of church and state.

Attorneys for Kathy Bricker claim that, in addition to the constitutional violation represented by Day of the Dead celebrations, her daughter has suffered from discriminatory treatment in the classroom. Apparently, in deference to the plaintiff's concerns, the fourth grader was separated from the classroom during Day of the Dead activities. As a result, the suit claims, "Petitioner's child will be, and is, harmfully affected by the activities of the Defendents . . . Specifically, the child has been separated from other children because of her religious views and those of the Petitioner. Defendant's activities have had the effect of singling out and inhibiting MS. BRICKER's religious views and those of her daughter." Whereas the "Petitioner is Christian," states the legal brief, "and is raising her daughter in a manner consistent therewith," the "'Day of the Dead' has its historical roots in Meso-American spirituality and religious practice."

In a letter to the principal of McNear Elementary School, demanding that teachers refrain entirely from Day of the Dead activities, attorneys for the plaintiff actually outline what would be to them an acceptable classroom presentation of this holiday. They state:

The only possible way that your institution could neutrally approach the situation would be through neutral allowance of all religiously relevant themes to be a part of the "celebration" of the Day of the Dead. As a matter of historical accuracy, this would require you to incorporate All Saints Day, which traditionally follows the Day of the Dead and Halloween ceremonial occasions. Moreover, you would also be required to show historical and cultural connections between Christianity and the Day of the Dead (as it has developed in Latino culture over history). Obviously, McNear Elementary has chosen only to take the portions of this religious holiday that somehow suit the institution's needs. This is unconstitutional conduct, smacks of censorship, and indicates a tendency toward cultural and religious revisionism.

It is significant that these charges, which precede the formal legal petition, were dropped from the petition itself. They reveal that the petitioner was motivated originally not merely by the presence of religious content in public school curriculum but specifically by the presence of what she considered non-Christian religious content. Of course the identification of what she and her legal counsel consider non-Christian elements is highly problematic. It seems to have been determined by popular opinion and their own religious preferences rather than by historical and ethnographic evidence.

The principal of McNear Elementary School, in response, sought to minimize the role of religion (Christian, Mesoamerican, or whatever) in her school and stressed instead the fundamentally cultural, secular nature of the Day of the Dead activities. The principal's declaration states, in part, that, "the activities in question are in line with the California content standards for history social science at the 4th grade level." Moreover, "the state standards require that students 'describe the social, political, cultural and economic life and interactions among people of California from the pre-Columbian societies to the Spanish mission and Mexican rancho periods'." Attorneys for the defense cited California Education Code Section 51511, providing that:

> Nothing in this code shall be construed to prevent, or exclude from the public schools, references to religion or references to or the use of religious literature, dance, music, theatre, and visual arts or other things having religious significance when such references or uses do not constitute instruction in religious principles or aid to any religious sect, church, creed, or sectarian purpose and when such references or uses are incidental to or illustrative of matters properly included in the course of study.

Attorneys for the defense conclude from this legal provision that the "challenged activities, including the cultural use of symbolic artifacts, craft activities, and dance, indisputably fall under the protective umbrella of Section 51511." Moreover, the defense brief states that the plaintiff claimed, but failed to demonstrate, any irreparable injury to the fourth grader that might have resulted from Day of the Dead activities.

In the end, the California Superior Court of Sonoma County issued an oral ruling in favor of the defense, that is, allowing McNear teachers to introduce the Day of the Dead into the school curriculum. Immediately upon issuance of this oral ruling, and without waiting for the entry of a written judgment by the court, the plaintiff filed an appeal. The Court of Appeals in San Francisco denied the plaintiff's request on the grounds that "the oral denial does not constitute an appealable order." On this technicality, the case died.

Anthropologists, sociologists and other academics might debate *ad infinitum* whether the cultural and religious domains are separable, whether religion is an inextricable part of culture or culture is fundamentally religious; or whether religion and culture even exist except as reified intellectual artifacts. If ever there could be a resolution to this debate, it might help the courts, the schools, parents, and children to resolve issues such as those that were raised in *Kathy Bricker vs. Petaluma City Schools*. But since no final resolution of this issue is likely to emerge— and, even if it did, probably would be ignored, misunderstood, or manipulated by legal powers—it is the prevailing popular conception of culture and religion that prevails in the courts. In the debate surrounding *Kathy Bricker vs. Petaluma City Schools*, "culture" is identified as essentially secular and "religion" is defined as sacred. To some observers, an *ofrenda* is an essentially sacred artifact, erected as a means of communicating with the dead. But to others, it is a cultural (hence, secular) object, a source of artistic creativity and an expression of ethnic identity. To some observers, sugar skulls represent cosmological beliefs about the after-life; to others, they are toys and candy and an excuse to learn how to follow a cooking recipe.

The Petaluma school controversy arose within a specific context, of course. The population of the city of Petaluma, at the time of the court petition, was about 15 percent Latino. In 2001, the Petaluma *Press Democrat* (Kovner 2001) reported on a diverse program of Day of the Dead activities throughout the last two weeks of October. These include a local men's choral group performing traditional Mexican music at the Petaluma Regional Library; the erection of six altars at the Petaluma City Hall and 11 window displays and exhibits in stores, restaurants, and art galleries around town. Also scheduled were poetry readings, photographic displays, and a showing, in City Hall, of the video, "La Ofrenda: The Days of the Dead." Apparently, too, the attack on the World Trade Center, which occurred on September 11, 2001, served as a major inspiration to residents of Petaluma to carry out a particularly vigorous Day of the Dead celebration that year (ibid.).

The program was such a huge success that the following year the city received some $4,000 in grants to help with the cost of setting up traditional altars, which were erected in 27 separate municipal locations, including, again, City Hall and the public library. City officials portrayed the Day of the Dead as a cultural counterpoint to Halloween, which is interpreted by Latinos and others as a pri-marily Anglo-American holiday. If you agree with this point of view, celebrating the Day of the Dead, whether in or outside of the schools, is a civic responsibility. It provides equal time for exposure to Latino culture, a means of learning about ethnic difference and diversity, and an opportunity to enhance respect and artistic appreciation for traditions other than one's own. Of course, for Catholics—particularly Latino Catholics—Day of the Dead celebrations assume a direct religious meaning. In Petaluma, the St. Vincent de Paul Church sponsors an outdoor enactment of the "Raising of the Cross," presided over by the parish priest. The church also puts on a dance performance by the Ballet Folklorico Netzahualcoyotl.

Religion inevitably filters in to community and school Day of the Dead celebrations, because this holiday in essence is a religious event. Even where religious elements of the Day of the Dead are scrupulously excised from the celebration, however, the ethnic politics of the celebration raises heated controversy. In response to the Bricker petition, one Mexican American reported anonymously (Lynne 2002),

> I . . . am appalled at the "Day of the Dead" "festivities" in the Bay Area community and its schools . . . The core of those promoting these events are actually white, non-Hispanic liberals and a handful of "Latino artists." What they celebrate is a caricature of the true "Dia de los Muertos" holiday. These people celebrate as if it's Mardi Gras. They seem to leave out that in Mexico this solemn holiday is celebrated with Holy Mass, usually at the cemetery. Women recite the Holy Rosary for the Poor Souls in Purgatory. Men drink alcohol and reminisce; people crying is not a rare sight. Music is always muted. Dances performed, only by indigenous communities, are also solemn and part of a liturgy that has incorporated native customs. My family and all Latinos I know find the celebrations performed here as foreign . . . Liberals have taken a true religious observance and used it for their own nihilistic reasons.

With regard to the celebration of the Day of the Dead in Mexico, a number of the characterizations as expressed in this testimony are simply wrong. The testimony errs in generalizing and overlooking the enormously wide variety of Day of the Dead observances throughout Mexico, where class, regional, ethnic, political and age differences all influence specific ways in which people observe this holiday. As far as what is said about the United States is concerned, the writer of this testimony reveals a strong bias against white liberals and "Latino artists," who organize Day of the Dead activities. The quotation marks implicitly call into question the legitimacy of Latino artists, either as Latinos or as artists. The writer insists that his or her view of how the Day of the Dead is celebrated in Mexico—regardless of whether that view is accurate—is the way it should be celebrated in the United States. Allegedly inauthentic expressions of the holiday need to be suppressed.

It is clear that the McNear Elementary School controversy is about more than religion. At its heart is a struggle between conservative or fundamentalist Christians, on the one hand, and political and religious progressives, on the other, that cuts across ethnic lines. The battle seems so fierce because it concerns more than the celebration of a particular holiday. It is ultimately about the future of American society and culture.

School celebrations of Halloween have come under the same type of attack as the Day of the Dead, and for similar reasons. On September 30, 2003, officials at the University of Arkansas at Fort Smith banned the erection of campus Halloween displays that contain images of witches or devils. "Administrators said their decision to ban the likenesses reflects the values of the community," reports Aaron Sadler (2003a); "One critic of the move called the ban a 'witch hunt'" (ibid.). Sadler states further that Robin Mink, a student at the school, "said she thinks the institution is pushing an agenda that has more to do with Christian values than those of the community. 'They are dictating to us what we can and can't do and are using Christianity to do it,' she says. 'This is a public school'" (ibid.). A few days later, faced with serious student and community protest, the University backed down from its decision. Reports Sadler, "Participants at the University of Arkansas at Fort Smith's annual Halloween festival can come dressed as witches and devils after all" (Sadler 2003b). Kay Fisher, a student at the school "said she thought the school's initial decision insulted the public by associating Halloween with Satanism. 'They can't really assume that the people in Fort Smith are that stupid,' Fisher said. 'It's not worship of devils or evil, it's just simply a children's day'" (ibid.).

Although many people would share Kay Fisher's point of view, the incident at Fort Smith, Arkansas has been repeated throughout the country on numerous occasions. In 1989, a Palm Beach Post editorial (Crowley 1989) reported that the Levy County school superintendent banned Halloween celebrations:

> Mr. Irby sent his teachers a memo telling them no one would be allowed to wear a costume or do anything else to celebrate Halloween. He noted that recent court decisions have made it clear that no form of religious practice is allowed in public schools. Since witchcraft is a form of religion, Halloween must be banned from the schools. "It's a civil rights issue," Mr. Irby said. "I'm not saying that anyone who dresses up as a witch or celebrates Halloween practices witchcraft or condones witchcraft. I'm saying that because witchcraft has been recognized as a religion, we may violate someone's civil rights if we condone it in the schools." Parents are not happy. "This is the most ridiculous thing I ever heard," Denise Swift told reporters. "Halloween and Halloween carnivals have been a fun event for children through-out time."

In another part of Florida, Robert Guyer kept his children out of Alachua County's Hidden Valley Elementary School one Halloween and sued the school board on the grounds that "pointed hats, brooms and the like are symbols of Wicca, a variety of witchcraft and a religion. The lawsuit said some Wiccan adherents consider Halloween a religious holiday" (Anonymous 1994). When Guyer lost his suit, he appealed to the U.S. Supreme Court, which dismissed the case without comment (ibid.). Ironically, Wiccans themselves have brought legal action against public celebrations of Halloween. In Dunbar, West Virginia, two Wiccans settled out of court on charges that a Baptist church Halloween production in a city park was unconstitutional because it was disrespectful to Wiccans and promoted one religion over another (Associated Press 2000a, 2000b).

Consider, too, a Baltimore *Daily Record* story of October 25, 1995 reporting cancellation of school Halloween parties "because of complaints from some parents that the holiday is linked to satanic worship" (Anonymous 1995). One Maryland elementary school principal stated that "We'll do a parade, but we ask the children to dress up as book characters . . . We've taken the middle-of-the-road approach. We do the Halloween thing, but we work it out so that we don't look at the pagan worship side" (quoted in ibid.). Protests against the presumed religious content of Halloween celebrations has even extended to Canada, where "fears of 'devil worship' fuelled the controversy embroiling a Toronto public school that outlawed Halloween costumes in class . . ." (Wallace 2000). In Denver, Colorado, four-year old Zeke Tschumper, son of a parent who keeps her children home on Halloween, states blithely, "When my mom was little she wore a devil's costume on Halloween . . . But devils are bad" (quoted in Torkelson 1995:63a).

Legal battles that have arisen over Day of the Dead and Halloween are certainly not limited to educational settings. In fact, they generally revolve around whether these holidays incorporate specific religious content and, if they do, whether or not it is constitutional for publicly funded institutions—municipal buildings and parks as well as schools—to house their celebration. Nonetheless, it is evident that schools, from elementary through university level, are the primary battlegrounds. This circumstance among other things supports the view that the Day of the Dead as celebrated in the United States has become a largely child-centered holiday, to an extent traditionally unknown in Mexico. Especially in the southwestern portion of the country, the Day of the Dead may be considered the Latino equivalent of Halloween (just as Hannukah in the U.S. context, celebrated far beyond what it is in Israel, has developed into the Jewish child's Christmas). Halloween and the Day of the Dead are ethnic markers and, principally for this reason, are treated as separate school holidays, despite their historical links.

But the prevalence of school controversies and lawsuits derives from more than just the child-centeredness of these holidays. Plaintiffs tend to be conservative Christians, who fear for the religious contamination and moral impoverishment of their children. The Day of the Dead and Halloween to them represent holidays with pagan origins and practices, which in present day educational institutions not only survive; they actually thrive, protected and promoted by elected school boards, teachers and principals, and the courts. Conservative Christians are not merely interested in compliance with the constitutional requirement to separate church and state. They use constitutional provisions as an attempt to isolate children from what they perceive as foreign religious and cultural influences—influences that they consider fundamentally flawed. The legal petitions aimed at eliminating school celebrations of the Day of the Dead and Halloween are produced by indignant parents, convinced that the schools will steal and corrupt the hearts and minds of their children. Children are impressionable and parents know that as their children go, so too goes the nation. Those who support these school celebrations see them as preparation for a multicultural world in an era of globalization. Those who fight against them try—mostly, to this point, in vain—to hold back the tide.

8

CREATIVITY AND COMMUNITY

Should you happen to find yourself in New York City at the beginning of November—as I did in 2004—you might be surprised to discover that the Day of the Dead is very much alive in this unlikely extremity of the country. Here in the Northeast, far from Mexico, a demographically significant Mexican presence is indeed quite recent. This is all the more true when New York is compared with other parts of the United States, particularly California and the U.S. Southwest. The southwestern states are not only located adjacent to Mexico, thereby making them eminently accessible, but also actually belonged to Mexico—were part of Mexican territory—until 1848. Thus, the prominence of Mexicans in those regions is a result of the U.S. absorption of a people long present in the area as well as of a steady migratory stream that has been taking place over the past half century.

By contrast, until the mid-1990s, relatively few Mexicans lived within New York City proper. According to a *New York Times* report (March 3, 2005), from 1990 to 1999, the number of Mexicans in New York City quadrupled, from about 32,000 at the beginning of the decade to more than 122,000 by decade's end. In the year 2000, city demographers estimated a Mexican presence of nearly 200,000 within New York, making this group the city's fifth most numerous foreign-born population. And the 200,000 figure is probably an underestimate, given that minority and undocumented workers are often underreported in census counts. By the 1990s, Mexicans had become the New York's fastest growing immigrant population. Births to New York's Mexican-born mothers (6,408) were second only in New York City to births to native Dominicans. Through a process that social scientists term chain migration, in which early immigrants to a given area pave the way for others from the country of origin, most of the Mexican nationals in New York come from a single Mexican state, Puebla. It is therefore a combination of factors, including globalization, the impact of NAFTA, a growing fascination with Latin American culture among U.S. citizens, as well as the very presence of Mexicans within the United States, which accounts for much-heightened awareness of the Day of the Dead in New York and throughout the Northeast.

My first indication that the Day of the Dead was relevant to New Yorkers came with a *New York Times* full-page spread, which appeared on Sunday, October 24, 2004. The article dealt specifically with the Day of the Dead as celebrated in Mexico City, and was directed towards American tourists flying there for the holiday. Three days later, the normal Wednesday food section of the same newspaper highlighted Mexican Day of the Dead culinary specialties within New York itself. "Tasting the Day of the Dead in New York" listed a wide range of Manhattan restaurants, many of them very expensive, where gourmet Day of the Dead prix fixe menus were being served. At Starbucks, there suddenly became available for purchase organic coffee from Chiapas, served in paper cups decorated with Day of the Dead iconography. Art centers in suburban Westchester County, north of the city, offered craft workshops, where adults and children alike could attend lectures explaining the Day of the Dead and learn how to make crafts appropriate to the occasion. What is certain is that the vast majority of recently arrived Mexicans, working heavy hours seven days a week, could ill afford the time or money required to take advantage of these cultural resources. As I was to discover, the Mexican presence at public Day of the Dead celebrations was tiny when compared with that of other, especially non-Latino, groups.

On Sunday, November 30, 2004, I traveled to Fifth Avenue at 104th Street in Manhattan, the location of the Museo del Barrio, a museum normally devoted principally to Caribbean, rather than Mexican, themes. I was drawn there by an advertisement in the New York weekly, *Time Out*, announcing "Día de los Muertos: A Family Celebration." A mariachi band of Mexican musicians, dressed in full regalia, was playing at the Museum entrance. Inside, long tables were set with Mexican fruit drinks and typical foods, such as tamales and tostadas. Nearly an entire floor of the Museum had been turned into a crafts center, divided into three distinct activities. One large hall was devoted to the production of small cardboard objects that instructors termed "portable altars." This hall, which seemed to host principally African Americans, Anglos, and a few Asians, was filled with an ethnically diverse group of adults instructing more than 150 or so young children on how to construct miniature altars (see Figure 7.1), installed within decorated boxes. A second, smaller room was devoted to drawing and painting, with an emphasis on costumed skulls and skeletons after the fashion of José Guadalupe Posada (see Figure 8.1). In addition to art supplies, on the top of each crafts station rested reproductions of Posada's work. This room was filled with an ethnically diverse crowd of about fifty, somewhat older, children. A third, medium-sized room, hosting another fifty or so children, was dedicated to the art of *papel picado*, that is, traditional papercutting. Children of all ages, guided by adults, were busy fashioning designs out of colorful tissue paper. In yet another

Fig. 8.1   Posada workshop, Museo del Barrio Family Day, New York City,
October 30, 2004

room, a wall was lined with three Day of the Dead altars. Opposite this display,
and occupying an entire side of the hall, a Mexican artist had pasted a large cardboard *arbol de la vida*, or "tree of life." Visitors could write messages on pre-cut
paper leaves, which the artist then attached to the trunk and branches of the tree.

The crafts activities continued throughout the morning and into mid-afternoon.
On the first floor of the museum, a mariachi band played Mexican music and
visitors could line up to help themselves to abundant Mexican snacks. Around
2:30 p.m. that day, yellow school buses arrived at the Museo del Barrio to collect
Day of the Dead celebrants and transport them a mile and a half down Fifth
Avenue to the Guggenheim Museum, where a high-profile show, entitled "Aztecs,"
had just opened. If you managed to obtain a voucher showing that you had been
at the Museo del Barrio, the normal Guggenheim entrance fee of $15. would be
waived. Hundreds of visitors waited on line to see the exhibit, as the mariachi
band, situated now on Fifth Avenue right outside the Guggenheim, serenaded
the celebrants with emblematic Mexican songs such as "Cielito Lindo" and
"Guadalajara". Apart from these musicians, very few Mexicans were evident at
either of the two museums' activities. I was told that, even on a Sunday, most
were probably at work. Others, uprooted from homes in Puebla and elsewhere,
and far from family cemeteries, no doubt perceived no meaningful means to
celebrate what in Mexico would have been a major occasion. Says Julian

Zugazagoitia, director of El Museo del Barrio, "For some people, particularly new immigrants, the experience of going to the theater or a performance is not possible. They are working seven days a week, very heavy hours" (quoted in *New York Times*, December 8, 2004: page E1). In any event, there would be neither need nor motivation for Mexican natives to attend a principally instructional event such as was taking place at the Museo del Barrio.

In New York, as throughout much of the United States, the Day of the Dead was rapidly becoming an event designed around the needs of Anglo, African American, and Asian celebrants, as much as those of Latinos of diverse national origins. What is most notable is the focus in the Museo del Barrio celebration on familiar cultural icons—particularly altars, paper cutouts, and representations of skulls and skeletons. This festival, too, bore a completely non-sectarian, if not entirely secular, character. And, officially billed as "Dia de los Muertos: A Family Celebration," it centered on children, rather than adults.

Celebration of the Day of the Dead in New York pales by comparison with what it has become elsewhere in the country, particularly in the American southwest (see, e.g., Turner and Jasper 1994). After all, the Museo del Barrio, a center of Latino culture in the greater New York metropolitan area, has recognized the holiday officially only for the past half decade. Nonetheless, its very presence, in a region so remote both geographically and culturally from the Mexican border, signifies a transformation in the American consciousness of Mexico. Day of the Dead celebrations, in parks and plazas and on college campuses throughout the United States, are fast becoming a central feature of the Fall holiday season. Since the mid-1990s, places as unlikely as Detroit, Michigan (Sommers 1995), Toledo, Ohio (Sánchez Carretero 2003), and Washington, DC (Cadaval 1985) have seen Day of the Dead celebrations emerge and flourish. People of Mexican ancestry, as well as those representing virtually every major ethnic group in the United States, have appropriated the Day of the Dead to satisfy a variety of needs. For many celebrants, of course, the spiritual dimension remains paramount. But for countless others, the Day of the Dead responds to a combination of motives, including artistic expression, the promotion of commerce, preservation of health, community development, as well as the assertion of ethnic identity.

Day of the Dead celebrations in the United States vary substantially from one community to the other. Each town, city, or ethnic enclave develops a distinct emphasis, a different manner of representing themselves to themselves and to the world at large through this event. In some instances, the end product is a result of conscious deliberation among groups of organizers. In other cases, the holiday develops organically as a manifestation of collective will or a multitude of individual wills, with each party pursuing spiritual goals in his or her own way. Whatever the motivation, Day of the Dead celebrations north of the border are generally contested events, creating new rivalries and reviving old ones. Local groups tend to view the occasion as a means to advance public or private agendas, and they employ a variety of strategies to promote their point of view. In addition, Day of the Dead events in the United States often are designed in such a way that they strengthen primarily non-familial bonds—bonds with one's friends, political allies, local neighborhood, or wider ethnic community—rather than those within the family. Political causes are among the most popular. Hence, in November 2005, an organization in the state of Arizona called No More Deaths (www.nomoredeaths.org) sponsored what they called a "Day of the Dead Pilgrimage for Justice on the Border"—an eight-mile procession from Tuscon to San Xavier Mission "in memory of all the lives lost this year in Arizona's deserts." In essence, organizers drew on the Day of the Dead as an occasion to mobilize sentiment against "United States' militarized borders."

The Day of the Dead as observed in the San Francisco Bay Area—particularly in the cities of Oakland and San Francisco—provides an excellent example of divergent developments in how this holiday is celebrated within the United States. Both Oakland and San Francisco contain large, heterogeneous Latino populations. Some Latinos are recent arrivals to the States, while others descend from migrants who came to California several generations ago or more. Most of the Latino population in Oakland has roots in Mexico, although there are numerous community members from other parts of Latin America, particularly the Central American states. In San Francisco, the reverse is true. There the Latino population descends mainly from Central America, while there is a good representation of Mexicans as well.

No doubt many Latinos in these two cities, as elsewhere in the United States, celebrate the Day of the Dead in an exclusively private fashion, or not at all. Certainly, there are migrants and long-term U.S. residents from all over Latin America who do no more than attend the special Masses required of all Roman Catholics on All Saints' and All Souls' days. Generational splits on whether or how to observe the Day of the Dead commonly occur within the same family. One young woman from Guatemala City, who moved to California as a child, states that her mother—a "born again Christian"—seriously objects to her daughter erecting a Day of the Dead altar or participating at all in Day of the Dead activities. The daughter is what we might call a Day of the Dead activist, devoting a good part of her life to promoting this holiday, and yet her mother is completely averse to Day of the Dead celebrations. Hence, people sometimes define themselves in relation to this holiday to such an extent that it even becomes a point of contention.

Some Latinos are pro-Day of the Dead, others anti-Day of the Dead; or some are pro-Day of the Dead as celebrated in one particular fashion but in no other. Despite these controversies, the Day of the Dead in the San Francisco Bay Area—unlike in New York or the U.S. Northeast, for example—has become an eminently public occasion, characterized by a variety of high-profile cultural and civic proceedings. One curator at the Mexican Museum in San Francisco states:

if you don't have a cemetery, you can't do it the way they do it in Oaxaca. So, in a sense you take the core and then apply it to how it can be practiced where you are . . . You know, you had ofrendas, but they were made in the home, to people that you knew directly and who were connected to you. And taking that and putting it in an urban situation like San Francisco, and making it a public observance. To me, that was what made it different, that was the Chicano aspect of it. You aren't just bringing your own family together around a certain gravesite, or even a whole town to its own little cemetery. It was bringing the whole Chicano community together.

This astute commentator points to a significant difference between most Mexican and Chicano celebrations. The difference revolves around the role of the cemetery. The cemetery is without doubt the focus of Day of the Dead activities in Mexico, where communities of residents, all of whom share a single faith, bury their dead in a designated part of the city. In the United States—particularly in dense urban areas like the San Francisco Bay Area, Mexicans and people of Mexican descent possess no cemetery that they can call their own. Nor, because of city ordinances, would they be able to practice Day of the Dead rites in the way that they can do in Mexico. Hence, Chicanos have adapted to local circumstances and made the celebration more of a public, and less exclusively a family, affair.

Just as the Day of the Dead has received a big boost in Mexico through the efforts of governmental and cultural institutions (see Chapter 4), this holiday has become prominent in the Bay Area due to the vigorous efforts of community activists working on their own and in unison with civic and cultural groups. Day of the Dead proceedings in both Oakland and San Francisco are directed by highly effective leaders, who are imbued with strong personal feelings about the spiritual and emotional importance of this holiday. Without these leaders, it is doubtful that formal Day of the Dead activities would exist at all. During the 1970s, the Chicano who served as director of the Galería de la Raza in San Francisco founded and vigorously promoted Day of the Dead events. Nowadays, in the first decade of the 21st century, the Galería provides barely any support to Day of the Dead activities. For this development, Chicano respondents blame the current Galería director, a native of Colombia, who reputedly dislikes the Day of the Dead and does all he can to suppress its celebration. Effective leadership is essential if organized exhibitions, processions, and other events are to be launched and perpetuated.

Day of the Dead leaders are motivated not only by the desire to find an outlet for their own beliefs. They are also driven by a kind of missionary zeal, longing to educate the untutored segment of the American public as to the meaning of the Day of the Dead and its proper celebration. The Bay Area Day of the Dead is a holiday for an ethnically diverse society—a society, unlike that in most of Mexico—in which knowledge of the Day of the Dead cannot be taken for granted and needs to be explained. An official of the Mission Cultural Arts Center in San Francisco puts the matter succinctly: the Day of the Dead "has become an American holiday, yeah, just like Cinco de Mayo. That's an American holiday, not a Mexican holiday."

In the city of Oakland, Day of the Dead activities occur most prominently at two sites: the Oakland Museum of California and the Fruitvale Festival. The Oakland Museum is located on the outskirts of the city's downtown. It is a sprawling, multi-level concrete structure of modern design, incorporating strong horizontal lines and multiple courtyards that bring the outdoors inside, wherever in the Museum you might be. The Museum specializes in California art and artists and hosts extensive historical and photographic displays, in addition to the usual fine art exhibitions. The Museum seems particularly responsive to the multicultural character of the city in which it is housed.

Anyone who walks into the Oakland Museum during October and November will notice that the Day of the Dead occupies a special place on the Museum program. The gift shop is filled with Day of the Dead literature geared towards children and adults. Parents can buy their children Day of the Dead coloring books, based on the iconography of animated skulls and skeletons (see Chapter 4). A variety of miniature sculptures and toys, many of them imported from Mexico and fashioned with flexible wooden or plastic joints, are also available for purchase. Posters at the Museum announce craft workshops, film showings, roundtable discussions, and, most important, gallery exhibitions, all centered on the Day of the Dead. Every year, on a Sunday during mid-October, the Oakland Museum sponsors a Family Day upon which throngs of visitors converge. There are colorful outdoor productions by dance troups from around the Bay Area, performing folkloristic dances and recreating their versions of ancient rituals from throughout the Mexican Republic (see Figure 8.2). Multiple food stands and craft booths cater to visitors eager to acquire culinary experiences and artistic memorabilia reminiscent of those they might find in Mexico. Face painters decorate children and adults to appear as half-skeletal, half-living beings—a representation of the Aztec belief that life and death are part of a single, uninterrupted existential cycle (see Chapter 7, Figure 7.2). Altars dedicated, not to deceased individuals but rather to entire groups of people who died as a result of political folly, are dispersed throughout the temporary outdoor exhibition space that is carved out for Family Day celebrations. In October 2005 several prominent altars honored those who had died as a result of hurricane Katrina, and others highlighted American and Iraqi war casualties.

The Oakland Museum has been promoting the Day of the Dead since 1994. From that time on, Day of the Dead activities and exhibitions have steadily grown in number and elaboration, guided by two official bodies at the Museum: the Días de los Muertos Advisory Committee and the Latino Advisory Committee. One prominent education coordinator and member of the Días de los Muertos

Fig. 8.2 Ballet Folklorico de San Francisco performs at the Oakland Museum Days of the Dead Community Celebration, October 23, 2005

Advisory Committee at the Oakland Museum explained to us the origins of the Museum's involvement with this holiday. She was interviewed on July 23, 2004, almost exactly a decade after the Museum's first Day of the Dead celebration.

> In '94 was the first Days of the Dead. It was very informal at first, and it just drew so many people, because there was such a need for it. There was a lot going on in San Francisco, but there was not a whole lot going on in the East Bay, and members of the Committee were mostly from the East Bay, and they were like, "well, we don't want to have to go all the way over there, to cross the bridge to celebrate Days of the Dead. We want to have something over here that is ours." And, it felt like the Days of the Dead was going on a different route in the City [San Francisco] . . . There were mixed opinions. In some ways, as much as possible they wanted to stay as true to tradition as possible . . . There have been some opinions that some of that was lost in the hugeness of what takes place in the Mission [Mission District of San Francisco].

This testimony provides a first glimpse of variation in Bay Area Day of the Dead celebrations. In northern California, each holiday program, at least in part, develops as a reflection upon and intentional response to the policies and practices of neighboring communities.

True to her post as education coordinator, this commentator emphasizes the importance of teaching the Bay Area public about the Day of the Dead, so that the uninitiated can learn about its multiple benefits to themselves and their families.

> One of the objectives and goals from the [Días de los Muertos Advisory] Committee was that people had the tools to then learn about the Days of the Dead, so that they could practice it at home. So it wasn't just, "Oh, look at this show, this is pretty, this is exciting, and you know . . ." Basically you had Committee members who are very invested in what this tradition is all about, and they wanted to make sure that the visitors who came here left with knowledge and tools to then practice this tradition at home . . . And I think while people are apprehensive at first with the name, Days of the Dead—it sounds like Days of the Zombies or something—but I think once they are educated and understand what the tradition is, and how it functions in our society, then I think they embrace it a lot more. That's our purpose, to educate people so they understand what the tradition is.

Although this organizer defines the educational mission as one in which tradition is transmitted, she is well aware that "we are not in Mexico, we aren't in Latin America. We're in a public institution, and something that's considered very private, in terms of the process of the home, we are now putting in a public space." The public space is municipal space, which implies that the Museum is at least morally obligated to address itself to a variety of ethnic and religious communities. According to this commentator's estimate, sixty percent of the visitors to the Day of the Dead annual exhibition are Latinos. But in many ways it is towards the non-Latino groups, unfamiliar as they often are with this holiday, that the Museum's educational programs are directed. Says this respondent, "One of out basic functions is to educate so that people can then practice it at their homes on the Day of the Dead."

My own observations of Museum events over a period of five years confirm this respondent's testimony that the visiting public is "extremely diverse."

> When we give tours to the school groups . . . , we make it a point as much as possible to say the words in Spanish, and the ones who speak Spanish perk up: "I know how to say that!" It definitely becomes a way of exchanging and, actually, last year it was really neat, too, because it [the Museum program] was called Global Elegies. It was about showing how different traditions honor the Day of the Dead. So we had a Chinese American, a Vietnamese Buddhist American, so then the kids really got to have that exchange of cultures: "We do that, too!" or "We use paper in this way!" So it became a really neat exchange for students and people in general.

The Museum organizing committees are acutely aware of and responsive to the presence of an ethnically varied community.

One of the biggest issues, however, concerns not diversity within the wider community but rather diversity among Latinos themselves. Many observers perceive the Day of the Dead as a primarily Mexican celebration. In fact, the name given to the event—*Días de los Muertos*—Days of the Dead, in the plural originates in the belief that this term reflects the history of ancient Mexico better than does *Día de los Muertos* in the singular. A Museum catalog explains, "Although the celebration is popularly referred to as *Día de los Muertos*, we decided to use the plural form *Días* in recognition of its indigenous roots, when two distinctive feasts for the dead were held over an extended period of time and as part of the annual ritual cycle" (Henry 2005:8). As related in Chapter 2, this was indeed the Aztec practice at the time of the conquest, at least according to Fray Bernardino de Sahagún's account. Latino Advisory Committee organizers, therefore, adopted a name based on the desire to emulate to some degree ancient Mexican ritual practice.

But the popular perception that the Day of the Dead is fundamentally Mexican derives from more than the name that the Oakland Museum gives to the event. It is a product in part of the fact that Mexico is our closest Latin American neighbor, as well as the most populous Spanish-speaking country in the world. As stated elsewhere throughout this volume, the Day of the Dead is a pan-Catholic holiday, which people from many Latin American countries celebrate in ways that at least overlap with Mexican practices, even if they do not duplicate those practices. One Day of the Dead curator at the Oakland Museum, who was born and grew up in Guatemala, has struggled to overcome the Mexican-centeredness of the Museum celebration.

> Living in California there is definitely a Chicano presence, and a lot of times other Latino groups are kind of like pushed to the side . . . In Guatemala they also have Dia de los Muertos. They have the kites and other stuff, Mayan altars, and so, to me, it was like really bringing that voice to the table and really . . . pushing the boundaries of our identity and how the people who were at the table were looking at Days of the Dead . . . And it's not just Mexican-centric, it's like Oaxaca-style southern Mexico, because they weren't even being inclusive of Yucatan. It was very much about the Aztecs, the Nahua, south Mexico, the traditional thing.

Non-Chicano members of the *Días de los Muertos* Advisory Committee at the Oakland Museum fought for nearly a decade against what they perceived to be an ethnocentric, southern Mexican bias in the public presentation of the Day of the Dead.

After nearly a decade, their more inclusive interpretation of the Day of the Dead prevailed. The Advisory Committee began to shift perspective in 2002, with the guest curatorship of one of the principal curators at the Mexican Museum in San Francisco. With the Day of the Dead exhibition in 2002, says one commentator, this was the first year I felt there was definitely a Salvadoreño and Guatemalteco presence. And you could see that from the beginning because we had the kites and we had the traditional ofrenda, and . . . we had [artist] Claudia Bernardi who was talking about El Salvador, and she's actually from Argentina. And we had Víctor Cartagena who was also talking about El Salvador.

At the same time that the Oakland Museum celebration responds to ethnic diversity, it provides an outlet for pan-Latino identity (see Plate 8.1). In the words of one Oakland-based Latina, "for us immigrants it becomes a way of staying connected to . . . that sense of identity. It's like, 'Look at us, this is a tradition that goes back to the Aztecs and the Mayans.' You know, not in the form that it is now, but in its origins . . . So, there is a definite connection to that [tradition], and a definite embrace to where we come from."

Because of diversity, both intra- and intercultural, the spiritual aspect of the holiday needs to be approached cautiously. One Committee member reminds us that, "We are in a public space, you know." And yet meetings of the Day of the Dead Advisory Committee routinely begin with "the burning of sage and . . . talking stick sessions," a "Native American tradition," which is meant to "call the spirits home for the holiday." An Advisory Committee member reveals her own spiritual beliefs thus: "I do believe my grandmother comes to visit during Days of the Dead, my grandparents come to visit. You know, I believe that my ancestors are with me, and they speak to me, and they guide me." She will tell Museum visitors what she believes, but at the same time that "you don't have to believe what I believe!"

The Mexican Museum took an especially important step when it began to recognize Chicano Day of the Dead traditions, as well as those emanating from throughout Latin America. One Chicano member of the Latino Advisory Committee explains.

> I've done work on reservations and I can draw from learnings there. And the Chicanos, we are kind of like the Gypsies of the southwest. We have traditions to draw from and also we are evolving it by borrowing and sharing. Some don't like to hear it said that way, but we do borrow and share . . . With the Days of the Dead Advisory Committee at the Oakland Museum, some folks are very culture purists, and it's like, hey, "this is the way it's done in Michoacán, this is how it's done in Oaxaca, and this is how it should be!" But I've gone there and I've seen the whole spectrum of how it is done in Oaxaca. And so I'm saying, let's recognize it's our responsibility, so we can see more, to be more, and to draw the best of multiple traditions and advance that which does our families the most good.

With a doctorate in public health, and as a member of an underrepresented minority, this Committee member is perhaps especially sensitive to the issue of ethnic diversity. But he seems most concerned about the emotional payoffs that come with Day of the Dead practices.

Everyone seems to agree on one emotional benefit of the holiday: assistance in grieving. A member of the Advisory Committee tells of a woman who works at the Oakland Zoo and who learned about the Day of the Dead through Museum educational programs: "Her father passed away, and at her office she created this huge *ofrenda*. So she sent us pictures and she shared with us how healing it was to have this outlet." Another member of the Committee professes a particular interest in Day of the Dead practices as vehicles for healing. Referring to his healing workshops presented at the Oakland Museum during the Day of the Dead, he states that:

> Every year about forty to sixty folks come, of which it's pretty multicultural: one third Latino, one third African Americans/Asians, and a third dominant culture folks. So . . . I begin the session by asking folks, "Why did you come? What are your expectations?" And a good fifty percent are usually there because a son died, a brother died, a husband died, a friend died, or it's just that I've been thinking about my mother, my father, my grandmother, and I want to honor them. And "I assume it's alright to learn from your experience." So . . . , yes, we are drawing from our Chicano/Indigenous tradition. However, . . . I have really kind of worked to validate that people have their own traditions, whether it's Irish or African American or whatever . . . And here it's just our way, which may serve as a vehicle to connect more with your own way, an integration.

This Committee member's work extends well beyond the specific Day of the Dead season. He is interested in demonstrating the healing power of ritual *per se*.

His approach is to integrate Native American and Latin American healing traditions, his overall goal to create connections among living people as well as between the living and the dead. He accomplishes that goal by, first, asking the public in attendance to turn to those around them and tell them who they are, where they are from, why they have decided to come to the event.

> My concern is: let's use this to connect people. Um, the process, where we are from: "we're from Berkeley, from Hayward, from Oakland, from wherever. I came from Chihuahua, I came from El Salvador. Okay, we come from different places. And why are we here? I'm here for my dad, my mom, my brother, my father. I'm here to learn, I'm here because my friend brought me. Okay, well, we're here for all these different reasons, but the commonality is that we're here to honor those who have passed. So let's kind of get into that space.

This respondent estimates that three to four thousand people attend this event.

The actual ceremony starts with the burning of sage, "because when we burn sage, we mark the beginning of sacred time." Then prayers are offered—the leader himself chants them, or he invites the public to contribute their own prayers. Everyone faces each of the four cardinal directions in turn, first to the east.

> East is the direction of beginnings, also the direction of *el hombre*. Okay, so who are those men who have passed in our lives who we want to remember? South is the direction of health and well being and children and youth. We turn to the south. Who are those children or young people who have passed and we want to remember? Who are those that are ailing with their health that we also want to remember? Turn to the west, the direction of *la mujer*, the teachings of struggle and of love. Who are the women we want to remember? The north, the direction of elders. Who are the elders we want to remember? So you begin kind of helping connect people to who is it that we want to remember.

The ceremony ends with the scattering of marigold petals—an integral element in Mexican Day of the Dead *ofrendas*—in each of the four directions, as participants speak to their departed loved ones.

This ceremony is performed throughout the week prior to November 2, with the explicit goal of educating the pubic. The ritual leader aims to get people inspired enough to replicate the ceremony in home gatherings, designed to connect people to one another and to their deceased loved ones. For other respondents, Day of the Dead celebrations create "an alternative to how death is dealt with in the United States." Through the Day of the Dead, says one Advisory Committee member, people "could kind of talk about it versus clamming up and not talking about it at all. I think it kind of becomes, for some people, a way for them to work through grief."

Advisory Committee members at the Oakland Museum also instruct the public in the design and construction of Day of the Dead home altars. Some respondents advocate keeping altars on display throughout the year, to be modified periodically in response to each family's need to remember, grieve, and connect spiritually to departed ancestors and friends. Altars, in fact, provide the basis for the annual Day of the Dead exhibition at the Oakland Museum. Over the years new principles of display have emerged. In the words of one Oakland Museum curator, "Now we have an aesthetic of Days of the Dead." Artistic goals have overtaken religious ones in the design of altars. An altar that is mounted within the Museum, says one curator, is transformed into an installation. And the installations that have been constructed at the Museum tend to have an overtly secular cast, despite the inherent spirituality of any altar. Since the mid-1990s, altars have been erected in honor of those who have died in war, child homicide victims, and those who suffer from AIDS, among others. Latin American style altars usually predominate, although altars constructed by Asian, African American, and European artists, incorporating artistic motifs from those regions, regularly appear in the annual exhibition. Those who mount altar installations are all professional artists, and inevitably yield a self-conscious innovativeness and aesthetic variety normally lacking outside the museum context.

Elaborate altars, too, are the foundation of a second major Day of the Dead event in Oakland: the Fruitvale Festival. Fruitvale is the Oakland district that contains the highest concentration of Latinos, principally Mexicans. "You don't have to speak English in the Fruitvale," states one respondent. "You come to Oakland and you're in Mexico," says another. The lavishness and sheer joyfulness of the Fruitvale's Day of the Dead belie the economic and political marginality of Latinos who reside in that part of the city. Within the Fruitvale district, 24 percent of the population was living below the poverty line in 1999. According to a Ford Foundation report (www.fordfound.org/publications/ff), the Fruitvale is home to people born in an immense variety of countries, including Bosnia, Laos, Cambodia, the Philippines, Guatemala, Honduras, Thailand, Vietnam, Mexico, China, and Pakistan, among others. However, 53 percent of the district is Latino, and Spanish is spoken in 43 percent of the homes, according to a survey carried out in 1999. In fully 40 percent of Latino homes in the Fruitvale, Spanish is not only the preferred language, but also the only language of effective communication possessed by family members over 14 years of age. Only 51 percent of adults in the Fruitvale district hold a high school diploma; only 10 percent have a college degree. Residents, who in 1999 earned an average per capita annual income of under $12,000, overwhelmingly work in construction, manufacturing, retail, and food and service industries. Despite this portrait of poverty and social marginality, both the Fruitvale district and the Latino community itself have developed into models of community spirit and organization. This spirit is reflected perhaps nowhere so prominently as during Day of the Dead festivities.

The Festival, which always takes place on the Sunday preceding All Souls' Day, began slowly in the mid-1990s. The timing was intentional—a Sunday, rather than the actual holiday date of November 2, in an attempt to increase the public presence of Mexicans, who would be more likely to take Sunday off from work, rather than some other day. Originally, the celebration was held in a civic auditorium simply as a dinner dance in honor of the Day of the Dead. The celebration was sponsored by the Unity Council, a non-profit neighborhood organization, which was part of a national movement founded in 1964 by Arabella Martinez, then Assistant Secretary of the U.S. Department of Health. The San Francisco chapter of the Unity Council was originally devoted to improving life for Latinos throughout the San Francisco Bay Area. With time it became transformed into an organization focusing on the economic development of marginal neighborhoods and targeting immigrants from all over the world, rather than Spanish-speakers alone. Again, the choice of Sunday, rather than some other day of the week, as the day of celebration was designed to increase the attendance of working people.

One Fruitvale resident, herself a Latina of Nicaraguan descent and the first event coordinator for the Fruitvale Day of the Dead Project, explains its beginnings.

> This is 1997, and we knew that the Mission [in San Francisco] had the Day of the Dead . . . But they celebrate it the day of [that is, on the precise date of the holiday]. Consequently we very quickly put together something and the fact of the matter is that we only had 500 or 1000 people at it. And we didn't have any altars . . . By the second year we said, okay, let's do this again. We think this is a good idea for an event, so we got a cultural arts grant. We definitely knew that the idea was to create some altars, so we did three or four altars, or five altars, and we tried to make altars in the windows and encourage people. So we were able to get a cultural arts grant [from the city of Oakland] and really tap into artists in the area to create an altar pavilion that has a whole bunch of altars.

The Fruitvale Festival, in short, began with the construction of Day of the Dead altars, which have in fact become the major symbol of Day of the Dead celebrations in the United States.

This development should come as no surprise. Most observers would agree that, in Mexico itself, it is the cemetery vigil—the cleaning and decoration of tombstones, the picnic-like commensality that occurs at relatives' gravesites, the presence of musical bands serenading the deceased—that is the most salient feature of the holiday. As indicated earlier, throughout the United States, where cemeteries maintain strict and early hours of operation and bow to a host of stringent rules concerning noise and eating and public gatherings, the cemetery vigil is either severely restricted in form and content, or entirely prohibited. Altars, and to some extent processions, have correspondingly risen in importance within the American context.

From the beginning, the Fruitvale Festival organizers aimed to educate non-Latino groups about the Day of the Dead. Altars were their main instructional tool. One organizer recalls an early incident.

> I remember the first year there was an African American little boy who had been hit by a car. So we actually went to the family and said we want to create this altar, and the African American family was very touched by it. We used all the little trucks and all the little symbols of this child. So, again, a way to bring in the community. And we found that the altars attract artists, and people from Myanmar and other parts of Asia. The altars sometimes are personal, which are dedicated to something like your grandmother. And some are so intrinsic and artistic, they're beautiful, as you probably know. But there are some other ones dedicated to causes, like the immigrants who perish crossing the border, victims of lung cancer . . . The one year that was really special was right after 9/11. It seemed that there were a lot of altars dedicated to that.

From the start, as well, the Fruitvale Festival organizers decided to prohibit alcohol from the celebration. One respondent states, "I think that the Day of the Dead is beautiful because it eliminates the drinking component, which is a big problem in Hispanic festivals, too much partying."

By 2004, fewer than ten years after Oakland's first tentative Day of the Dead ball, an estimated 85,000 visitors attended what had developed into a full-blown Fruitvale Festival. The Festival site centers on a long avenue—coincidentally and appropriately called International Boulevard—which for this occasion is limited to pedestrians, and lined with elaborate altars, food stands, and performers. A large group of *concheros*—a nativistic group of dancers, prominent in urban Mexico and eager to revive (their version of) Aztec culture—also participate. Storefronts and building facades along the avenue are colorfully decorated. Neighborhood residents and visitors stroll at a leisurely pace, scrutinizing the artwork, reading explanatory signs and labels, and chatting with the proprietors and artists who have erected stands and altars along the route. So many people from outside the neighborhood itself attend the event that one artist and recent immigrant from Oaxaca declares, "if we continue at this rate, we're going to wind up the same as in Michoacán!" In 2005, the official Fruitvale Festival website (www.unitycouncil.org/ddlm/) announced that:

> The Día de Los Muertos Fruitvale Festival has been inducted by Congresswoman Barbara Lee into the United States Library of Congress as a "Local Legacy" for the State of California . . . Over 90,000 people are expected to attend. There will be 130 vendor exhibitors, and expanded arts and crafts displays with over 40 altars ranging from local merchants to non-profit organizations and public agencies. Food vendors will line the streets offering up their goods and services.

As suggested in this Internet bulletin, the Fruitvale Festival early on became defined as a vehicle for economic development. The Main Street program, a non-profit organization funded by the National Trust for Historic Preservation, provided the initial financial impetus. A member of the Unity Council in Fruitvale explains:

> The Main Street program is something across the nation where they help business neighborhoods grow, and mostly in the Midwest, like in small town America, they take dying communities and then revitalize them. And what they do is help them improve their store fronts. This agency [the Unity Council] had Main Street funding, which means they helped businesses in the Fruitvale grow . . . That led to the fact that they had to have these community meetings as part of the Main Street program. So, you had to involve the community. So you invite community store owners and businesses, vendors and citizens, to help design this whole project. So the whole town was involved, the whole Fruitvale district was involved, because that was the effort, and then the artists were involved.

From modest beginnings, the Fruitvale Festival has grown to the point where there is substantial sponsorship from Latin television and radio stations, most notably Telemundo. There is support, as well, from the *Oakland Tribune*, in the form of free advertising. Then, too, there are contributions from large corporate sponsors such as Citibank, Clorox, Safeway, Alameda County Transit, even the Port of Oakland. And, to ensure security at the Festival, the city of Oakland provides a grant ($20,000 in 2004) for increased police services.

Anyone who visits the Fruitvale Festival will note that the majority of people in attendance, whether as participants or visitors, are Latinos. If only because of its pan-Hispanic origins, the celebration addresses Latino identity, and incorporates symbols from Latin America—particularly Mexico—to a disproportionate extent. States one Oakland artist from Mexico, the Fruitvale Festival

> is the best way to arrive at community, because there's an appreciation, a respect towards Mexican culture, or indigenous culture. And we should be a little better informed about this aspect [of the holiday], too. It's just that he who comes here [from Mexico], he who comes to wash dishes, to work like a pack animal, also brings his culture, right? Bringing his culture, he can also teach. The people who settle there are very humble, and they spend all their time working, but they also possess a great culture, and it's well that it should be recognized . . . Because now he's not just a wetback, who only arrives to be exploited, but he's someone who leaves something within this [U.S.] culture.

But the Fruitvale Festival speaks not only to Mexicans and other Latinos. The event also draws a substantial multicultural crowd and performs important functions for those groups as well. The ethnically diverse nature of the event is a source of obvious pride to Festival organizers. One organizer states, "When I first started it was pure Latino. Now, we have Afro-Americans coming in, we have Central Americans, we have Laotian, Hmong populations coming in, Chinese, or Afro-Americans coming in celebrating Martin Luther King, or their favorite teacher, or their mother that was a teacher." Organizers are also proud that Festival participants cut across class lines. My respondent continues, "This is an opportunity not just for me to have pride, or the Unity Council, but it's for our people. For people at all levels, from the rich merchant to the poor person in the street that just arrived from Mexico. What else is it? It's family. This is a family event." According to this respondent, the Festival "becomes a vehicle for outreach, for people that have a cause, or people that have a need, or people that have a product, or a non-profit, . . . or the Hispanic community, like Clínica de la Raza, like your Diabetes Association, your Chiapas support group, the Battered Women's Association."

Community organizers credit the Fruitvale Festival with not only building a sense of community among diverse groups, but also with raising the quality and public image of the neighborhood that they all share. States one organizer,

We are trying to revitalize the district, so whenever we talk about Fruitvale, we can say, it's where Dia de los Muertos is held. Pretty much around the country people talk about it. The National Trust for Historic Preservation wrote this one article on the Day of the Dead as a way to revitalize your neighborhood. And actually the California Main Street gave us an award one year for a promotion of our Day of the Dead festival. So, if you call the National Main Street Center and say, "Oh, what's a good ethnic event?", they're immediately going to say the Fruitvale Dia de los Muertos Festival . . .

Another organizer states that, through attending the Festival:

People discover that Fruitvale is not such a bad place. And they also discover, gosh, there are people that walk the streets in Oakland . . . That's what our whole purpose is, to turn around economic development in the neighborhood and make is a safe place, a viable place for the community, so people can walk safely in the streets . . .

Certain features of the Oakland Day of the Dead replicate the significant spiritual, economic, and artistic elements found elsewhere. What is special about the Fruitvale celebration, however, is its emphasis on community—community building, community integration, and community pride. Events at both the Oakland Museum and International Boulevard are designed to demonstrate the social, spiritual, artistic, and commercial value of Mexican culture to people of diverse national backgrounds, religious congregations, and occupational groups (see Plate 8.2). In celebration of the Day of the Dead, a rapidly changing, multicultural society establishes—albeit only momentarily—points of unity and connection, and hope for a healthy, prosperous, and secure future. One young Asian American artist, and organizer of Day of the Dead activities in San Francisco, unabashedly expresses her admiration for the Fruitvale Festival across the Bay: "What is really beautiful about the Fruitvale is that it can reach so many people. If you put up 'Day of the Dead in California' on Google, their site comes up. It's really a great way to get their community together . . . It's like a huge event for their community. And it gets tons of people from all over the Bay Area to come that are Mexican or not." In that respect, claims this artist, the Oakland celebration contrasts radically with the one in San Francisco. Indeed, from an outsider's point of view, everything about the two holiday celebrations seems different. Events in San Francisco always occur on November 2, the very Day of the Dead, which often falls during the work week, thereby limiting the attendance of poor working people or anyone who needs to arise early the next day. This aspect of the celebration, combined with the fact that it takes place from about 5:00 p.m. onward late into the night, cuts down significantly on the presence not only of laboring people but also small children, who normally retire to bed early. For these reasons, as much for the character of the celebration itself, the Day of the Dead in San Francisco is, in the words of one organizer, "sort of just local to San Francisco."

Despite this difference from Oakland, the San Francisco celebration is driven by a dedicated group of community activists, just as events proceed in Fruitvale across the Bay. The founders and leaders of the San Francisco celebration are responsible for organizing two main activities, both of which take place in the Mission District on the Day of the Dead: (1) a procession, with an associated ritual billed as pre-Columbian; and (2) the Marigold Project, which is a park installation consisting of elaborate altars. The San Francisco Day of the Dead, unlike the one in Oakland, has evoked strong contention among organizers. As a staging platform for competing ideas about ritual and ethnic identity, the San Francisco celebration exudes a strong ideological spirit, which eclipses any concern for community harmony and economic development that organizers might hold.

José Saragosa, the name I give to an immigrant who came to the United States from Mexico as a small child, helped found Day of the Dead celebrations in San Francisco in the early 1990s. Nowadays, at the turn of the 21st century, he leads the annual Day of the Dead procession and associated rituals. Saragosa claims that, because of the incorporation of special rituals, the San Francisco Day of the Dead procession is unique. Every year in the month of June he and the other members of the Colectivo de Rescate Cultural (Cultural Rescue Collective)—a group which he heads—examine the Aztec calendar and other ancient documents "to literally go back 2,500 years and count from there forward to see which aspect god or goddess is honored on November 2." One year, he indicated, the chosen deity was the sun god and principal Aztec deity, Quetzalcoatl. In 2004, the goddess Colixatuil was selected. And because Colixatuil is known as the goddess with the skirt of reeds, she is associated symbolically with rivers, water, growth, and the color green. Colixatuil, the color green, and other similarly selected symbols therefore became the theme of the procession in that year. States José Saragosa, "They [the themes] are all based on the chronology as outlined by the Aztec calendar. It's not something that someone says, 'OK, we're going to have this as a theme.' It's a theme that has been established by tradition, rather than someone coming to make it up."

Despite José Saragosa's self-assured declaration of selection criteria, the annual choice of a ceremonial theme has become a source of serious conflict among Day of the Dead activists. Saragosa defends the elevation of the goddess Colixatuil as central symbol to the 2004 celebration. In his words:

> We have always had Colixatuil, because whenever there were rampages, and when Indians would go from one culture to another to rampage a town, the images that survived were the images of Colixatuil. For some reason they respected that goddess . . . If you go into any museum, you are going to notice that it's the image

of women, of Colixatuil, that has survived all along . . . She is a cyclical woman who is destroyed every day and rises again in the evening without end . . . So, how we link all that to the present, by also dedicating this year's procession [he reads from Day of the Dead informational literature] "to the individuals who have met an untimely death, especially as a result of violent crimes and unnecessary war." Because a lot of the destruction of the matriarchal cultures came through unnecessary wars. And what are we having now? Unnecessary wars and thousands of people slaughtered. So there has to be a link in whatever ritual we do to present times.

In José Saragosa's view, the theme of the year should infuse not only the procession and night-long ritual over which he presides, but also every Day of the Dead public event throughout the city of San Francisco.

He seems disturbed that other organizers have chosen alternative paths, most notably the Marigold Project and art gallery exhibitions. States Saragosa, "They don't want to follow the theme. [The Marigold Project] becomes an art free-for-all. So, a lot of the stuff that gets done at the park has nothing to do with what I've just told you—about doing research, about finding out what the culture was, about how to tie it in with contemporary themes." Saragosa's rivals harbor their own complaints. Organizers of the Marigold Project, for example, accuse procession organizers of sexism. The main perpetrator, in their view, is Saragosa himself. He defends himself against this accusation by pointing out that accusations derive from the fact that "Aztec culture is traditionally known as sexist—and, so, if you look at Aztec culture, there are your centrists, your leftists, your right wing."

There is also the problem of the ethnicity of the participants. José Saragosa, for example, objects to the central involvement of whites in the Marigold Project. "Most of the altars in the park are done by white people," he points out. "I think they have maybe one or two Latin people involved." "It's a severe problem," he believes, because by now they should have more than half of the people at the park "doing what we're doing." "Because in the Colectivo [the procession organizers] we have maybe five or six white people. The rest are all Latino, and very young . . . What is the long term vision? . . . What are we doing to bring in the younger crowd . . . ?"

José Saragosa is displeased not only with rival organizers in San Francisco. He also objects to activities in Oakland. Consider his estimation of the Fruitvale Festival: "It's very folkloric! Extremely folkloric . . . A lot of the dancers that dance don't participate in ritual. What I mean by the dancers who lead the ritual procession in San Francisco is [that] we do an all night ritual, that lasts literally all night until the sun comes up to consecrate the symbols that lead the procession, instead of just showing up because the tourists are coming, to watch them put on their feathers and dance around with drums. Or putting on these altars that really have no connection to anyone else other than the persons who died. None to the larger society. You see some reaching out, but very, very, very little, unfortunately, really little."

The altars of which Saragosa speaks are those erected each year in Garfield Park under the auspices of the Marigold Project. The Project founder and principal organizer, an Asian American, here called Samantha, explains the origin of the name Marigold Project. According to her, the Day of the Dead "is a time when families . . . make special altars, I think, in Oaxaca. Well, the marigolds—the dead follow their scent to the altars, so you leave a trail of marigolds around the altar so the dead know where to go." Every year, organizers of the Marigold Project, relying on mailing lists provided by two San Francisco community organizations—the Mission Cultural Arts Center and the Galería de la Raza—announce a call for altar proposals. Five proposals are selected, one for each of the four cardinal points, plus one at the center. "We have done altars for social causes," explains Samantha, "such as disease of war, aging, stuff like that. In the past there were altars by elements: earth, water fire, wind, and center. People would apply through our website, or with written proposals. And we sort of go through them and pick and choose which we think are best."

In 2003, there was erected what Samantha calls a "passage altar . . . about African Heritage and Culture. They focused on the slave trade and how many people died in the process throughout the passage and the inhuman conditions and the whole process of what it's taken for African Americans to get where they are today." For Samantha, the Marigold Project "is a very community and spiritually based event. It is non-denominational and open to everyone and everyone has it in common. I mean we all know people who have died, we are all going to die in our lives, and this is bringing light to that, to celebrate that, and share it, too, even when it is painful." Clearly, Samantha is much less concerned than is José Saragosa about a Latino presence or specifically Latino themes in Day of the Dead public celebrations.

Samantha confirms the muted presence of Latinos at Garfield Park on the Day of the Dead.

> The criticism that it's gotten . . . is that it really has turned into less Mexican people and more of a white or urban celebration, which is probably true. I'm not going to dispute that's happened. I think part of it is just that the complexion of the Mission has changed. If you're putting up posters and handing out post cards, sending it out to e-mail lists, and all these people may or may not be Mexican or Spanish at all, then you are starting from the local community, it's a community event.

When the Day of the Dead falls on a weekend, there are perhaps 10,000 visitors to the Park, estimates Samantha. On weekdays the number drops dramatically. And always, it is a draw for locals, not for people outside San Francisco. For Samantha, the altar installation acts as "a galvanizing community event . . . So many people come to it, different races, different cultures, different everything. It's really the only thing holding us together, that we are human and we are dying, that we experience death or are going to experience death sometime in our lives."

It is generally late at night that observers gather in Garfield Park to view the altar installation. Visitors first watch the Day of the Dead procession, which starts around 7:00 p.m. and winds through the Mission, ending about two hours later (see Plate 8.3). The visitors then wander over to the Park. At first the atmosphere is quiet, meditative, as people slowly gravitate from one altar to another. By 10:30 or so, the Park is filled with the sound of drummers and acoustic instruments. "So part of it turns into a party," states Samantha, "just like it probably does in some parts of Mexico . . . People are covered in flowers, their faces are painted, they are in costume. And they are just dancing and enjoying each other."

Although Samantha imagines that some similarity exists between Mexico's Day of the Dead and San Francisco's, she does not strive to replicate in San Francisco events that normally unfold in Mexico. For one thing, she says, "Since we don't have any graveyards in San Francisco, we transform a park into a graveyard." For another, the San Francisco Day of the Dead "is going to take on its own identity. I don't want to take over its original identity . . . For me, I am about building community. I am a community activist and a community organizer . . . and I definitely say [to Chicano colleagues] . . . that I don't mean to dilute the celebration, because I know what it means to you, has meant to you and people from Mexico for years. But, it's changing into something else, you know. I mean, we don't say that this is a traditional Day of the Dead. It's called San Francisco's Day of the Dead."

San Francisco's Day of the Dead means connectedness says Samantha. It is a:

> way to remember that you aren't really alone in your experience of the city . . . If you sort of open yourself up, there is community to be found. You don't always have to work so hard to find community. It is there, and you just have to open yourself up to that experience. You just have to figure out the right way to get people together, talking with each other.

Suzanne Morrison, a Day of the Dead researcher, declares that "the annual Day of the Dead procession and related exhibits are concrete embodiments of intercultural dialogue and cooperation . . . [W]hat once maintained an ethnic boundary has become a means of crossing borders and providing face-to-face encounters with diversity" (Morrison 1992:533). This observation perhaps seemed more apt in the early 1990s, when Morrison was writing, than it does a decade later. For Samantha, as for many Day of the Dead organizers, the Day of the Dead in San Francisco provides the perfect arena for gathering separate communities together into one. If community building means simultaneous attendance at an event, such as the exhibition at Garfield Park, then Samantha has been successful. If it means central coordination of disparate activities and a focus on neighborhood economic development and social vigor, a good deal of work remains to be done.

More than community building, the San Francisco Day of the Dead in effect emphasizes aesthetics, an arena for artistic expression in performing and visual arts. As in Oakland, the Day of the Dead provides practitioners of fine art—be they Latino or not—an outlet for demonstrating their creativity and exhibiting their works. A curator at the San Francisco Mexican Museum dates this development in Day of the Dead exhibitions to the mid-1970s, when the Mexican Museum exhibited an *ofrenda* to Frida Kahlo.

> That's when you have this shift from the altars being more ofrenda-like, in the tradition of remembering someone who has died and doing offerings for that specific person, to . . . an ofrenda installation, an art piece. Still, it's having this same kind of intent of honoring someone, but it's more, the aesthetic becomes a lot more important.

In 1992, Suzanne Morrison, in a doctoral dissertation on San Francisco's Day of the Dead, filled two tightly packed pages with a list of Day of the Dead activities carried out in the preceding year. Many of these activities include arts and crafts exhibitions and workshops. For example, on October 5, the Galería de la Raza held what they termed a "Family Art Day for Day of the Dead." Two weeks later, the Galería held a craft demonstration by master sugar skull maker Miguel Angel Quintana, brought to San Francisco from Puebla especially for the occasion. The Student Art Gallery at San Francisco State University ran a "Día de los Muertos" show from October 22 through November 14. From October 25 through the month of November, the Mission Cultural Center exhibited art under the title, "Rooms for the Dead." This partial list gives only the faintest idea of the exhibition opportunities for those who created Day of the Dead installations, paintings, and crafts in 1991, not only in San Francisco but also throughout the Bay Area. The list would be many times longer now, at the beginning of the 21st century.

Curators at the Mexican Museum hope to educate the viewing public to a new, more flexible notion of the *ofrenda*, to stretch their conception of *ofrenda* beyond the stereotypic displays of candles, flowers, and food. With this goal in mind, in 1997 the Galería de la Raza in San Francisco asked a well-known Chicana curator to produce a Day of the Dead exhibition entitled "electronic memories," which used computers and videos to create *ofrendas*. She decided to place one traditional ofrenda on display:

so people could still see the reference point, but then see how a computer program can function as an ofrenda as well . . . And I think that's an important thing that spaces such as the Galería and even museums can do. You really think what an ofrenda is. As long as that space is there, artists can go about creating something different than what you expect an ofrenda to look like.

Other Chicano leaders from the Bay Area agree. A founder and former co-director of the Galería de la Raza echoes this curator's sentiments:

> We can't go to the graves or the cemeteries, it's a whole different urban environment. The Mission, it's a hybrid, the Day of the Dead here is a hybrid. We're not living in Mexico, so people who have these illusions that they want to see reproductions of Oaxaca in the Mission, it's not gonna happen. Even the evolution of artists doing the altars and rooms and installations have become very sophisticated. They are using computers, they are using projections. It's a very different approach to the Day of the Dead.

Chicano leaders understand that within the U.S. context, the Day of the Dead will evolve into something different from what it has been in Mexico. They understand, too, that in Mexico the celebration has not even been the way people conceive it to be—a set of uniform, formulaic and standardized practices. And, in the United States as in Mexico, it will respond to the needs and desires of the people who choose to adopt it as their own. In the words of one San Francisco organizer from the Chicano community,

> Well, wherever there are Mexicans, people have latched onto the Day of the Dead. We get calls here all the time from cities, from cultural affairs departments, from museums, saying we have a huge Mexican community here, we want to do a Day of the Dead, what can you tell us. We always say the same thing: "go talk to the community, and ask them how they want it to be, or what they want, and number two, how they want to celebrate it." Because they might be from different parts of Mexico, and they may not celebrate it in the same way, and I can't give you the whole spectrum of how it is celebrated, and to me it's more meaningful if the community itself does it, and if they are the ones driving it, and putting it together.

After all, continues this respondent, in Mexico itself there exists not only regional diversity in the celebration of the Day of the Dead, but also diversity through time, an evolution over "hundreds and hundreds of years." Elaborating, she states, "So I kind of figure they'll keep doing it, too, they'll take some of the American and Halloween stuff and just keep right on doing it, as they have been doing for thousands of years." Another Chicano leader from San Francisco also knows that the Day of the Dead has evolved in Mexico. Years ago, he says, "a lot of Mexicans were ignoring the Day of the Dead." But, as he points out, "It's becoming a big tourist attraction," so more people now pay attention to it.

As always, controversy over Day of the Dead involves how it should be presented to children in schools. "I have seen those little Day of the Dead kits," says one Chicana artist, "and I think that's too formulaic." While she clearly believes that the Day of the Dead can help create and provide sustenance to Chicanos throughout the United States, she insists that the needs of all school children must be respected. If the Day of the Dead is presented in school, she states, "I don't want it to be just like . . . you've got to celebrate the Day of the Dead or you are not spiritual or whatever . . . I don't want someone who comes from another culture like the Chinese to think, 'Oh, I'm not doing the right thing, my culture doesn't really do it the right way, the way people should be doing it'." As we have seen in the previous chapter, within the American school context there exists a never-ending tension to respond to competing, often contradictory interest groups: satisfying the needs of ethnic communities, satisfying the needs of territorial (neighborhood, municipal) communities, satisfying the needs of a multiethnic, globalizing society. The problem that Day of the Dead activists face in the United States today is yet another version of problems that school administrators confront. The story of how the Day of the Dead has become absorbed within the United States demonstrates that globalization and ethnic diversity have produced a complicated array of circumstances that have transformed both the shape and the content of this holiday. This holiday, more than any other in the San Francisco Bay Area today, offers an opportunity for ethnic groups to reaffirm their identity, for political groups to disseminate information and promote social goals, for communities of health providers to rally the public in support of disease prevention and control, and for artists to display the products of their creative energies.

The Day of the Dead in the United States, as in Mexico, also provides an outlet for spiritual sentiments and for the mourning of deceased loved ones, be they public figures or members of the family. But, unlike in Mexico, the principal site of mourning is neither the cemetery nor the home. It is rather a multiplicity of public spaces, places such as art galleries, museums, and streets, where like-minded people gather simultaneously to share their grief and revel in festival feasts and fun.

PART 5

CONCLUSION

9

MEXICAN VIEWS
OF DEATH

From what we read and hear, there exists a unique Mexican view of death. Scholars, journalists, critics, and writers from both Mexico and the United States tell us so. With few exceptions (e.g., Carmichael and Sayer 1991:10), commentators convey the impression that Mexicans develop a close relationship, not necessarily to deceased relatives, but rather to an abstract entity known as Death. It is said that Mexicans live side by side with death and are therefore able to confront death honestly and directly. They scorn death, they mock death, they are disdainful and irreverent in face of death. Whether valid or invalid, this national portrait has at least one unmistakable consequence: it furthers the cause of Mexican national identity. It delineates yet one more trait that all Mexicans share and that differentiates them from others. The portrait classifies the Mexican people into a single type. It portrays a pan-Mexican uniformity at the expense of variations by class, ethnicity, age, religious affiliation, and place of residence. Moreover, it is a timeless portrait, extracted from historical context and protected from the vicissitudes of politics, economics, and demographics. For these reasons, it reads suspiciously like a stereotype. It therefore needs to be scrutinized and, if necessary, challenged.

Octavio Paz's *The Labyrinth of Solitude*—which over the past half century has provided the most influential interpretation of Mexican national character—summarizes a range of popular opinions on how Mexicans relate to death. The following famous passage from the book (Paz 1961:57–58) is worth citing at length:

> The word death is not pronounced in New York, in Paris, in London, because it burns the lips. The Mexican, in contrast, is familiar with death, jokes about it, caresses it, sleeps with it, celebrates it; it is one of his toys and his most steadfast love. True, there is perhaps as much fear in his attitude as in that of others, but at least death is not hidden away: he looks at it face to face, with impatience, disdain, or irony . . . The Mexican's indifference toward death is fostered by his indifference toward life . . . It is natural, even desirable, to die, and the sooner the better. We

kill because life—our own or another's—is of no value. Life and death are inseparable, and when the former lacks meaning, the latter becomes equally meaningless. Mexican death is a mirror of Mexican life. And the Mexican shuts himself away and ignores both of them. Our contempt for death is not at odds with the cult we have made of it.

Paz claims, in other words, that Mexicans not only blur the familiar European distinction between life and death, but they also embrace death, as if it were some sort of welcome friend. It is not too much to say that Paz believes that Mexicans actually like the idea of dying, or at least live easily in its presence, while Europeans and Anglo-Americans do not. For Paz, Mexicans accept death stoically; Europeans, by contrast, cannot easily or bravely confront the prospect of dying. Certainly, my awkwardness at the Tzintzuntzan burial in 1967, as reported in Chapter 1, seems to confirm this point of view. Implicit in Paz's analysis is an image of the macho Mexican, a person allegedly unwilling to demonstrate fear and imbued with a hard, indifferent exterior in the face of danger. Throughout *The Labyrinth of Solitude*, it is the isolated individual, hermetically sealed against insult and injury, which emerges as the most common personality type.

For Paz, loneliness and solitude conspire to make the Mexican unfeeling, guarded, and defended, in matters of death and life. Paz composed *The Labyrinth of Solitude* as a lengthy essay. It is a thought piece rather than a carefully documented scholarly treatise. Regardless of whether he accurately represented the full range of Mexican beliefs and attitudes, the impact of his forceful prose is undeniable. Its lyrical beauty and rhetorical power helped establish his role as authoritative spokesman for his people. Given the almost instantaneous popularity of *The Labyrinth of Solitude*, Paz's views on Mexican national character soon constituted a kind of intellectual orthodoxy that flourished during the 1960s and the 1970s. Consider the words of several representative Mexican scholars writing at that time. Psychologist Rogelio Díaz Guerrero states that a man's virility can be proven "when he convincingly affirms or demonstrates that he is unafraid in the face of death" (Díaz Guerrero 1968:15). Literary critic Juan M. Lope Blanch claims that "there is in Mexico a true obsession with death" (Lope Blanch 1963:8) and that "Man, the true 'macho,' should fear nothing, not even death. Or at least overcome his natural fear, giving evidence of his boldness [*arrojo*]" (ibid.). Anthropologist Luis Alberto Vargas writes that "The Mexican of today continues to be anguished by the prospect of death, the same as all humanity, but in contrast to other peoples, he does not hide behind death, but rather lives with it, makes it the object of jokes and tries to forget it by transforming it into something familiar" (Vargas 1971:57). Folklorist Gabriel Moedano Navarro says that, "although the cult of death is a trait that appears among every people, there is nowhere in the world where it exists so rootedly and with so many profound manifestations as in Mexico" (Moedano Navarro 1960–61:32). Finally, an UNAM museum catalogue published in the mid-1970s states that for Mexicans death is "Triumphant or scorned, venerated or feared, but always and at every moment, walking inevitably alongside us" (Anonymous 1974–75:1).

Scholars working outside Mexico have reinforced these lugubrious impressions. Patricia Fernández-Kelly sees the Mexican view of death as "bitter gaiety that philosophically recognizes . . . that the definitive character of death can only be successfully confronted with gestures of indifference and scorn" (Fernández-Kelly 1974:533). Barbara Brodman devotes a entire book to what she calls "the Mexican cult of death" and believes that "A much noted psychological manifestation of this cult is the Mexican's strikingly fatalistic and stoic nature" (Brodman 1976:40). Judith Strupp Green writes that, "the Mexican Indian seems to be on . . . familiar, accepting, even humorous terms with death" (Green 1969:1). And Douglas Day makes the almost shocking statement that "In ways that frequently startle the foreigner, death seems to lack meaning to the Mexican. It comes easily, matters little" (Day 1990:67). In case after case, there emerges a familiar cultural construction: Mexicans fail to distinguish life and death and seem unperturbed by death, while Western Europeans are squeamish before the reality of death, repulsed by the idea of death, and differentiate markedly between life and death.

These longstanding ideas persist in the Mexican national press. Consider a 1995 report on the Day of the Dead published in *Excelsior* (October 28, 1995): "It cannot be denied that this festival involves the typical idiosyncratic feeling of the Mexican, which causes him to joke at death, co-exist with it, look at it straight on, an attitude opposite that of other peoples, such as Europeans, who regard death with profound respect and treat death with serenity . . ." A photograph published the same year in *El Universal* (October 31, 1995) bears a caption referring to "the ludic spirit with which the Mexican confronts death." A year later, a Mexican journalist reported that his compatriots address death by the pronoun *tu*, thereby establishing a familiar relationship with death (*Excelsior*, October 27, 1996).

At the risk of oversimplifying, we might list the recurrent themes thus:

(1)   Mexicans are obsessed with death;
(2)   Mexicans fear death;
(3)   Mexicans do not fear death;
(4)   Mexicans are stoic in the face of death;
(5)   Mexicans defy the prospect of death in order to appear manly;
(6)   Mexicans are fond of, and even crave, death;
(7)   Mexicans play with death;
(8)   Mexicans are surrounded by and live side by side with death;
(9)   Mexicans express a fatalistic acceptance of death;
(10)   Mexicans perceive life and death as indivisible.

Presented in this kind of blunt, condensed form, the Mexican view of death appears highly contradictory. It is pointless to try to resolve the contradictions, however, for authors, with few exceptions, fail systematically to defend their points of view. Rather than take the list of claims at face value, as representing the Mexican state of mind, we would do well to interpret it as a construction of national character, as a projection of views about Self and Other.

It has long been recognized (e.g., Barth 1969:9–38; Sumner 1906:1–74) that people construct collective identities through differentiating their own group from others. Not all aspects of culture enter into this differentiation. For historical and cultural reasons, particular elements become especially salient identity markers. Applying this perspective to Mexico, we might say that over time the meaning of death and the nature of mortuary rituals have become central to the construction of what it means to be Mexican. In a multicultural context, such as that which prevails on the North American continent today, national identity is shaped by commonly accepted binary oppositions. Contrasting views of death are just one among many ways in which Anglo-Americans and people of Mexican ancestry draw distinctions between the two groups. Expressing the Chicano point of view, a leading Chicana curator and community leader in San Francisco, states that "Appropriation of an indigenous past and the rediscovery of myth, legend, cultural tradition, and spiritual thought have long been components of political liberation movements throughout the world. In the United States, much of the aesthetic inherent in Chicano/Latino art is drawn from the pre-colonial past. It is an attempt to articulate an experience of cultural difference, of being 'the other,' to come to terms with a history of oppression, exploitation, and domination" (Romo 2000:33).

And yet, when we examine mortuary customs among diverse peoples, Mexicans, Mexican Americans, and the majority Anglo population seem to share like-minded attitudes towards death. Just consider colonial New England tombstones, with their prominent skull bas-reliefs (Deetz 1977:64–91). By contrast, skulls almost never appear on Mexican tombs, past or present. In the United States today, the Vietnam War Memorial, with its seamless list of fallen heroes, functions as a potent national symbol. The emotional power of the Memorial underscores the important role of death in this country. In fact, as Benedict Anderson says, throughout the Western world "No more arresting emblems of the modern culture of nationalism exist than cenotaphs and tombs of Unknown Soldiers;" "void as these tombs are of identifiable mortal remains or immortal souls," he continues, "they are nonetheless saturated with ghostly *national* imaginings" (Anderson 1983:17). Thanks to best-selling author Jessica Mitford, Americans have become aware of the enormous expense and extravagance of their funerals. The American way of death, as she calls it, belies the view that people in the United States hide from death and do everything possible to deny its existence (Mitford 1963). Finally, the hospice movement, growing in popularity throughout the United States, provides evidence of a resignation to and direct confrontation with the reality of death. This movement suggests at least as much acceptance of death as prevails in Mexico. Perhaps Mexico and the West are not so divergent after all.

After all, there are certainly few Mexicans who actually yearn to die, who face illness and death with rigid, fatalistic stoicism, and who fail to distinguish life from death. Probably most Mexicans would agree with the anthropological respondent in Oaxaca, who stated, "Death is a moment that cuts off one's life. It's a natural moment" (quoted in Norget 2005:215). At the same time, there are a good number of Europeans who yearn to die (suicides are statistically more common there than in Mexico), and who face illness and death stoically. Just consider the growing support in the United States for euthanasia. And the current popularity of New Age and Asian philosophies has no doubt given many Anglos the perception that death is a mere extension of life. In other words, even if we assume that the stereotypes of Mexican views of death are accurate, it is likely that numerous Anglo-Europeans share these views. Scholars and critics would benefit from reading the anthropological literature on mortuary beliefs and ceremonials. Mexican and Anglo-European perspectives on death positively pale when compared with the obsessive concerns about mortality found among the peoples of Indonesia (Hertz 1960), Madagascar (Bloch 1971), and other cultures remote from North America (see Huntington and Metcalf 1991).

It is clear as well that Mexicans constitute a highly complex society. In their attitudes toward death, they vary not only individually but also by class, ethnicity, and region. Just consider what Robert Laughlin says of the Tzotzil Indians in Chiapas: "Death, 'the end,' is not accepted impassively by the Tzotzil but is always a sudden surprise that shakes every man's uneasy security. Generally it is deemed premeditated murder. No matter how solicitously the lifeless body is equipped for its journey to the afterworld, the dread finality of death is a constant concern" (Laughlin 1969:191). The Tzotzil, at least by this account are hardly stoic in the face of death; they neither crave death nor feel comfortable with it. Nor do their indigenous neighbors in Chiapas, the Tzeltal. States Eugenio Maurer Avalos, "In contrast with Western Christianity, Tzeltal traditional religion does not regard death as a step to a better life, but rather as a point at which 'it's all over.' This matter-of-fact view of death as a sad reality underscores the premise that true happiness is to be found in this life, here on earth" (Avalos 1993:233).

This author underscores this point even more forcefully when discussing Tzeltal avoidance of Extreme Unction:

> The resistance of Indians and others to this custom derives from the premise that this sacrament allowed the dying person to die "with grace," or to "die well." The very idea of "dying with grace" is antithetical to Tzeltal spiritual premise that the only true life worth living is here on earth and in this life. The point of being is to "live well in harmony," not to "die well." To die is in fact the ultimate disjunction with harmony. (Avalos 1993:244)

It would be difficult to encounter an approach to death more at odds with the Mexican stereotype than this. We need not invoke economically and politically marginal Indian groups, however, to challenge the stereotype. James Lockhart, speaking of the very Nahuas during the colonial era, states that there is little evidence among them of a "concern with salvation and the afterlife" (Lockhart 1992:255). Continues Lockhart, "The entire set of funeral rites at once defined the individual's relation to his surroundings, above all his social surroundings, and by their final seal allowed his relatives and fellow citizens to adopt a different stance toward him" (ibid.).

Although cases such as these demonstrate the futility of generalizations, the stereotypical portrait of Mexican attitudes toward death is in fact both accurate and inaccurate: accurate in the sense that it describes at least some of the true feelings of at least a portion of the Mexican people, inaccurate in that the portrait is a one-sided exaggeration that fails to take into account the full range of emotions that every human being experiences when confronted by death. What is lacking in the discussions of Mexican attitudes toward death is the recognition of ambivalence or uncertainty. When Brodman refers to "The Mexican's attitude toward death, his indifference toward it as well as his fascination with it . . ." (Brodman 1976:39), she describes feelings that are virtually universal. Who, we might ask, is not sometimes indifferent towards death and at other times fascinated with it? To be sure, there are societies that have elaborated death rituals to the point where they occupy an enormous amount of time, energy, and resources. But can we be so sure that if we could quantify Mexican investment in death-related thought and behavior the result would differ from a similar survey carried out, say, in Italy, Japan, Kenya, Israel, or Peru?

True, Anglo-Europeans spend a good deal of time, energy, and money trying to prolong their life span, but, when they can afford it, so do Mexicans. Studies in medical anthropology bear abundant witness to the fact that Mexicans yearn to preserve health and prolong life. Mexicans, when they fall ill, are no more willing to throw in the gauntlet than anyone else. Experience shows that when they command the resources to combat illness and stave off death, those resources will be summoned. How, then, can writer Edna Fergusson have claimed that "Mexico is probably the only country in the world where a person may look forward with some pleasure to his own death, his own funeral, his own grave . . ." (Fergusson 1934:199)? Or Edward Tinker have written long ago with confidence that "the Mexican mind accepts death with philosophy, even nonchalance" (Tinker 1961:20)?

As for the question of whether Mexicans do or do not fear death, I know of no systematic treatment of the issue. However, logic dictates that Mexicans are as varied in their attitudes as are peoples everywhere: some fear death, others do not. Much is made in the literature of a Mexican playfulness and jocularity in the face of death. This quality indeed stands out at times, notably during the Day of the Dead. However, the symbolic meaning and psychological consequences of this ludic attitude have yet to be deciphered. It would seem to indicate a direct confrontation with death, a psychological escape from death, or some combination of the two. Surely, Mexicans are like everyone else in expressing an ambivalent response to death, a simultaneous fascination with and repugnance from it. What differs from society to society is not the existence of mixed feelings, but rather the cultural means through which these feelings are projected.

If we examine the origins of Mexican attitudes toward death, authors seem to be divided into two incompatible camps. On the one hand, there exists a prevalent belief that views of death are an inheritance from the Indian past. This perspective is inherent in Paz's *Labyrinth*, for example, with its persistent references to ancient Aztec philosophy. Frances Toor, whose *Treasury of Mexican Folkways* introduced thousands of foreign readers to Mexican popular culture, writes that, "The Mexicans, fatalists that they are, accept death uncomplainingly but also bravely. They fraternize, play, joke with death even while they weep. In their blood is the spirit of adventure of their conquerors . . . Also in them is the blood of their ancestors, who met death of their own volition for the sake of their gods" (Toor 1947:s236). More recently, another commentator (Anonymous 1974–75:1) has stated that:

> The rites of the ancient Mexicans expressed a vision of death, heroic and sacrificial, as a source of renovation, fertility, and transcendence. Later, Christian sentiment which was imposed during the colonial era made of death a permanent dance of death [*danza macabra*]: fear and craving for the final judgment. Both concepts fused in the synthesis of the Mexican; the contemporary popular display is expressed in a syncretism in which ostensible fear has been lost and death is no longer restorative of life but rather a familiar and everyday part of life.

Pre-Columbian culture patterns, reinforced by the alleged Spanish penchant for morbidity, are usually blamed for the almost inhuman stoicism attributed to Mexicans in the contemporary era.

But can personality traits be transmitted rigidly throughout millennia, despite cataclysmic upheavals in politics, economics, culture, and religion? Obviously not. The only possible explanation for such cultural tenacity is biological, the persistence of what I have termed the eternally morbid Mexican. For a nation as culturally rich and historically cataclysmic as Mexico, it is impossible to accept an interpretation of national character that ignores variation through space and time. There is, however, one proposition that lends itself to critical examination. I speak of the belief that, when death is a common occurrence, a daily reality, people become callous in the face of death, possibly even morbidly attracted to death. Where survival cannot be taken for granted, people are likely to treat death with nonchalance and familiarity. Nancy Scheper-Hughes advances this thesis in her study of the Brazilian northeast, where high infant mortality rates have apparently hardened mothers against pain and outward expressions of loss. *Death Without Weeping* (Scheper-Hughes 1992) is her title, designed to describe the typical maternal reaction upon the death of their children. Likewise, Patricia Fernández-Kelly states that, "Death is a permanent concern, a daily presence, especially in a country such as Mexico in which problems ranging from the difficulty of providing medical services to the persistence of ignorance and oppression accentuate its meaning" (Fernández-Kelly 1974:531). Hence the "indifference and scorn" (ibid.:531) which she attributes to Mexicans who are faced with death. Here at last is a testable scenario: that is, the constant confrontation with death inures people against feelings of sadness and loss.

As a corollary to this thesis, we might hypothesize that when death becomes less prevalent, the cultural and emotional involvement with death declines as well. Certainly, Mexican statistics, at least throughout the 20th century, show a precipitous drop in mortality rates (Narro *et al.* 1984:636–646). Crude death rates were understandably highest during the Mexican Revolution (1910–20), a decade of widespread bloodshed, when they varied between 46.6 and 48.3 per thousand per year. Aside from this anomaly, death rates have declined steadily from 34.4 thousand per year in the period 1895–99 to 12.5 in 1955–59 (Mitchell 1993:81). By 1975–80, the mortality rate had gone as low as 7.3; in 1985–90, it was down to 5.9, and between 1990 and 1995 it declined to 5.5 (United Nations Economic Commission for Latin America and the Caribbean 1993). The decline of infant mortality rates has been equally dramatic (Narro *et al.* 1984:636–646). Again, excepting the revolutionary years, which experienced somewhat greater infant mortality than had existed previously, the average rates declined steadily from 226 in the late 1890s to 78 in 1955–59. By the early 1970s, this figure had been reduced to 68.4 and in the late 1980s dropped dramatically to 41.3. Infant mortality rates for Mexico in 1990–95 were at an all-time low of 35.2 (United Nations Economic Commission for Latin America and the Caribbean 1993:14).

Another significant indication of mortality trends in Mexico is life expectancy at birth, which is itself a function of crude death rates and infant mortality rates. Here, again, Mexicans have experienced marked improvement over the course of the 20th century (Narro *et al.* 1984:636–646). In 1930, overall life expectancy at birth was 36.8. By 1950, it had increased to nearly 50. And by 1990–95, it had risen to 70.3, nearly double the figure six decades before (United Nations Economic Commission for Latin America and the Caribbean 1993:14). Hence, the relevant indices—aggregate mortality rates, infant mortality rates, and life expectancy at birth—all demonstrate that death has touched Mexicans to a lesser and lesser degree over the course of the past half century or more. The precipitous drop in mortality rates and corresponding increase in life expectancy over the course of the 20th century should have had some effect on Mexican attitudes toward death. And yet, judging from the literature, attitudes have remained immutable, not only during the 20th century but also over the course of centuries, even millennia.

Of course, they have not remained immutable nor are they at all times and places the same. Even within the same community, people approach death in contextually specific ways. Let us return for a moment to the burial of the Tzintzuntzeño, who was struck by lightning in June 1967, as reported in Chapter 1. The wake was solemn and subdued. As I entered the home of the deceased, an occupant asked that I respectfully take off my hat. Each visitor carried a candle for the deceased. By the time I arrived, dozens of candles illuminated the casket and cadaver. The single-roomed house was crowded with mourners. Because that part of town lacked electricity, pools of candlelight fell on the crestfallen faces of the relatives, neighbors, and *compadres* in attendance. A villager led the mourners in reciting responsive prayers. Although there was no wailing, women wept silently and the atmosphere was heavy with sadness. Well into the night, the victim's family served *atole*, which warmed us against the cold damp air and seemed to raise collective spirits temporarily. The next morning, four men carried the casket about one kilometer's distance to the cemetery. Immediately after I took a few miserable photographs, the casket was lowered into the grave. Everyone appeared tormented by the cruel fate of a healthy man in the prime of life suddenly being snatched from their midst.

The same cemetery during the Day of the Dead could not present a greater contrast. As reported in Chapter 4, Tzintzuntzan, which the state government selected for touristic promotion in the 1970s, has since celebrated the Day of the Dead with an exuberance that would have been unrecognizable only a generation before. Floodlights illuminate large parts of the cemetery for the benefit of television cameras. The highway that runs through town suffers among the worst traffic jams that I have ever experienced. Middle-class visitors from Guadalajara, Mexico City, and Morelia stomp through the graveyard while munching on snacks, snapping pictures, and listening to portable radios. At considerable expense, they attend staged performances of the classic Spanish drama, "Don Juan Tenorio". For a large fee, they can also view a presentation of *pirekuas*, allegedly traditional Tarascan dances, performed on an esplanade in front of five *yácatas*, the famous circular bases of Tarascan temples. Citizens of Tzintzuntzan who maintain vigil over the tombs of their ancestors seem utterly unshaken by an atmosphere that many outsiders would consider inappropriately chaotic, noisy, even joyful.

Despite a long, rich ethnographic tradition in Mexico, there exist very few detailed accounts of wakes and funerals. Those that do exist, however, paint a very different picture than that portrayed by national stereotypes. Consider Ralph Beals' description from the 1940s of the Tarascan village of Cherán. Following a funeral, he says, "the parents of the surviving spouse may remain very sad. If it appears they may be made ill of 'sadness,' the relatives visit the survivors frequently, talking to them of things which they think will alleviate their condition and giving consolation. If this does not improve matters, they seek a curer who gives medicines" (Beals 1946:208–209). When a Tzotzil of Chiapas dies, says George Collier, "the first order of business is the funeral" (Collier 1975:90). "Family members," he says, are "grief stricken" (ibid.). William Madsen (Madsen 1960:209–210) describes a typical wake for adults in Milpa Alta, just south of Mexico City:

> Male visitors sit on board benches put up against the walls; the women sit on the floor on straw mats . . . When thirty or forty guests have arrived, the prayermaker kneels at the head of the coffin and the dead man's widow sits at the foot of it. The prayermaker leads a rosary chant and the people say responses . . . Weeping in grief, the dead man's wife and children clap their hands loudly. As the clapping dies down, the prayermaker sings a final farewell to the dead man. Guests rush up to embrace the family and beseech them not to weep so much.

Miguel Covarrubias observed the death of one of his friends in Juchitán. As she died, she sighed deeply, which "was regarded as a sign that the soul had left her body" (Covarrubias 1954:391). States Covarrubias:

> A violent reaction shook the members of the household, strangely calm and collected before, particularly the women, her daughters and sisters, who gave vent to wild outbursts of despair and screams of "jewel of my heart!", "my little mother!" . . . Soon the neighbors and distant relatives came to the house to embrace and sympathize with the mourners, as well as to deposit their alms (ibid.).

At the burial, says Covarrubias, "it is the custom for the nearest women relatives of the deceased to give a final and most violent display of despair" (ibid.:393). On the particular occasion which Covarrubias witnessed, "one of the old lady's daughters had to be restrained from throwing herself into the open grave (ibid.).

Anthropologist Kristin Norget records the testimony of a man from Oaxaca, who on the Day of the Dead in November 1990 explained why funerals, as opposed to the Day of the Dead, are so replete with grief. In the words of this repondent, "Funerals are sad because you know that you're not going to see the *difunto*, and so you feel his absence. You feel the sadness because, physically, he isn't there. He's in the coffin; he is still, now, unmoving. But you still see him. When you go to the cemetery you know that when you put him in the ground, you aren't going to see him anymore" (quoted in Norget 2005:196). It is not only the immediacy of death—the fact that it has just occurred—but also the palpable, concrete presence of the inert cadaver that no doubt produces a predictably somber tone at Mexican funerals.

Even this brief review is sufficient to demonstrate that all over the Mexican Republic—whether in Michoacán, the Isthmus of Tehuantepec, or the State of

Mexico—mourners react to the death of loved ones in a manner that defies national stereotypes. In none of these descriptions can we detect evidence of stoicism, humor, playfulness, and disdain in the face of death. It is true that alcoholic drink is an integral part of many wakes and that live music often accompanies funeral processions and burials. True, too, there exists a certain lightheartedness at funerals honoring small children—*angelitos*—said to go directly to heaven without having to pass through Purgatory. And yet, as I have stated previously, the lightheartedness seems to me only relative, as compared with the mood at funerals for adults.

In the 1930s, Elsie Clews Parsons described the funeral of an *angelito* in the Zapotec village of Mitla. The night of the death, the wake was accompanied by lively music and dancing. States Parsons, "The theory is that unless people are gay the 'little angel' will not go directly to God" (Parsons 1970[1936]:148). And yet, she continues:

> the next afternoon I find the wake mournful enough. It is much like that of an adult except that more children are present, there are fewer candles, and the corpse lies on a table alongside the altar . . . All the children present and a few women crowd around the infant, crying . . . A few fireworks are set off behind, and a gay march is played, which to one at least makes the little procession all the sadder. (Parsons 1970:149)

Throughout Mexico, the mood is similar to that experienced by Parsons. Joviality and gaiety at a child's funeral exist more in people's minds, in their descriptions of events, than in their actual behavior. Those ethnographers who bother to register how mourners react emotionally to a death—be it of a child or an adult— all convey the profound, overt grief experienced by survivors. Moreover, this grief is not limited to particular ethnic groups. Tarascans, Zapotecs, Nahuas, Indians and meztizos alike, share this fundamental human response.

Observers who insist that Mexicans hold a unique relationship to death conveniently overlook the emotional texture of funerals. And yet their viewpoint is not entirely without foundation. Mexicans, in fact, sometimes do seem to disdain death, play with death, and confront it directly while still holding it at a distance. It is just that these attitudes do not predominate. Rather, they are largely confined to a particular time of year: the Day of the Dead.

The Day of the Dead, without doubt Mexico's most famous holiday, is also its most commercial holiday. And, in my opinion, it is the enormous popularity and commercial promotion of the Day of the Dead that are largely responsible for creating the essentialist image of a macabre Mexican. Consider once more some of the main features of this annual celebration, as portrayed in this book. As analyzed in Chapter 4, Day of the Dead preparations in October lure large numbers of foreign visitors to Mexico to witness what to them are colorful, exotic, and entertaining ritual performances and artistic displays. Decorated breads, paper cutouts, and plastic toys, most of them humorous variations on the death theme, are evident everywhere. Whimsically sculpted toys and candies made of sugar, amaranth seed dough (*alfeñique*), and papiêr-maché are prominently displayed for sale at parks, plazas, and stores all over the Republic. Toys and figurines, both edible and not—most taking the form of animated skulls and skeletons—are ubiquitous during the Day of the Dead. They adorn every imaginable public space, from tombstones and supermarkets to open-air markets and storefront windows. The *calavera* tradition in the plastic arts, as we have seen, has enjoyed a long history, combining pre-Columbian and colonial European representations of death. But, except for the year-round sale of toy skulls and skeleton figurines to tourists, it is principally during the Day of the Dead that this artistic tradition flourishes. No Mexican adorns a grave with candy skulls or presents a *calavera* to a friend when a family member dies and is buried. It is not only in the plastic arts, however, that the Day of the Dead demonstrates a ludic quality. As detailed in Chapter 5, short poetic epitaphs known as *calaveras* mock the shortcomings of their victims. During this time of year, too, newspapers and broadsides fill their pages with rhymed ridicule. These satirical poems victimize public figures—politicians, athletes, literati, and movie and television personalities, among others. They represent a distillation of public opinion—that they have been and continue to be the collective, anonymous voice of the Mexican people.

For reasons both historical and cultural, the Day of the Dead—which, after all, is the Mexican version of the pan-Roman Catholic celebration of All Saints' and All Souls' days—has become much more salient in Mexico than anywhere else. It has developed traits that have become intimately associated with Mexico, particularly *calaveras* in their literary and plastic forms as well as the pervasiveness of humor, music, and a ludic spirit. The Day of the Dead, in fact, has become an international symbol of Mexico, promoted by intellectuals, journalists, government officials and even influential Mexicans. Town governments award prizes for the best altar and gravestone decoration. In these contests the presence of so-called "foreign elements," such as jack o'lanterns and witches riding on broomsticks, immediately disqualify the contestants (Plate 9.1). Anthropologist Juan Luis Ramírez Torres, an astute observer of what this holiday has come to mean, puts the matter thus:

> It is commonly asserted that the Mexican laughs at death, a strange adage designed for touristic appeal, but which does not correspond exactly to cultural expressions found among the Mexican people . . . Among the contemporary ways of rendering tribute to those who have preceded us in life . . . the most "authentic and pure" customs . . . are sought; for this reason, in schools and government offices there is installed an *ofrenda* striving to be the "most faithful possible" to that pursued

purity. Those in charge of erecting [the *ofrenda*] search in libraries, interview specialists on the matter, investigate, that is, look for identities, primordial origins —the earliest genes—and, once this collection of material is gathered, they set up floral arrangements, pile platters with food, pour *pulque*, burn *copal*, evoke ancestry. (Ramírez Torres 1994:43)

In the 1990s, the Archbishop of Coahuila fueled this campaign by prohibiting the celebration of Halloween, which he interprets as an entirely pagan, commercial holiday. All of these efforts, of course, attract tourists to the Day of the Dead. They present urban, middle-class Mexicans with a vision of their supposed past, they offer artisans unparalleled opportunities for profit, and they allow foreigners a low-cost window into exotic customs and beliefs.

Although the popularization of the Day of the Dead has increased in velocity and intensity since 1994, when NAFTA came into effect, the holiday began to expand much earlier. Malcolm Lowry's novel, *Under the Volcano*, first published in 1947, and later released as a film, takes place against the backdrop of the Day of the Dead. The enormous popularity of this book, which has gone through multiple editions in many languages, as well as the enormous success of the movie version, probably did as much as Octavio Paz's *The Labyrinth of Solitude* to make this holiday famous. When the world thinks of the Mexican view of death, it thinks of the Day of the Dead. What is more, many Mexicans themselves believe that they are unique in their attitude toward death. In fact, neither the direct confrontation with mortality that I witnessed at the funeral graveside in 1967 nor the humor and banter that characterize the Day of the Dead are restricted to Mexico. In fact, humor is a common component of death rituals cross-culturally (Apte 1985; Metcalf and Huntington 1992). Irish wakes are perhaps the most famous example of this phenomenon (see, e.g., Ó'Súilleabháin 1967) and the graveside behavior of poor people in many countries, including Mexico, reflects the extreme fragility of life that for them is a given part of their existence.

The image of the morbid, death-obsessed Mexican, as promoted through the Day of the Dead, has become integral to Mexican national identity. It represents the essence of being Mexican, particularly in the increasingly complex dialogue between Mexico and the Anglo United States. Alleged Mexican attitudes towards death are cultural capital. They are among the most effective ways to create and maintain ethnic and national boundaries in an era of globalization, when boundaries are being broken as never before. They help to define Self and Other—and, as has long been true, to sell a good many candles, flowers, candy figurines, newspapers, and miniature *calaveras* as well. This contemporary attitude is no doubt also an inheritance of the long historical process—chronicled by Claudio Lomnitz (2005) with such fine-grained precision—through which Mexican power-holders have co-opted and promoted death-related matters as a means of constituting the nation and increasing their own governmental control.

A good number of celebrants in the United States also draw upon the Day of the Dead as cultural and political capital. The holiday, to these civic leaders, make this holiday part of a larger project of creating community or reinforcing ethnic identity, be it specifically Mexican or pan-Latino identity. North of the border, the Day of the Dead for many citizens has come to symbolize a healthy, normal—rather than exotic and unusual—approach toward death. The Day of the Dead, to these followers, represents the kind of acceptance of death that they perceive to be lacking in Anglo society and culture. They perceive the Day of the Dead as good therapy: the holiday provides an outlet for grief, an emotion better expressed openly through ritual than suppressed and hidden. Others in the United States, however, interpret the holiday in purely religious terms as a Roman Catholic ritual which, following the principle of separation of church and state, deserves no public funding. From its inception during the early colonial era in 16th-century Mexico to the present day, the Day of the Dead has undergone constant modification, at the mercy of political and religious agendas as much as economic and social circumstances. Globalization is only the most recent in a long line of changing conditions affecting the shape, content, and interpretation of this key Mexican ritual. The Day of the Dead is and always has been what celebrants and observers want it to be. As a holy occasion, it presumably benefits from its status as an eternal verity. But, like most eternal verities, it has been and will continue to be subject to an endless process of controversy and change.

REFERENCES

Aguirre Soronda, Antxon
  1989 El fuego en el rito funerario vasco. *In* La religiosidad popular, vol. 2 of Vida y muerte: la imaginación religiosa. Carlos Alvarez Santaló, María Jesús Buxó, and Salvador Rodríguez Becerra, eds. Pp. 344–584. Barcelona: Anthropos.

Ainsworth, Catherine Harris
  1973 Hallowe'en. New York Folklore Quarterly 29:163–193.

Ajofrín, Francisco de
  1958 Diario del viaje que por orden de la sagrada congregación de propaganda fide hizo a la América septentrional en el siglo XVIII. Vicente Castañeda y Alcover, ed. Madrid: Real Academia de la Historia.

Amades, Joan
  1956 Costumari Català: el curs de l'any, Vol. V. Barcelona: Salvat.

American Art Association
  1922 The Notable Collection of Miss Susan Minns of Boston, Mass . . . Illustrative of "The Dance of Death." New York: American Art Association.

Ancona, George
  1993 Pablo Remembers: The Fiesta of the Day of the Dead. New York: Lothrop, Lee and Shepard.

Anderson, Benedict
  1983 Imagined Communities: Reflections on the Origin and Spread of Nationalism. London: Verso.

Anonymous
  1756 Relación de lo acaecido en la ciudad de Granada el día Primero de Noviembre de 1755. . . . México, DF: Biblioteca Mexicana.
  1963–64 Masterworks of Mexican Art: From Pre-Columbian Times to Present. Los Angeles: Los Angeles County Museum of Art.
  1974–75 "Introducción". La Muerte: expresiones mexicanas de un enigma, 1. México, DF: Museo Universitario, Universidad Nacional Autónoma de México.
  1994 Justices Reject Wiccans' Appeal of "Halloween" Case. Legal Intelligencer, December 6, p. 3.
  1995 Some Schools Change Focus of Halloween Parties. Daily Record (Baltimore), October 25.

Appadurai, Arjun
  2002 Disjuncture and Difference in the Global Cultural Economy. *In* The Anthro-
        pology of Globalization: A Reader. Jonathan Xavier Inda and Renato Rosaldo,
        eds. Pp. 47–64. Minneapolis: University of Minnesota Press.
Apte, Mahadev L.
  1985 Humor and Laughter: An Anthropological Approach. Ithaca: Cornell University
        Press.
Arellano, Ignacio, and Victoriano Roncero, eds.
  2002 Poesía satírica y burlesca de los siglos de oro. Madrid: Espasa Calpe, Colección
        Austral.
Ariès, Philippe
  1974 Western Attitudes Towards Death: From the Middle Ages to the Present.
        Baltimore: Johns Hopkins University Press.
Armstrong, Anne Elizabeth
  1992 The Boon of Merrimient: Halloween Programs in the Los Angeles City Depart-
        ment of Recreation and Parks. Unpublished doctoral dissertation, University of
        California, Los Angeles.
Arora, Shirley
  1980 "To the Grave with the Dead . . .": Ambivalence in a Spanish Proverb. Fabula
        21(3–4):223–246.
Associated Press
  2000a Witches Seek to Halt Churches Baptist-Flavored Halloween Production.
          October 17.
  2000b Wiccans, Dunbar settle Lawsuit over Church's Halloween Production.
          October 26.
Avalos, Eugenio Maurer
  1993 The Tzeltal Maya-Christian Synthesis. *In* South and Meso-American Native
        Spirituality: From the Cult of the Feathered Serpent to the Theology of
        Liberation. Gary Gossen and Miguel León-Portilla, eds. Pp. 228–250. New
        York: Crossword.
Bakewell, Liza
  1995 Bellas Artes and Artes Populares: The Implications of Difference in the Mexico
        City Art World. *In* Looking High and Looking Low: Art and Cultural Identity.
        Brenda Jo Bright and Liza Bakewell, eds. Pp. 19–54. Tucson: University of
        Arizona Press.
Barrett, Ward J.
  1976 Morelos and its Sugar Industry in the Late Eighteenth Century. *In* Provinces of
        Early Mexico: Variants of Spanish American Regional Evolution. Ida Altman
        and James Lockhart, eds. Pp. 63–95. Los Angeles: UCLA Latin American Center
        Publications.
  1977 La hacienda azucarera de los Marqueses del Valle. México, DF: Siglo XXI.
Barrett, Ward J., and Stuart B. Schwartz
  1975 Comparación entre dos economías azucareras coloniales: Morelos, México y
        Bahia, Brasil. *In* Haciendas, latifundios y plantaciones en América Latina. Enrique
        Florescano, ed. Pp. 532–572. México, DF: Siglo XXI.

Barth, Fredrik, ed.
  1969   Ethnic Groups and Boundaries. Boston: Little, Brown.
Bartra, Roger
  1987   La jaula de la melancolía: Identidad y metamorfosis del mexicano. México, DF: Grijalbo.
Basso, Keith
  1979   Portraits of "The Whiteman": Linguistic Play and Cultural Symbols Among the Western Apache. Cambridge: Cambridge University Press.
Bastien, Joseph
  1978   Mountain of the Condor. St. Paul, MN: West.
Beals, Ralph
  1946   Cherán: A Sierra Tarascan Village. Washington, DC: Smithsonian Institution Institute of Social Anthropology.
Beezley, William H.
  1987   Judas at the Jockey Club and Other Episodes of Porfirian Mexico. Lincoln: University of Nebraska Press.
Beezley, William H., Cheryl Martin and William E. French, eds.
  1994   Rituals of Rule, Rituals of Resistance: Public Celebrations and Popular Culture in Mexico. Wilmington, DE: SR Books.
Behar, Ruth
  1986   Santa María del Monte: The Presence of the Past in a Spanish Village. Princeton: Princeton University Press.
Beidler, Lloyd M.
  1975   The Biological and Cultural Role of Sweeteners. *In* Sweeteners: Issues and Uncertainties. Robert R. White, ed. Pp. 11–18. Washington, DC: National Academy of Sciences.
Ben-Amos, Dan
  1984   The Seven Strands of Tradition: Varieties in its Meaning in American Folklore Studies. Journal of Folklore Research 21:97–132.
Benavente, Fray Toribio de [Motolonía]
  1951   History of the Indies of New Spain. Frances Borgia Steck, trans. Washington, DC: American Academy of Franciscan History.
Berrin, Kathleen, ed.
  1988   Feathered Serpents and Flowering Trees: Reconstructing the Murals of Teotihucan. San Francisco: Fine Arts Museums of San Francisco.
Bialostocki, Jan
  1986   The Image of Death and Funerary Art in European Tradition. *In* Arte funerario, Vol. I. Louise Noelle, ed. Pp. 11–32. México, DF: Universidad Nacional Autónoma de México.
Bloch, Maurice
  1971   Placing the Dead: Tombs, Ancestral Villages, and Kinship Organization in Madagascar. New York: Seminar Press.
Bouissac, Paul
  1976   Circus and Culture: A Semiotic Approach. Bloomington, IN: University of Indiana Press.

Brandes, Stanley

1975   Migration, Kinship, and Community: Tradition and Transition in a Spanish Village. New York: Academic Press.

1977   Peaceful Protest: Spanish Political Humor in a Time of Crisis. Western Folklore 36(4):331–346.

1979   Dance as Metaphor: a Case From Tzintzuntan. Journal of Latin American Lore 5(1):25–43.

1980   Metaphors of Masculinity: Sex and Status in Andalusian Folklore. Philadelphia: University of Pennsylvania Press.

1981   Cargos versus cost-sharing in Mesoamerican fiestas, with special reference to Tzintzuntan. Journal of Anthropological Research 37(3):209–225.

1983a   The posadas in Tzintzuntzan: structure and sentiment in a Mexican Christmas festival. Journal of American Folklore 96(381):259–280.

1983b   Humor, agresivitat i salut mental a la Peninsula Iberica [Humor, aggression and mental health in the Iberian Peninsula]. Quaderns de l'Obra Social 16:9–13.

1988   Power and Persuasion: Fiestas and Social Control in Rural Mexico. Philadelphia: University of Pennsylvania Press.

1997   Sugar, Colonialism, and Death: On the Origins of Mexico's Day of the Dead. Comparative Studies in Society and History 39(2):266–295.

1998a   Iconography in Mexico's Day of the Dead: Origins and Meaning. Ethnohistory 45(2):181–218.

1998b   The Day of the Dead, Halloween, and the Quest for Mexican National Identity. Journal of American Folklore 111(422):359–380.

2002   Staying Sober in Mexico City. Austin: University of Texas Press.

2003   Is There a Mexican View of Death? Ethos 31(1):127–144.

Bricker, Victoria R.

1973   Ritual Humor in Highland Chiapas. Austin: University of Texas Press.

Brodman, Barbara

1976   The Mexican Cult of Death in Myth and Literature. Gainesville: University Presses of Florida.

Buechler, Hans

1980   The Masked Media: Fiestas and Social Interaction in the Bolivian Highlands. The Hague: Mouton.

Burga, Manuel

1976   De la encomienda a la hacienda capitalista: el valle de Jequetepeque del siglo XVI al XX. Lima: Instituto de Estudios Peruanos.

Burgoa, Fray Francisco de

1674   Geográfica Descripción de la parte septentrionla América, y Nueva Iglesia de la Indias Occidentales. México: Juan Ruyz.

Burkhart, Louise M.

1989   The Slippery Earth: Nahua-Christian Moral Dialogue in Sixteenth-Century Mexico. Tuscon: University of Arizona Press.

Cadaval, Olivia

1985   "The Taking of Renwick": The Celebration of the Day of the Dead and the Latino Community in Washington, D.C. Journal of Folklore Research 22(2–3): 179–193.

Cantor, Sidney M., and C. Cantor
1977   Socioeconomic Factors in Fat and Sugar Consumption. *In* The Chemical Senses and Nutrition. O. Kare and O. Maller, eds. Pp. 429–446. London: Academic Press.

Carmichael, Elizabeth, and Chloë Sayer
1991   The Skeleton at the Feast: The Day of the Dead in Mexico. Austin: University of Texas Press.

Carrasco, David
1992   Toward the splendid city: knowing the worlds of Moctezuma. *In* Moctezuma's Mexico: Visions of the Aztec World. Pp. 99–148. Niwot, CO: University Press of Colorado.

Carrillo Hocker
2003   Días de los Muertos Curriculum Packet. Unpublished booklet. Oakland: Oakland Museum of California.

Casas, Fray Bartolomé de la
1992[1552]   The Devastation of the Indies: A Brief Account. Herma Briffault, trans. Baltimore: Johns Hopkins University Press.

Casas Gaspar, Enrique
1947   *Costumbres españolas de nacimiento, noviazgo, casamiento y muerte.* Madrid: Escelicer.

Chaney, Edward F.
1945   La Danse Macabre des Charniers des Saints Innocents a Paris. Manchester: Manchester University Press.

Childs, Robert V., and Patricia B. Altman
1982   Vive tu Recuerdo: Living Traditions in the Mexican Days of the Dead. Los Angeles: Museum of Cultural History, University of California at Los Angeles.

Clark, James M.
1950   The Dance of Death in the Middle Ages and the Renaissance. Glasgow: Jackson, Son & Co.

Coe, Michael D.
1975   Death and the ancient Maya. *In* Death and the Afterlife in Pre-Columbian America. Elizabeth P. Benson, ed. Pp. 87–104. Washington, DC: Dunbarton Oaks Research Library and Collections.
1988   Ideology of the Maya tomb. *In* Maya Iconography. Elizabeth P. Benson and Gillett G. Griffin, eds. Pp. 222–235. Princeton: Princeton University Press.

Collier, George
1975   Fields of the Tzotzil: The Ecological Basis of Tradition in Highland Chiapas. Austin: University of Texas Press.

Contreras, Eduardo
1990   Una ofrenda en los restos del Templo Mayor de Tenochtitlán. *In* Trabajos arqueológicos en el centro de la Ciudad de México. Eduardo Matos Moctezuma, ed. Pp. 403–414. México, DF: Instituto Nacional de Antropología e Historia.

Cook, Sherbourne F., and Woodrow Borah
1971   Essays in Population History: Mexico and the Caribbean. Vol. 1. Berkeley: University of California Press.
1979   Essays in Population History: Mexico and California. Vol. 3. Berkeley: University of California Press.

Cornides, A.
  1967   All Souls Day. *In* New Catholic Encyclopedia. New York: McGraw-Hill.
Corona Núñez, José, ed.
  1977[1541]   Relación de las ceremonias y ritos y población y gobierno de los indios de
       la provincia de Michoacán. José Tudela, transcription. México, DF: Balsal.
Covarrubias, Miguel
  1954   Mexico South: The Isthmus of Tehuantepec. New York: Knopf.
Crowley, Brian E.
  1989   Public Schools Can't Celebrate Halloween? Los Angeles Daily Journal, October
       9, p. 6.
Curet, Francesc
  1953   Visions barcelonines, 1760–1860. Vol. III (Els Barcelonins i la Mort). Barcelona:
       Dalmau i Jover.
Curiel Méndez, Gustavo
  1987   Aproximación a la iconografía de un programa escatológico franciscano del
       siglo XVI. *In* Arte funerario, Vol. 1. Louise Noelle, ed. Pp. 151–160. México, DF:
       Universidad Nacional Autónoma de México.
Davidman, Rachel, ed.
  1993   Días de los Muertos: Curriculum Packet. Unpublished MS. Oakland, California:
       Oakland Museum of California.
Davies, Nigel
  1977   The Toltecs Until the Fall of Tula. Norman: University of Oklahoma Press.
Davis, Natalie Zemon
  1975   Society and Culture in Early Modern France. Stanford: Stanford University Press.
Day, Douglas
  1990   A Day with the Dead. Natural History, p. 67.
Deetz, James
  1977   In Small Things Forgotten: The Archaeology of Early American Life. New
       York: Anchor Books/Doubleday.
Díaz Guerrero, Rogelio
  1968   Estudios de psicología del mexicano. México, DF: F. Trillas.
Díaz Viana, Luis
  1981   El paso de fuego en San Pedro Manrique (el rito y su interpretación). Revista de
       Folklore 12:3–9.
Diehl, Richard A.
  1983   Tula: The Toltec Capital of Ancient Mexico. London: Thames and Hudson.
Dundes, Alan
  1971   "A Study of Ethnic Slurs: The Jew and the Polack in the United States." Journal
       of American Folklore 84:186–203.
Dunn, Richard
  1972   Sugar and Slaves: The Rise of the Planter Class in the English West Indies,
       1624–1713. Chapel Hill: University of North Carolina Press.
Durán, Diego
  1964   Aztecs: the History of the Indies of New Spain. Doris Hayden and Fernando
       Horcasitas, trans. New York: Orion.

Epton, Nina

    1968   Spanish Fiestas: Including Romerías, Excluding Bullfights. London: Cassell.

Espinosa, Aurelio M.

    1918   All-Souls Day at Zuñi, Acoma, and Laguna. Journal of American Folklore 31(122):550–552.

Fagg, John Edwin

    1965   Cuba, Haiti, and the Dominican Republic. Englewood Cliffs, NJ: Prentice-Hall.

Fergusson, Edna

    1934   Fiesta in Mexico. New York: Knopf.

Fernández-Kelly, Patricia

    1974   Death in Mexican Folk Culture. American Quarterly 25(5):516–535.

Fine, Gary A.

    1976   "Obscene Joking Across Cultures." Journal of Communication 26:134–140.

Florescano, Enrique, ed.

    1975   Haciendas, latifundios y plantaciones en América Latina. México, DF: Siglo XXI.

Foster, George M., assisted by Gabriel Ospina

    1948   Empire's Children: The People of Tzintzuntzan. Smithsonian Institution Institute of Social Anthropology Publication Number 6. Mexico, DF: Smithsonian Institution.

Foster, George M.

    1960   Culture and Conquest: America's Spanish Heritage. Viking Fund Publications in Anthropology, No. 27. New York: Wenner-Gren Foundation.

    1967   Tzintzuntzan: Mexican Peasants in a Changing World. Boston: Little, Brown.

    1981   Old Age in Tzintzuntzan. In Aging, Biology, and Behavior. James L. McGaugh and Sara B. Kiesler, eds. Pp. 115–137. New York: Academic Press.

Freeman, Susan Tax

    1978   The Pasiegos: Spaniards in No Man's Land. Chicago: University of Chicago Press.

Freud, Sigmund

    1974   Jokes and their Relation to the Unconscious. James Strachey, trans. New York: W.W. Norton (originally published 1905).

Fuente, Beatríz de la

    1974   Arte Prehsipánico funerario: el occidente de México. México, DF: Universidad Nacional Autónoma de México.

Furtado, Celso

    1977   The Early Brazilian Sugar Economy. In Haciendas and Plantations in Latin American History. Robert G. Keith, ed. Pp. 63–71. New York: Holmes & Meier.

Gabriel Llompart, C.R.

    1965   Pan sobre la tumba. Revista de Dialectología y Tradiciones Populares (Madrid) 11:96–102.

Gaillard, Jacques

    1950   Catholicisme. Paris: Presse Catholique.

García Canclini, Nestor

    2001   Culturas híbridas: estratégias para entrar y salir de la modernidad. Buenos Aires: Paidos.

Garciagodoy, Juanita
    1998   Digging the Days of the Dead: A Reading of Mexico's Días de Muertos. Niwot,
            CO: University Press of Colorado.
Geertz, Clifford
    1973   Deep Play: Notes on the Balinese Cockfight. *In* The Interpretation of Cultures.
            Pp. 412–453. New York: Basic Books.
Gibson, Charles
    1964   The Aztecs under Spanish Rule: A History of the Indians of the Valley of
            Mexico, 1519–1810. Stanford: Stanford University Press.
Gombrich, Ernst H.
    1972   Symbolic Images: Studies in the Art of the Renaissance. London: Phaidon.
Gonzales, Michael J.
    1985   Plantation Agriculture and Social Control in Northern Peru, 1875–1933. Austin:
            University of Texas Press.
González, Rafael Jesús
    2005   Introduction to El corazón de la muerte: altars and offerings for Days of the
            Dead. Pp. 14–43. Berkeley: Heyday Books.
Gonzalez-Crussi, Frank
    1993   The Day of the Dead and Other Mortal Reflections. New York: Harcourt Brace.
Goodwin, Sarah Webster
    1988   Kitch and Culture: The Dance of Death in Nineteenth-Century Literature and
            Graphic Arts. New York: Garland.
Green, Judith Strupp
    1969   Laughing Souls: The Days of the Dead in Oaxaca, Mexico. San Diego: San
            Diego Museum of Man.
    1979   Days of the Dead in Oaxaca, Mexico: An Historical Inquiry. *In* Death and Dying:
            Views from Many Cultures. Richard A. Kalish, ed. Pp. 56–71. Farmingdale, NY:
            Baywood.
Greenwood, Davydd
    1977   Culture by the Pound: An Anthropological Perspective on Tourism as Cultural
            Commoditization. *In* Hosts and Guests: The Anthropology of Tourism. Valene
            L. Smith, ed. Pp. 129–138. Philadelphia: University of Pennsylvania Press.
Gundersheimer, Werner L.
    1971   Introduction to The Dance of Death, by Hans Holbein the Younger. Pp. ix–xiii.
            New York: Dover.
Gutmann, Matthew
    1993   Primordial Cultures and Creativity in the Origins of "Lo Mexicano." Kroeber
            Anthropological Society Papers 75–76:48–61.
Haberstein, Robert W. and William M. Lamers
    1963   Funeral Customs the World Over. Milwaukee: Bultin.
Handler, Richard, and Jocelyn Linnekin
    1984   Tradition, Genuine or Spurious. Journal of American Folklore 97:273–290.
Harlow, Ilana
    1997   Creating Situations: Practical Jokes and the Revival of the Dead in Irish
            Tradition. Journal of American Folkore 110(436):140–168.

Hassig, Ross

    1988   Aztec Warfare: Imperial Expansion and Political Control. Norman: University of Oklahoma Press.

    1992   War and Society in Ancient Mesoamerica. Berkeley: University of California Press.

Henry, Barbara

    2005   Preface to El Corazón de la Muerte: Altars and Offerings for Days of the Dead. Pp. 8–13. Berkeley, CA: Heyday Books.

Herrera, Hayden

    1983   Frida: A Biography of Frida Kahlo. New York: Harper and Row.

Hertz, Robert

    1960[1907]   Death and the Left Hand. Rodney Needham and Claudia Needham, trans. Aberdeen: Cohen and West.

Holbein, Hans, The Younger

    1971[1538]   The Dance of Death. A Complete Facsimile of the Original 1538 Edition of Les simulachres & historiees faces de la mort. New York: Dover.

Hoyos Saínz, Luis de

    1944   Folklore español del culto a los muertos. Revista de dialectología y tradiciones populares 1:30–53.

Hoyt-Goldsmith, Diane

    1994   The Day of the Dead: A Mexican-American Celebration. New York: Holiday House.

Huerta, María Teresa

    1993   Impresarios del Azúcar en el Siglo XIX. México, DF: Instituto de Antropología e Historia.

Huntingon, Richard, and Peter Metcalf

    1991   Celebrations of Death: The Anthropology of Mortuary Ritual. 2nd edition. Cambridge: Cambridge University Press.

Inda, Jonathan Xavier, and Renato Rosaldo

    2002   Introduction: A World in Motion. In The Anthropology of Globalization: A Reader. Jonathan Xavier Inda and Renato Rosaldo, eds. Pp. 1–34. Malden, MA: Blackwell.

Ingham, John M.

    1986   Mary, Michael, and Lucifer: Folk Catholicism in Central Mexico. Austin: University of Texas Press.

Isaacs, Susan, and Robert Royeton

    1982   Witches, Goblins, Ghosts—Why Your Child Loves Halloween. Parents 67 (October):66–69.

Jacobson-Widding, Anita

    1991   The Fertility of Incest. In The Creative Communion: African Folk Models of Fertility and the Regeneration of Life. A. Jacobson-Widding and W. van Beek, eds. Pp. 47–74. Stockholm: Stockholm Studies in Cultural Anthropology 15.

Johnston, Tony and Jeanette Winter

    1997   The Day of the Dead. New York: Harcourt, Brace.

Karp, Ivan, and Steven D. Lavine, eds.
  1991   The Poetics and Politics of Museum Display. Washington, DC: Smithsonian Institution Press.
Kertzer, David
  1988   Ritual, Politics and Power. New Haven: Yale University Press.
Kinsbruner, Jay
  1987   Penny Capitalism in Spanish America: The Pulperos of Puebla, Mexico City, Caracas, and Buenos Aires. Boulder, CO: Westview.
Klor de Alva, J. Jorge
  1988   Sahagún and the Birth of Modern Ethnography: Representing, Confessing, and Inscribing the Native Other. *In* The Works of Bernardino de Sahagún: Pioneer Ethnographer of Sixteenth-Century Aztec Mexico. Klor de Alva, Nicholson and Quiñones, eds. Pp. 31–52. Albany: State University of Albany, Institute for Mesoamerican Studies.
Klor de Alva, J. Jorge, H.B. Nicholson, and Eloise Quiñones, eds.
  1988   Introduction. *In* The Works of Bernardino de Sahagún: Pioneer Ethnographer of Sixteenth-Century Aztec Mexico. Pp. 1–12. Albany: State University of New York at Albany, Institute for Mesoamerican Studies.
Koestler, Arthur
  1964   The Act of Creation: A Study of the Conscious and Unconscious in Science and Art. New York: Dell.
Kovner, Guy
  2001   City Organizes Expanded Day of the Dead. Press Democrat (Petaluma, California). October 17, p. 1.
Krull, Kathleen, and Enrique O. Sánchez
  1995   Maria Molina and the Days of the Dead. New York: Macmillan.
Kubler, George
  1969   Studies in Classic Maya Iconography. New Haven: Connecticut Academy of Arts and Sciences.
  1970   Period, Style, and Meaning in Ancient American Art. New Literary History 1–2:127–144.
  1973   Science and Humanism among Americanists. *In* The Iconography of Middle American Sculpture. New York: Metropolitan Museum of Art.
Laughlin, Robert M.
  1969   The Tzotzil. *In* Handbook of Middle American Indians, Vol. 7. Evon Vogt, ed. Pp. 152–194. Austin: University of Texas Press.
Legman, Gershon
  1968   Rationale of the Dirty Joke: First Series. New York: Grove.
  1975   No Laughing Matter: Rationale of the Dirty Joke: Second Series. New York: Breaking Point.
LeRoy Ladurie, Emmanuel
  1979   Carnival in Romans. Mary Feeney, trans. New York: G. Braziller.
Limón Rojas, Miguel
  1984   The Concept of Death in Mexico. Speech delivered on October 25, Museo Nacional de Artes e Industrias Populares, Instituto Nacional Indigenista. Excelsior, November 2.

Lipp, Frank J.
    1991   The Mixe of Oaxaca: Religion, Ritual, and Healing. Austin: University of Texas Press.

Llabrés Quintana, Gabriel
    1925   Los panetets de mort. Correo de Mallorca, October 1925.

Lockhart, James
    1992   The Nahuas After the Conquest. Stanford: Stanford University Press.

Lomnitz, Claudio
    2005   Death and the Idea of Mexico. New York: Zone.

Lope Blanch, Juan M.
    1963   Vocabulario mexicano relativo a la muerte. México, DF: Centro de Estudios Literarios, Universidad Nacional Autónoma de México.

Lorenzo Pinar, Francisco Javier
    1991   Muerte y ritual en la edad moderna: el caso de Zamora (1500–1800). Salamanca: Universidad de Salamanca.

Luján Muñoz, Luis
    1987   Contribución al estudio de la iconografía de la muerte en Guatemala: El rey San Pascual. *In* Arte Funerario, Vol. 1. Louise Noelle, ed. Pp. 161–170. México, DF: Universidad Nacional Autónoma de México.

Lynne, Diana
    2002   District sued over "Day of the Dead". World Net Daily <www.worldnetdaily. com>, October 30.

MacCannell, Dean
    1976   The Tourist: A New Theory of the Leisure Class. New York: Schocken Books.

McNeill, William H.
    1976   Plagues and Peoples. New York: Doubleday.

Macazaga Ramírez de Arellano, and César Macazaga Ordoño, eds.
    1977   Posada y las calaveras vivientes. México, DF: Editorial Innovación.

Madsen, William
    1960   The Virgin's Children: Life in an Aztec Village Today. Austin: University of Texas Press.

Mancera, Pablo
    1974   Las plantaciones azucareras en el Perú, 1821–1875. Lima: Biblioteca Andina.

Martin, Cheryl E.
    1985   Rural Society in Colonial Morelos. Albuquerque: University of New Mexico Press.

Matos Moctezuma, Eduardo, ed.
    1986   Los dioses se negaron a morir: arqueología y crónicas del templo mayor. México, DF: Secretaría de Educación Pública.
    1992   Aztec history and cosmovision. *In* Moctezuma's Mexico: Visions of the Aztec World. David Carrasco and Eduardo Matos Moctezuma, eds. Pp. 3–97. Niwot, CO: University Press of Colorado.

Mead, Margaret
    1975   Halloween: Where has all the Mischief Gone? *In* Aspects of the Present. Margaret Mead and Rhoda Metraux, eds. Pp. 201–207. New York: William Morrow.

Metcalf, Peter, and Richard Huntington

1992   Celebrations of Death: The Anthropology of Mortuary Ritual. Second edition. Cambridge: Cambridge University Press.

Mintz, Sidney W.

1984   Sweetness and Power: The Place of Sugar in Modern History. New York: Viking.

Mitchell, B.R.

1993   International Historical Statistics, the Americas, 1750–1988. New York: Stockton Press.

Mitford, Jessica

1963   The American Way of Death. New York: Simon and Schuster.

Moedano Navarro, Gabriel

1960–61   La ofrenda del Día de los Muertos. Folklore Americano, p. 32. Lima: Organo del Comité Interamericano de Folklore.

Morales Cano, Lucero and Mysyk, Avis

2004   Cultural Tourism, the State, and Day of the Dead. Annals of Tourism Research 31(4):879–898.

Moreno Villa, José

1986   Lo mexicano en las artes plásticas. México, DF: Fondo de Cultural Económica. Museo Nacional de Arte.

Mörner, Magnus

1975   En torno a las haciendas de la región de Cuzco desde el siglo XVIII. *In* Haciendas, latifundios y plantaciones en América Latina. Enrique Florescano, ed. Pp. 346–392. México, DF: Siglo XXI.

Morrison, Suzanne

1992   Mexico's "Day of the Dead" in San Francisco, California: A Study of Continuity and Change in a Popular Religious Festival. Unpublished Ph.D. dissertation, Graduate Theological Union, Berkeley, California.

Museo Nacional de Arte

1994   Juegos de ingenio y agudeza: La pintura emblemática de Nueva España. México, DF: Patronato del Museo Nacional de Arte.

Narro, José R., et al.

1984   Evolución reciente de la mortalidad en México. Comercio Exterior 34(7): 636–646.

Narvaez, Peter, ed.

2002   Of Corpse: Death and Humor in Folklore and Popular Culture. Logan, UT: Utah State University Press.

Norget, Kristin

2005   Days of Death, Days of Life: Ritual in the Popular Culture of Oaxaca. New York: Columbia University Press.

Nutini, Hugo G.

1988   Todos Santos in Rural Tlaxcala: A Syncretic, Expressive, and Symbolic Analysis of the Cult of the Dead. Princeton: Princeton University Press.

Ochoa Zazueta, Jesús Angel

1973   La muerte y los muertos: culto, servicio, ofrenda y humor de una comunidad. México, DF: Sep-Setentas.

Ó'Súilleabháin, Seán

    1967   Irish Wake Amusements. Cork, Ireland: Mercier Press.

Parsons, Elsie Clews

    1917   All-Souls Day at Zuñi, Acoma, and Laguna. Journal of American Folklore 30(118):495–496.

    1970[1936]   Mitla: Town of the Souls. Chicago: University of Chicago Press.

Pasztory, Esther

    1988   A reinterpretation of Teotihuacán and its mural painting tradition. In Feathered Serpents and Flowering Trees: Reconstructing the Murals of Teotihuacán. Kathleen Berrin, ed. Pp. 45–77. San Francisco: Fine Arts Museums of San Francisco.

Paz, Octavio

    1961   The Labyrinth of Solitude: Life and Thought in Mexico. Lysander Kemp, trans. New York: Grove.

Peterson, Jeanette Favrot

    1993   The Paradise Garden Murals of Malinalco: Utopia and Empire in Sixteenth-Century Mexico. Austin: University of Texas Press.

Poleszynski, Dag

    1982   Food, Social Cosmology, and Mental Health: The Case of Sugar. Tokyo: United Nations University.

Quigley, Christine

    1996   The Corpse: A History. Jefferson, NC: MacFarland.

Radcliffe-Brown, A.R.

    1965   Structure and Function in Primitive Society. New York: Free Press.

Ramírez, Fausto

    1988   Tipología de la escultera tumbal en México, 1860–1920. México, DF: Universidad Nacional Autónoma de México.

Ramírez Torres, Juan Luis

    1994   Ofrenda a los muertos: regeneración de la esperanza y la vida del México reciente. La Colmena: Revista de la Universidad Autonoma del Estado de Morelos 4:43–45.

Ramos, Samuel

    1962   Profile of Man and Culture in Mexico. Peter G. Earle, trans. Austin: University of Texas Press.

Robicsek, Francis, and Donald Hales

    1988   A ceramic codex fragment: the sacrifice of Xbalanque. In Maya Iconography. Elizabeth P. Benson and Gillett G. Griffin, eds. Pp. 260–276. Princeton: Princeton University Press.

Romo, Tere

    2000   A spirituality of resistance: Día de los Muertos and the Galería de la Raza. In Chicanos en Mictlán: Día de los Muertos in California. Tere Romo, ed. Pp. 30–41. San Francisco: Mexican Museum.

Ruby, Jay

    1995   Secure the Shadow: Death and Photography in America. Cambridge, MA: MIT Press.

Sadler, Aaron
    2003a UAFS Drops Witch Watch. Times Record (Fort Smith, AR).
    2003b Halloween Ban Casts Spell on Campus. Times Record (Fort Smith, AR).

Sahagún, Fr. Bernardino de
    1978 General History of the Things of New Spain. Arthur Anderson and Charles E. Dibble, trans. Santa Fe, NM: School of American Research.

Sánchez Carretero, Cristina
    2003 The Day of the Dead: Dying Days in Toledo, Ohio? *In* Holidays, Ritual, Festival, Celebration, and Public Display. Cristina Sánchez Carretero and Jack Santino, eds. Pp. 173–190. Alcalá de Henares (Spain): Universidad de Alcalá, Instituto de Estudios Norteamericanos.

Sandstrom, Alan R., and Pamela Effrein Sandstrom
    1986 Traditional Papermaking and Paper Cult Figures of Mexico. Norman: University of Oklahoma Press.

Santino, Jack, ed.
    1993 Halloween and Other Festivals of Death and Life. Knoxville: University of Tennessee Press.

San Vicente, Luis
    1999 The Festival of Bones/El Festival de las Calaveras. John William Byrd and Bobby Byrd, trans. El Paso, TX: Cinco Puntos.

Sayer, Chloë, ed.
    1993 Mexico: The Day of the Dead. Boston: Shambhala Redstone.

Scheffler, Lilian
    1976 La celebración del día de muertos en San Juan Totolac, Tlaxcala. Boletín del Departamento de Investigación de las Tradiciones Populares 3:91–103.

Schele, Linda
    1988 The Xibalba shuffle: a dance after death. *In* Maya Iconography. Elizabeth P. Benson and Gillett G. Griffin, eds. Pp. 294–317. Princeton: Princeton University Press.

Scheper-Hughes, Nancy
    1992 Death Without Weeping: The Violence of Everyday Life in Brazil. Berkeley: University of California Press.

Smith, C.
    1967 Feast of All Saints. *In* New Catholic Encyclopedia. New York: McGraw-Hill.

Sommers, Laurie Kay
    1995 Fiesta, fe y cultura: Celebrations of Faith and Culture in Detroit's Colonia Mexicana. East Lansing, MI: Casa de Unidad Cultural Arts and Media.

Spranz, Bodo
    1973 Los dioses en los códices mexicanos del grupo Borgia: una investigación iconográfica. México, DF: Fondo de Cultura Económica.

Sumner, William Graham
    1906 Folkways: A Study of the Sociological Importance of Usages, Manners, Customs, Mores, and Morals. Boston: Ginn.

Super, John C.
    1988 Food, Conquest and Colonization in Sixteenth-Century Spanish America. Albuquerque: University of New Mexico Press.

Taylor, William B.
    1976   Town and Country in the Valley of Oaxaca. *In* Provinces of Early Mexico: Variants of Spanish American Regional Evolution. Ida Altman and James Lockhart, eds. Pp. 63–95. Los Angeles: UCLA Latin American Center Publications.
    1987   The Virgin of Guadalupe in New Spain: An Inquiry into the Social History of Marian Devotion. American Ethnologist 14:9–33.

Tinker, Edward Larocque
    1961   Corridos and Calaveras. Austin: University of Texas Press.

Toor, Frances, et al., eds.
    1930   Las obras de José Guadalupe Posada, grabador mexicano. México, DF.
    1947   A Treasury of Mexican Folkways. New York: Crown.

Torkelson, Jean
    1995   Halloween Creates Devil of a Controversy. Rocky Mountain News (Denver), October 22, Spotlight Section, p. 63a.

Tuleja, Tad
    1994   Trick or Treat: Pre-Texts and Contexts. *In* Halloween and Other Festivals of Death and Life. Jack Santino, ed. Pp. 82–102. Knoxville: University of Tennessee Press.

Turner, Kay, and Pat Jasper
    1994   The Day of the Dead: The Tex-Mex Tradition. *In* Halloween and Other Festivals of Death and Life. Jack Santino, ed. Pp. 133–151. Knoxville: University of Tennessee Press.

United Nations Economic Commission
    1993   United Nations Statistical Yearbook for Latin America and the Caribbean. Santiago de Chile: United Nations Economic Commission for Latin America and the Caribbean.

Van Gennep, Arnold
    1947–53   Manuel de Folklore Français Contemporain, Vol. 1, parts 3–6. Paris: A. Picard.

Vansittart, E.C.
    1990   All Souls' Day in Italy. The Antiquary (London) 36:326–330.

Vargas, G., Luis Alberto
    1971   La muerte vista por el mexicano de hoy. Artes de Mexico 145:57.

Violant y Simmora, Ramón
    1956   Panes rituales, infantiles y juveniles, en el nordeste y levante español. Revista de Dialectología y Tradiciones Populares 12:300–359.

Viqueira, Juan-Pedro
    1984   La Ilustración y las fiestas religiosas populares en la Ciudad de México (1730–1821). Cuicuilco (Revista de la Escuela Nacional de Antropología e Historia) 14–15:7–14.

Wallace, James
    2000   "Devil Worship" Fear Killed Halloween Students Barred from Wearing Costumes. Toronto Sun, November 2.

Wark, Robert R.
    1966   Introduction to Rowlandson's Drawings for the English Dance of Death. Pp. 1–13. San Marino, CA: Huntington Library.

Westheim, Paul
    1983   La Calavera (3rd edition). México, DF: Fondo de Cultura Económica.

Whyte, Florence
    1931   The Dance of Death in Spain and Catalonia. Baltimore: Waverly Press.

Winning, Hugo von
    1987   El simbolismo del arte funerario de Teotihuacán. *In* Arte funerario, Vol. 1. Louise Noelle, ed. Pp. 55–63. México, DF: Universidad Nacional Autónoma de México.

Wolf, Eric, and Sidney Mintz
    1977   Haciendas and Plantations. *In* Haciendas and Plantations in Latin American History. Robert G. Keith, ed. Pp. 36–62. New York: Holmes & Meier.

Wolfenstein, Martha
    1954   Children's Humor: A Psychological Analysis. Glencoe, IL: Free Press.

Wollen, Peter
    1989   Introduction. *In* Posada: Messenger of Mortality. Julian Rothenstein, ed. Pp. 14–23. Boston: Redstone Press.

Newspapers and Broadsides

Calaveras Encanijadas (Mexico City)

El Chivo (Oaxaca)

El Condor (Tijuana)

El Imparcial (Oaxaca)

La Jornada (Mexico City)

La Jornada Morelos (Cuernavaca)

El Metiche (Mexico City)

El Mexicano (Ciudad Juárez)

México Hoy (Mexico City)

Milenio (Mexico City)

Nacional (Mexico City)

La Opinión (Veracruz)

Reforma (Monterrey)

Unión de Morelos (Cuernavaca)

INDEX